About the Author

Marilee Sprenger is an international presenter and trainer. She is an adjunct professor at Aurora University and a member of the American Academy of Neurology, the Learning and the Brain Society, and the Cognitive Neuroscience Society.

Marilee has applied brain research in classrooms, staffrooms, and boardrooms. She has been both an educator and a business leader and believes that understanding the brain is helpful on a personal and professional level.

Marilee has authored six books on the brain and has published numerous articles online and in journals.

Dedication

I would like to dedicate this book to the memory of my father, Lee Broms, who was the first to model true leadership to me. I miss you, Dad.

Author's Acknowledgments

When I first started doing trainings and presentations in this area 17 years ago, there were many skeptics. But the wealth of knowledge about the brain keeps growing, and more people are interested as they want to live longer and more productive lives.

I want to thank the many neuroscientists who work to help us understand the brain, and the translators who help all of us understand the research and its applications.

I want to thank the people at Wiley for making this project a reality. First, I wish to thank Mike Baker for believing in this idea and getting it off the ground. Traci Cumbay had the monumental job of being my project and copy editor. You are blessed with patience and kindness, Traci. My technical editor, Dr. Robert Sylwester, has always been a wonderful friend and mentor. Thanks, Bob, for your kind assistance. I want to thank the publicity and marketing people who will help make this book a success.

I also want to thank my dear friend, Mary Jane Sterling, author of many *For Dummies* books. She saw my work fitting in the *For Dummies* format. Now we can be Dummies together!

I wouldn't be doing any of this if my mother, Mollie Broms, hadn't been the businesswoman that she was. She raised a family, ran a business, and volunteered her precious time. She has been an inspiration. I want to thank my husband, Scott, a man who lives to make me and his customers happy. A wonderful leader, Scott read every word and offered his wisdom. I also want to thank my children for their patience as I shortened vacations and gave up opportunities to be with my grandchildren in order to meet my deadlines. To my son, Josh, his wife, Amy, my daughter, Marnie, and her husband, Thabu, I look forward to watching your families grow as well as your business careers. I will make up any time I missed being with you, Jack and Emmie.

Publisher's Acknowledgments

We're proud of this book; please send us your comments at http://dummies.custhelp.com. For other comments, please contact our Customer Care Department within the U.S. at 877-762-2974, outside the U.S. at 317-572-3993, or fax 317-572-4002.

Some of the people who helped bring this book to market include the following:

Acquisitions, Editorial, and Media Development

Project Editor: Traci Cumbay

Acquisitions Editor: Mike Baker

Copy Editor: Traci Cumbay

Assistant Editor: Erin Calligan Mooney

Editorial Program Coordinator: Joe Niesen

Technical Editor: Robert Sylwester

Senior Editorial Manager: Jennifer Ehrlich

Editorial Supervisor and Reprint Editor: Carmen Krikorian

Editorial Assistants: David Lutton, Jennette ElNaggar

Art Coordinator: Alicia B. South

Cover Photos: © Image Source

Cartoons: Rich Tennant (www.the5thwave.com)

Composition Services

Project Coordinator: Sheree Montgomery

Layout and Graphics: Ashley Chamberlain, Samantha K. Cherolis, Joyce Haughey, Melissa K. Jester

Proofreaders: Rebecca Denoncour, Evelyn C. Gibson

Indexer: Joan K. Griffitts

Publishing and Editorial for Consumer Dummies

Diane Graves Steele, Vice President and Publisher, Consumer Dummies

Kristin Ferguson-Wagstaffe, Product Development Director, Consumer Dummies

Ensley Eikenburg, Associate Publisher, Travel

Kelly Regan, Editorial Director, Travel

Publishing for Technology Dummies

Andy Cummings, Vice President and Publisher, Dummies Technology/General User

Composition Services

Debbie Stailey, Director of Composition Services

Contents at a Glance

Table of Contents

Part IV: Training and Developing Brains 237

Chapter 16: No Train, No Gain: Understanding the Value of Training 239

Chapter 17: Ensuring that Employees Are Fit to Be Trained. 251

Introduction

*B*ecoming a leader can take a lifetime, or just as long as it takes you to read this book. *The Leadership Brain For Dummies* is designed to equip you with everything you need to become the leader you want to be.

Although you can find many books on leadership and many books on the brain, no book has connected the subjects like this one. Neuroscience offers you an opportunity to maximize your brain and the brains of those you depend on to shape your future.

In this book you get the *how* and the *why*. You find out how to be a great leader, great listener, great decision-maker, and great at handling yourself and others. But that information is only part of the picture. Understanding *why* you should do these things by using specific strategies that are compatible with how the brain works is the rest of the story. Knowing *why* makes you more likely to use these strategies again and again.

Although business fads come and go, the brain is here to stay. Apply the best from neuroscience to your organization to create a climate and a culture in which everyone is happy — you, your employees, and your customers or clients.

About This Book

Leadership is an art and a science. This book shows you where the two meet and complement each other. It's meant to engage your brain without taxing it. I want you to think about who you work for and who you work with to consider what you may do to make your experience and theirs a better one. With that purpose in mind, I have put together lists, stories, and tips to help you lead your own brain as well as the brains of others. The book you hold in your hands is not typical, and it's certainly not a textbook. You can jump around however you like, not worrying that you've missed critical information from an earlier chapter. I define new terms wherever they show up or direct you to their definitions so that you're never at a loss for information. If an example or explanation from a previous chapter may support your understanding of a topic, I let you know how to find it.

This book is designed to be personalized by you — read it as questions arise or leadership challenges present themselves to you. Turn to any topic that interests you at any time that you want to find out about it. I've worked hard to make sure that you are always be at home within these pages.

Conventions Used in This Book

I use the following conventions throughout the text to make things consistent and easy to understand:

- ✔ All Web addresses appear in monofont.
- ✔ New terms appear in *italic* and are closely followed by an easy-to-understand definition.
- ✔ **Bold** highlights the action parts of numbered steps and key words in bullet lists.

When this book was printed, some Web addresses may have needed to break across two lines of text. If that happened, no extra characters like hyphens indicate the break. So, when using one of these Web addresses, just type in exactly what you see in this book, as though the line break doesn't exist.

The brain is a funny thing, and leadership should be fun. For these reasons, I have added humor where I think it is appropriate. Leaders should add humor to their leadership style because the brain responds to humor and it actually allows the brain to use some of its higher levels in order to "get the joke."

Foolish Assumptions

The brain makes many assumptions. Mine is no different. I assume that you have picked up this book for one of two reasons: like me, you're enthralled with research on the brain and want to know how it relates to everything, or you're intently looking for new information about leadership — a fresh approach that motivates and inspires you. Either way, I assume that you will find information and strategies that you can apply right away.

I also assume that you would like to know what's going on inside the heads of other people in your life — at work and at home. Finally, you're a little worried about your own brain, and you want to know what to do to keep your business brain in business!

What You're Not to Read

The beauty of *The Leadership Brain For Dummies* is that you don't have to read the whole book to come away with quite a bit of easily applicable information. You can skip the shaded boxes of text called sidebars, which contain stories or examples that relate to information in the chapter. Sidebars help you connect more with some of the ideas in the chapter, but they don't contain new ideas and so are skippable.

How This Book Is Organized

The Leadership Brain For Dummies is organized into five parts. The following sections give you a description of each part.

Part 1: Leadership Is All in Your Head

Part I links leadership and the brain by giving you an overall feel for the connections between the way the brain runs and the way your organization runs. It covers some brain basics, such as how the brain makes connections and changes, how it's structured, and what it needs to learn and be productive. The fact that leaders are made and not born is a tribute to the brain's ability to learn and change.

This part also describes a great leader who uses knowledge about the brain to share a vision and mission, and to motivate others. And it describes a not-so-good leader. Although negativity is not the point here, the brain needs examples to avoid as much as those to emulate, and so I give you both.

Part II: Tapping Into the Brain of a Leader

Part II shows you how to develop leadership traits. Discovering your intelligence strengths through self-knowledge and a written assessment helps you determine the style of leadership that feels right and put employees into the right positions. You find out about emotional intelligence and becoming an emotionally intelligent leader. As you assess yourself in relationship to your self-awareness, social awareness, and handling relationships, you see the importance of empathizing with your employees and all of your organization's stakeholders.

Additionally, you find out how the brain makes decisions in this part of the book. Can you think your way to the top? Good decision-making skills combine both cognitive and emotional intelligences.

Part III: Working with the Brains You Have

Rather than shaking up an organization by firing employees, a leader is better off first taking a close look at the current staff. Retraining often is a better option than rehiring, and this part of the books shows you how to find and foster the skills employees have to offer.

Understanding some major differences between the sexes and among different generations helps you get employees into the positions where they're most likely to thrive and offer them the most optimal working conditions to ensure that they do.

This part of the book also deals with the importance of teams, filling you in on how they develop and how they grow. Creating goals that appeal to the whole brain makes a difference in how your teams approach those goals and whether they reach them.

Part IV: Training and Developing Brains

In this part, I examine the importance of training and the consequences of not training, and I give you brain-compatible training techniques to increase learning and memory.

I explain what the brain needs to be ready to learn and ready to work, and I show you how to make your training dollars count by ensuring that the information sticks in employees' brains.

Finally, I show you how to conduct meetings that make a difference. Communicating with a diverse workforce means differentiating some of your meeting and communication strategies.

Part V: The Part of Tens

This section is part of the rich format of every *For Dummies* book. In it you find chapters devoted to quick bits of advice on the brain and leadership. First, I dispel some of the more common myths about the brain. I then offer you ten tips on leading with the brain in mind. Finally, I show you ten ways to develop your brain for leadership and living a better life.

Icons Used in This Book

Every *For Dummies* book uses icons — those little pictures in the margins that catch your eye as you peruse the book. Here's what they are and what they mean:

This icon flags bits of information that deserves a second look, making it easier for you to return to again and again.

Although you're likely to find the detailed technical information you find next to this icon interesting, you don't need it to understand the main points of the book.

Whenever I give you information that will save you time or money or make your job easier, I flag it with this icon.

Stop and read information that appears next to this daunting icon to avoid leadership pitfalls and mistakes.

Where to Go from Here

Pick a chapter, any chapter. Each one is its own little book. You won't need to go back to fill in missing pieces from earlier chapters. Looking for information about how to make a team function smoothly? Go straight to Chapter 14. Want new ways to make your meetings more interesting and effective? Chapter 20 has what you need. And if you're an overachiever or just insatiably curious, by all means turn the page and keep going until you get to the back cover.

The best leaders never stop wondering, reading, and seeking answers. You are obviously one of them! I'm grateful for the opportunity to help you on your quest.

Part I
Leadership Is All in Your Head

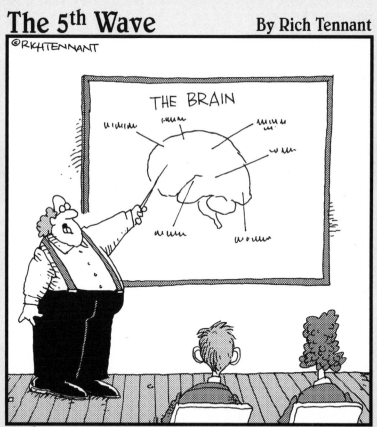

The 5th Wave   By Rich Tennant

"Information is moved via neurotransmitters from neuron to neuron via the synapses into the brain where it is then retrieved by the memory via a slap on the back of the head."

In this part . . .

Here, I show you some basics of the brain, including how the brain's structure and function is similar to the structure and function of your business. Your brain has a CEO that makes decisions, plans for the future, and celebrates success. I tell you about what the brain needs to be at its best, as well as methods for making sure you're leading your best.

Chapter 1

Connecting Brain Science to Leadership Principles

In This Chapter

▶ Looking into leadership

▶ Connecting neuroscience and leadership

▶ Building teams with the brain in mind

▶ Training effectively for any brain

*I*n this book you find out how your brain works and how to work it to improve your decision-making, training, and hiring so that you create a workplace where people are happy and productive.

In order to survive and thrive through humans' long history, the brain had to be social. Humans needed people around them to help them conquer whatever dangers they might face. Today's world looks a lot different from that of even a century ago, but you still need people to help you prosper. Being social means establishing relationships. Relationships often require leadership.

The leadership brain learns how to be self-aware and self-confident. This brain knows how to persuade and convince others that her idea is the best. At the same time, the leader takes others' feelings and ideas into consideration.

The good news from neuroscience is that you can learn how to be a leader. This book shows you how.

The Leadership Brain For Dummies helps you become the leader you want to be.

Defining Leadership

Leadership is the ability to bring like-minded people together to get remarkable things done. Because humans are a social species and natural hierarchies develop, the concept of leadership emerged. Someone has to be in charge, share a vision, and lead others toward the goals.

Leadership depends on relationship-building. A leader can lead only through her ability to build relationships between and among employees, customers, investors, and any other stakeholders.

Knowing and amending your leadership style

Different approaches to leadership give you the opportunity to be the leader you want to be when you want to be it. You can find your leadership style by reading Chapter 6. The style you naturally use or the one you cultivate may change according to circumstances, which is as it should be. When you need to take charge because you're dealing with new employees who need more guidance, you might adopt the authoritarian style. But perhaps in your heart you really favor group decision-making; you can then use that style in other situations, when it's a better fit.

As a leader, you are many different things to different people. You have a lot of hats to wear, but there's only one brain under those hats, and you get to know it better in Chapter 5, which shows you how leadership and the brain interact.

Providing feedback

As you find out in Chapter 4, feedback is food for thought. Feed the brains of your employees by providing the necessary information to keep them on task and keep your vision in sight. Without feedback, people lose self-confidence and motivation.

Feedback begins with the senior leadership team, but it goes much beyond that. Rather than relying on a trickle-down effect, leaders must provide feedback to each and every person in the organization. You find suggestions in Chapter 20 to communicate with employees throughout your organization.

Developing high emotional intelligence

Your ability to have good relationships with others gets you farther in business and in your personal life than your IQ. It's not how smart you are that counts, but rather how you are smart.

Leaders use their emotional intelligence to handle relationships. When leaders are aware of what they feel and how their feelings affect the work environment, they can choose to handle those emotions in such a way that they use their intuition but don't become overwhelmed by emotion. Emotional intelligence includes the ability to understand and work with what another person is feeling. For instance, the possibility of lay-offs looms in your organization. How are your people feeling? Stress levels must be high. As their leader, you have to let employees know how much you value their contributions, exactly how things stand, and what your decision-making process relies on.

Real power is the ability to control your own brain. You need to understand how the brain works, how powerful your emotions are, and how you can use your self-awareness to prevent reflexive actions.

Chapter 8 highlights the importance of self-awareness, self-management, social awareness, and social management.

Ensuring a safe working environment

One of the basic responsibilities of a leader is providing a safe and appealing work environment. Employees face stressors in their lives every day; relieving them of the stress that an unsafe environment may cause is imperative to having happy, productive employees.

Safety in the workplace includes both physical safety and emotional well-being. After you have the safety factor covered, making the work environment fun as well as inspirational invites cooperation. Caring enough to provide an attractive, safe working environment and put the needs of your staff ahead of your own needs is a key leadership quality.

Chapter 12 tells you how to create a safe and appealing work environment.

Communicating effectively

Effective communication is a hallmark of a great leader. You need to share your vision with passion and commitment. Creating a picture for all to see requires you to make your message simple enough for all to grasp and complex enough to make it interesting. When you paint your picture and employees or customers see it, their brains connect this vision to their own previously stored networks of information to reinforce your words.

But communication doesn't happen in just one direction. Listening to the needs, desires, and dreams of your employees is essential. And you listen and make connections between their statements and your dream.

Chapter 4 emphasizes good communication skills.

Making decisions with heart and head

Decision-making is based on prior experiences. Your brain asks, "What worked in the past?" or "In what similar situations was a decision made that was good? Or bad?"

Your emotions are very much involved in the decision-making process. The neurotransmitter dopamine is very active in your reward system. The dopamine neurons remember whether an experience or a decision made you feel good. Those chemical memories help you make every decision. If you made a bad decision, your amygdala, the raw emotional center in the brain that I discuss in Chapters 2 and 8, reacts immediately to the situation.

Good leaders make decisions based on what their emotions tell them as well as on the facts. The right hemisphere of your brain explores the challenges and possibilities in a novel situation in which you must make a decision. But your logical left hemisphere recalls routines and previously established processes that have worked in the past. Decision-making is a whole-brain activity. Good decision-making always takes into account both cognitive skills and emotional intelligence.

Chapter 9 discusses the art and science of decision-making.

Leadership on the Brain

Emerging science connects the brain to leadership: Promising leaders can access different levels of the brain in a conscious way in order to share their vision and achieve their goals. Understanding how the brain functions enables you not only to work within the bounds of your own brain but also understand and work with, rather than against, the brains of others. Leading in a brain-compatible manner helps you accomplish your goals much faster.

Balancing novelty and predictability

Both predictability and novelty make the brain happy. Knowing what is going to happen next lowers stress in the brain, but too much predictability leads to boredom. In Chapter 3, I show you how creating an environment that contains enough predictability makes it easier for the brain to concentrate on such areas as creativity, problem-solving, and decision-making.

Because the brain remembers patterns and seeks patterns to make sense of its world, familiarity breeds security. If your teams are in an environment in which it is okay, actually encouraged, to ask "dumb" questions or make mistakes, then their brains can run wild with ideas. Some research suggests that solving problems in a more creative way may lead to better solutions, and so an atmosphere in which the brain can relax and wander may lead to more innovations.

Grasping the chemical element

If you want to understand human nature, you need to know something about neurotransmitters, the chemicals in your brain. For instance, serotonin has long been known as a neurotransmitter related to emotion. If your serotonin levels are low, you're more likely to become angry or aggressive. What's more, you're less likely to be able to control your reactions.

Because serotonin is produced by the food you eat, eating right — and especially eating breakfast — helps you control emotional responses.

Your chemical levels can also be affected by social behavior, culture, and genetics. In Chapter 2, I share information about the functions of some of the chemicals in your brain, as well as ways to make the most of them.

Sculpting brains — yours and theirs

That three-pound lump of tissue in your skull is flexible and vulnerable. This is good news and one of the most promising research findings in neuroscience. This flexibility enables the brain to recover from some traumas and break old habits. It also means you can change your brain.

Chapter 4 shows you how to train your brain and explains that the brains of your current and future employees are indeed very trainable. You have to appreciate the fact that you *can* teach an old dog new tricks!

In Chapter 19, you discover the differences between training new employees and those who have been with you for awhile. Both brains respond to training, but they do so in different ways. Finding out how to address those differences goes a long way toward making training stick.

Do you want the leader's brain?

People often confuse the roles of leader and manager. After you understand the brain, you will see that there are cognitive skill differences between the two. If you look at the function of the left hemisphere as described in Chapter 2, you see that one of its responsibilities is to handle routine procedures that have been previously established. This is the role of the manager. The manager manages what has previously been set up.

The leader, on the other hand, delegates the established processes to managers. New challenges, new problems, and unidentified situations are handled by the right hemisphere of the brain. The leader and the leadership team deal with these novel situations and create procedures to handle them.

A manager can be a leader, of course, and a leader may also be a manager. But in talking about the brain, the leadership role is much like the right hemisphere's role, and the manager's role is akin to the left hemisphere's role. To run efficiently both the productive brain and the productive organization utilize both roles.

If you develop a leadership brain, you learn to recognize situations using your sensory systems and your emotions. Then you use your brain's CEO, the prefrontal cortex, along with your gut feelings to respond. If the situation is novel, your right hemisphere, and the right hemispheres of your leadership team, use their creative, holistic, spatial approach to create the response. In familiar situations, your left hemisphere relies on previously established processes.

You can develop yourself into the kind of leader you want to be.

Different strokes for different brains

Move over IQ, new intelligences are in town, and their number keeps growing. In Chapter 7, I share information about nine different ways of being smart. If you have a brain, you have some of each of these kinds of intelligence:

- ✔ Verbal/linguistic
- ✔ Mathematical/logical
- ✔ Musical/rhythmic
- ✔ Visual/spatial
- ✔ Bodily kinesthetic
- ✔ Naturalist
- ✔ Interpersonal
- ✔ Intrapersonal
- ✔ Philosophical/moral/ethical

I find that leaders and employees alike enjoy finding out more about themselves. And so Chapter 7 not only offers you a definition and examples of these intelligences, it provides an assessment for you. Knowing your strengths and weaknesses and helping your followers learn theirs is part of good leadership. This information may help you understand why you like something and why you're uncomfortable with some people, tasks, and environments.

Using Brain Science to Build Your Team

Information on the brain suggests ways you can change the brains of those you train. The person others consider the best may not be the best choice for your particular situation. Knowledge and skills are important, but employees also need to know how to build and maintain those relationships that keep your company thriving.

When you need to add to your team, former General Electric CEO Jack Welch recommends that you look at the best employees you have and find people just like them.

As a leader, you are called on to make hiring decisions that affect the entire organization. Whether you promote current employees or hire new ones, understanding how the brain functions helps you make those decisions.

Understanding male and female brains

Definite variations exist in male and female brains. The brain is highly influenced by its experiences; therefore, some of the characteristics you see in males or females may be from environmental influences or in combination with the brain differences.

Chapter 13 helps you address the common differences between male and female brains. For example, knowing that females tend to prefer eye contact while males may not can affect the way you share your vision and the values of your company.

Women *can* read maps and men *do* ask for directions. But there are some differences that may affect how they perform at work — not how well they perform, but rather how they do things differently.

Bridging the generation gap

Several generations often are at work in one organization. Becoming familiar with the work ethic, needs, and expectations of each of these generations can make the climate of your workplace less stressful for all.

As a leader involved in business in this technological world, you must catch up and keep up with the challenges of working with several generations. Your organization can be part of a global economy and become more successful with the assistance of the younger generations and the loyalty and values of the older generations. Find out in Chapter 15 how to take advantage of the characteristics of all employees.

Goal setting and goal getting

Whether rewards are tangible (like bonuses) or intangible (good feelings of accomplishment), goals help the brain focus. Part of the leader's job is to keep people centered on the mission of the organization. As your teams go through developmental stages from infancy to wisdom, their goals keep them on track. Chapter 14 shows you how to create goals that intrigue the right hemisphere and the left hemisphere of the brain.

Celebrate each accomplishment! Every step along the way to reaching a goal is cause for celebration. As a leader, you must shift your focus from your success to the successes of your employees.

Training with the Brain in Mind

One of the goals of most organizations is to have a staff of highly trained employees. Brain science has effectively shown that the way information is presented, rehearsed, and reviewed influences the effectiveness of that training. For instance, using emotion in training helps trainees store information more effectively.

CEOs cringe at the thought of having employees away from the job for one to three weeks for training. They soon realize, however, that good training is worth it. The results of training include

✔ Brains that see the big picture.

✔ Brains that have changed to use a new process or product.

> ✔ Brains that can see and share your vision.
>
> ✔ Brains that can work together as training creates relationships.
>
> ✔ Brains that can see beyond their own jobs.

In Chapter 16, I talk about mental maps — pictures of how people see the world and how things should work. Training provides the opportunity to change the mental maps of your employees so that they more closely match your own vision.

Supporting trainees' bodies and brains

As a former educator I can tell you that I would have loved nothing more than to have a classroom full of students who were ready to learn. Their parents thought they were ready, and most of the students thought they were ready. But they weren't ready because their bodies and their brains weren't fit enough to learn. It takes proper nutrition, the right amount of sleep, and regular exercise to truly make the brain ready for learning or training.

In Chapter 17, I share information about how proper nutrition affects the brains of your trainees as well as your employees and yourself. The amount of sleep your people get each night has an impact on what and how much they remember from the previous day's training. And exercise is key to getting blood and oxygen to the brain for optimal work.

You can take steps to make your trainings more productive. Lowering your trainees' stress levels through proper nutrition, rest, and exercise is a beginning. Get the most out of your training dollars by ensuring that your people are fit to be trained.

Making training stick

The most memorable and productive trainings are those that engage your brain. This engagement can be through emotional connections, humor, fun, or through personal connections to your life.

If you can answer the following question for each of your employees and trainees, you can head them in the right direction: What's in it for me? Both the CEOs of major corporations and every classroom teacher knows that if employees and students can see a connection to their lives, they will buy in to the learning.

Motivation comes from a desire or a need. See to it that your vision and your training goals fit into one of these two categories.

In Chapter 18, I share with you ways to make trainings stick. The emotional component, the memory systems involved, and the climate of the training make a big difference in how much information employees retain.

Training must also involve the support of both leaders and managers. Employees and new hires need to feel that they're part of something bigger — that their contributions are appreciated and make a difference.

Chapter 2

The Science behind the Brain

*I*n the past 20 years, scientists have been able to look at the brain through specialized imaging technology. Looking at the brain in action is a far cry from the old way: looking at brains during autopsy, finding lesions, comparing the area of the lesion to the behavior of the patient, and making a diagnosis. The 1990s were the Decade of the Brain, and the 21st century promises to be the Century of the Brain. Walk into any book store or up to a magazine stand during any month and you find cover articles about the brain. Curiosity about the brain peaked with the horror stories about Alzheimer's disease, and the baby boomers want to know how to keep their brains young and in good shape.

Interest in the brain goes beyond worrying about memory. The wonderful applications of brain research have reached classrooms and boardrooms around the world. New words and new worlds are being adopted to help us use brain science, psychology, and cognitive science at home, in school, and in our global economy.

Brain functions and leadership functions are similar. Brains and leaders both need to know where they are, where they may go, whether they are going in the right direction, how to get there, and how to remember the experiences to apply them in the future.

Humans have brains to help them plan and move. Understanding the brain means understanding yourself, your loved ones, and the people with whom you work. As scientists continue to study the brain (and they have a very long way to go), you'll get more information to apply to your life. But caution is key — this complex organ continually surprises researchers. The famous quote by Lyal Watson, the South African biologist who wrote *Supernature,* says, "If the brain were so simple we could understand it, we would be so simple we couldn't."

In this chapter you find out about the structures of the brain, their functions, and the ways they work together.

Organization: The Business of Business and the Business of the Brain

As a leader, you have to take care of what goes on within your business and what goes on outside your business — that is, your employees and their work on the inside and your customer service, sales, and satisfaction on the outside. Your brain also has internal control centers as well as external controls. Just as you organize and coordinate what is happening inside and outside in order to make the best decisions and act on necessary problems and situations, your brain coordinates internal messages about what's going on within your body as it monitors external information in order to respond in an appropriate way. Both leaders and brains must be experts at executing appropriate actions and reactions.

Starting at the bottom

Some neuroscientists talk about the brain's organization from the top down, while others like to start at the bottom. The bottom of the brain consists of the brain stem and the cerebellum, along with a few smaller structures. The pons and the medulla run your body, keeping you breathing and your heart beating. For the most part, the bottom of the brain runs on an involuntary system. Like the inner workings of most companies, these processes are expected and go unnoticed unless something goes wrong.

Executive functions take place in the top layer of the brain, the *cortex*. There decisions are made, planning is completed and executed, and challenges are addressed. Like the orchestra leader, the top of your brain keeps all of the pieces playing together to create a masterpiece. Similarly, leaders, senior leadership teams, and employees work together to address the needs and desires of the organization.

Moving forward to make connections

The four lobes of the brain are arranged so that the sensory lobes are located in the back of the brain. As you look at the words on this page, the occipital lobe in the back of your brain takes in that information. Then those words are brought forward in the brain to the frontal lobes, where the information is defined and you determine the meaning of those words. Perhaps they are a call to action or you make a connection between those words and information you have previously stored in memory. The temporal lobes hold onto the new information and link it with the old.

Left, right, left (hemispheres)

According to Elkhonon Goldberg, clinical professor of neurology at New York University School of Medicine, as new information enters the brain through the sensory lobes in the back and then is brought forward for thoughtful reflection, your brain decides which hemisphere is going to first process it. Familiarity and novelty come in to play now. If the information is novel, it is processed by the right hemisphere, which is organized to deal with novel challenges in order to come up with a creative response. When the information is familiar — a challenge that the brain has responded to before and now has an established routine in which to deal with — the left hemisphere first processes it.

At some point, both hemispheres are involved in responding to incoming stimuli. Just as in the reading example above, information starts in one hemisphere and then is moved to the other. Both hemispheres contribute to cognitive processing. In your organization, you have departments or teams for established routines, but when novel challenges arise, you probably have specialized teams or the senior leadership team to deal with the challenge first.

Separating the Mind from the Brain

Some people compare the brain to a computer. Although this is not a very accurate analogy, the correlations are helpful when talking about the mind and the brain. If the brain is the hardware, then the mind is the software.

Does the brain matter?

The brain is often described as your gray matter. *Gray matter* refers to the top layer of the brain. This layer isn't actually gray but brownish-pink while it's alive, but its name comes from preserved brains. Brains that have been preserved and sliced for research purposes look as though the tissue around the outside of the brain is gray, and the inner lining appears white.

Separating gray matter and white matter helps with some understanding of brain function. The gray matter consists of the neuron cell bodies in the brain, and the white matter is made up of the cells' nerve fibers that are coated with a white fatty substance called *myelin*. Myelin assists in the transmission of information in the brain.

The mind is what the brain does

Neuroscientist Susan Greenfield, theorizes that the mind may be the "personalization" of the brain. According to many researchers, the brain's functions, such as feeling, thoughts, problem-solving, and communicating create the mind. But the mind also constructs the brain. The feelings, thoughts, experiences, and memories that build that personal mind also change the structure and the function of the brain.

As you read this book, your brain is changing. Brain cells are organizing themselves to take in this information, consider the importance, and then decide whether to dispose of or keep the learning.

In this book, I refer to the organ of learning as the brain as many neuroscientists have chosen to do. Some call it the mind/brain, but I consider brain more active than mind. In making this decision, I created networks that automatically cause me to refer to the mind/brain as the brain without giving any thought to the decision. If I focus on changing that pattern in my brain, I would consciously have to try for several weeks before I fully adopted the change, but I would be able to change my brain . . . or change my mind, if I wanted to!

Discovering the Chemicals and Structures that Power Your Brain

You ask your team leader what new sales techniques were taught at the regional meeting. You have caught him a little off guard in the elevator without his notes. Watching closely, you see his brain working. His right hemisphere processes this novel challenge. He imagines himself back at the meeting. He pictures the room and the trainer. In his mind, he sees the trainer demonstrating the strategy. The left hemisphere takes over as he remembers the process. "Oh, yes!" he thinks to himself. He looks at you and begins to share what he learned. His brain was making connections. He found the information by tracing his steps and thinking about locations and events. The connections had been made at the meeting, and so by visualizing the meeting room, he found triggers to reconnect to those networks he had set up in his brain.

The upcoming sections explain how your brain makes connections and processes information.

Neurons old and new

Brain structures are made up of cells that continually interconnect with other brain cells — even at night while you sleep. The brain learns by making connections among brain cells. The brain cells attributed with learning are called *neurons.* You are born with about 100 billion neurons, and most of them stay with you throughout your life.

The brain also includes cells called *glia,* or *glial cells.* Glia actually means glue, and in some instances holding things together is what they do. Glia are sometimes called housekeepers or nurturing cells. Not long ago, glia were believed to have nothing to do with actual learning, but recent research supports that indeed glia may perform some important functions for making connections and retrieving memories. Your brain has about ten times more glial cells than neurons.

Twenty years ago the widely held thought was that the brain produces no new neurons. Studies suggest that under certain conditions, the brain does produce more of these cells. Throughout our lives we lose neurons for a variety of reasons, and so replacing some of them seems to make sense. The process of creating new neurons is called *neurogenesis.* If you're interested in stimulating this process in your brain, try learning something new, exercising, and avoiding stress.

Your brain works by communicating among neurons. Each neuron has three main parts: dendrites, the cell body, and an axon. (See Figure 2-1.) Communication happens like this:

1. **The axon in the sending neuron releases a chemical messenger to convey information.**

2. **The sending neuron moves the chemical messenger through its dendrites, and the amount of electricity within the cell body changes.**

3. **Electricity travels down the axon.**

    Most axons are coated with a substance called myelin. Glial cells within myelin aid in transmission of messages.

4. **The electrical impulse forces chemicals called neurotransmitters out of the vesicle and through the end of the axon into a space called a *synapse*.**

5. **Neurotransmitters swim in the synapse until they find a dendrite of another neuron to attach themselves to.**

6. **The process begins again.**

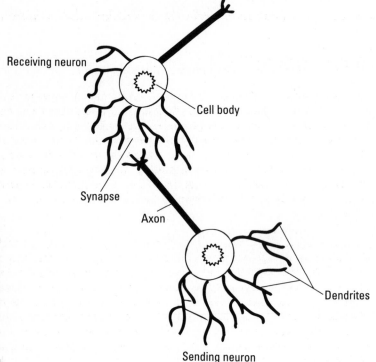

Figure 2-1:
Messages
travel
through
neurons via
neurotrans-
mitters.

As you use your brain for learning, socializing, and generally taking in information from different sources, your neurons change. Dendrites grow as you learn. When you are born some neurons have few or no dendrites. As your brain begins taking in information, dendrites grow. Your axons change, as well. As neurons are used, axon terminals begin to grow to send out more messages.

The visual system is one of the better understood systems in the brain. When a baby begins to see, the visual part of her brain stores the patterns she sees. Neurons connect to form a pattern like her mother's face. The baby begins with a fuzzy outline, and as her vision continues to develop fine points such as eyebrows and nostrils are added until her brain stores the complete picture.

New brain, new tricks?

At a presentation on the brain, a neuroscientist was explaining that the brain is the only organ that doesn't replace all its cells. Our bodies replace other cells every few days or months. You get brand new skin, but your new skin looks like the old skin because of your genetic blue-print. Your brain, however, does not replace cells at that rate. What would happen, the neuroscientist asked, if your brain did?

A reply came from the back of the room, "Well, I guess you could hide your own Easter eggs!"

Neuroplasticity

Your thoughts can change your brain. That's a pretty impressive statement, and worthy of explanation. Your thoughts and your actions can change the structure and function of your brain. Going back to the computer analogy, the brain is not as hard-wired as was once thought. The process of changing the brain is called *neuroplasticity*. Scientists shorten that by saying the brain is plastic. In response to the environment, neurons change their activity and reorganize pathways. Neuroplasticity occurs throughout the normal development of the brain and for adaptive purposes when the brain tries to repair after an injury.

The brain's plasticity enables you to learn and remember. Perhaps you decide to learn how to play bridge. You have played other card games before, and so your brain contains *networks* (neurons that have connected to each other) for basic card information: 52 cards in a deck, four different suits, two red, two black, and the numbering system for each. As you learn to play the new game, your brain connects the rules to your previously stored card networks. Learning the new game is therefore much easier for you than for someone who has never played cards before and has no card networks. As you continue to learn bridge, your card networks grow and your brain changes.

Better living through brain chemistry

Chemicals that the brain produces are called *neurotransmitters*. These are the messengers that go between the sending neuron and the receiving neuron. Neurons exchange neurotransmitters to communicate with each other. They do their job at the synapse by either causing a neuron to fire or preventing the firing. (*Firing* is the word given to the action of a neuron when it is activated to send a message to another neuron.) Some of the neurotransmitters are *excitatory* — that is, they cause the neuron to fire when they attach themselves to the dendrites. Other neurotransmitters are *inhibitory* and keep the neuron from firing. A large number of different excitatory and inhibitory neurotransmitters are in involved in the decision to fire or not to fire. If more excitatory than inhibitory neurotransmitters attach themselves to the neuron, the neuron fires and sends the message on.

When neurons fire together, they are said to *wire* together. The more often a message is sent through a network, the faster and stronger that wired network becomes. If you go back to the bridge analogy, as you continue to take lessons and practice how to count the number of points in the hand you're dealt, the stronger the network that is set up for counting points becomes. Think of any task or skill that you have learned. You started out slowly and tentatively, but as you learned and practiced you got better.

Dozens of neurotransmitters have been identified. For the purpose of this book, only a few are important. I tell you about them in Table 2-1.

Table 2-1:	Common Neurotransmitters
Neurotransmitter	*Function*
Acetylcholine	Used to operate muscle movements; plays a critical role in memory
Dopamine	Released as part of the reward system in the brain as well as to control muscle movements; assists with focus
Endorphins	Brain and body's natural painkiller; known to cause the "runner's high"; laughing, social contacts, and music encourage the release of this chemical
Norepinephrine	Sometimes called noradrenaline; acts in our brains the way adrenaline acts in the body; affects moods; serves as major alert chemical for the stress response
Serotonin	Assists in transmission of messages; enhances mood; calms

Chemical messengers determine your moods, behavior, and what you remember. The foods that you eat, the activities in which you participate, your relationships, whether you love your job, your co-workers, and your life all determine the chemical balance of your brain. Yes, some genetics play a role in this as well. For instance, low levels of serotonin resulting in anxiety or depression may be related to some genetic factors. Some research suggests that eating right and exercising can increase those levels and you may be one of the lucky depressives who can control your feelings without drugs. However, anti-depressants do save lives both literally and figuratively. Some people have difficulty maintaining a normal chemical balance. Only you and a professional can determine your needs.

How the brain loves

Oxytocin is a hormone that acts as a neurotransmitter in the brain. Along with the chemical phenyethylamine, oxytocin and dopamine give you the feelings of excitement, passion, or euphoria when you're falling in love, whether you're experiencing a crush on someone you hope will become your significant other or falling in love with your new baby.

You may have witnessed an office romance or attraction that affects your employees' focus and concentration. Or perhaps one of your workers falls in love and you observe more of a desire to get work done and go spend time with this person. Sometimes love makes a worker better at the job and easier to get along with. Happiness can have that affect. If the romance matures, less of the "love chemicals" are released, but the good feeling remains. If the relationship ends suddenly, and your employee gets dumped, the feelings of despair cause a sudden depletion in the love chemicals and may cause a problem in the office. You may want to give the employee some time to regain a chemical balance. As a leader, knowing how the chemical system works in such situations may help you be more understanding of both types of situations.

From rocky roads to superhighways

As networks of neurons are set up via their chemical messengers, they initially are slow and sometimes clumsy. An assembly line at any factory begins in the same fashion. Perhaps you remember the *I Love Lucy* episode in which Lucy and Ethel work at a candy factory. After the candy is chocolate-coated a conveyor belt brings the candy to Lucy and Ethel. They are to take each piece, wrap it in paper, and then place the wrapped candy back on the belt for the next destination, where it will be boxed for shipment.

Having total focused attention is a must for this type of work, and the Lucy character is anything *but* focused. She wraps the first few pieces of candy and thinks she is doing a great job. The manager sees that Lucy and Ethel are doing well and turns up the speed on the conveyor belt. Lucy desperately tries to wrap the candy but ends up eating the pieces, hiding them, and even putting them down her uniform to get rid of enough so that she can wrap a few to send on their way. Ethel performs the same ridiculous actions.

Lucy never developed the opportunity to set up a strong network in her brain for wrapping candy quickly. Her initial network was working but hadn't had enough time to gain strength through repetition. Her candy-wrapping network was similar to a trail just being blazed to become a road. The path is overgrown and rocky, but eventually with enough traffic it begins to get smooth. As more and more people use the road, more lanes are necessary to keep up with the demand. Eventually such a busy road becomes a superhighway. Our everyday habits and procedures began in this rock fashion but became smooth and speedy with repetition. They turn into superhighways where connections are made in milliseconds.

Starting the day

You awaken at 6 a.m. to the sound of your alarm clock. Norepinephrine is released in your brain to make you get up and go. You jump out of bed and dress for your morning run. Before you leave, you grab a protein bar because you know your brain does not store energy and you want to run on more than just fumes. You fill your water bottle so you can keep your brain and body hydrated, and you step outside. The day is warm and wonderful, and as you breathe in deeply dopamine is released in your brain as you look forward to some great exercise. As you run, endorphins are slowly released in your brain. You begin to experience the "runner's high" as your somewhat stressed body begins to feel no pain. You finish your run at about 7:10 a.m. feeling good because the exercise also caused more dopamine to be released, not only in your reward pathway but also in your frontal lobe. This release helps you keep better focus throughout the day. After a shower, you dress for work and as you admire yourself in the mirror and feel good about your accomplishment, your brain releases serotonin. After eating a breakfast of fruit, yogurt, and steel-cut oatmeal, you head to the office satisfied with your accomplishments thus far and looking forward to a productive day.

The result would have been different for Lucy and Ethel if the leadership in the candy factory had trained its employees properly. Training creates the correct connections and provides practice so that employees know how to respond.

Use it or lose it

Blooming and *pruning* refer to the processes that go on in the brain in which neurons develop new connections while losing others.

This organ, which keeps us alive by regulating our heartbeat and respiratory system, is constantly active. Connections are being made even while we sleep. Neurons are firing all of the time, albeit more slowly some of the time.

Imagine that a baby's brain has formed a pattern for recognizing the baby's mother. And then the baby's mother is not around for a long period of time. The network that was set up in the baby's visual system would not be activated, and that pattern would slowly fade. The neurons used for that pattern may be recruited to be used for another pattern, and slowly the mother's face pattern would be disassembled. The dendrites would be pruned away. The synapses disappear, and the baby would no longer recognize Mommy.

Keeping your brain forever young

Dr. David Snowdon of the University of Kentucky discovered an order of nuns living in Mankato, Minnesota, who lived to a very ripe old age. Many were in their nineties or older when they died. Snowdon autopsied the nuns' brains and discovered a lot about the brain from this work.

For example, one of the nuns who died was in her late nineties. She watched television shows like *Jeopardy!* and answered a lot of the questions. She gardened and interacted with the other nuns and seemed quite happy, and although she had a few memory lapses, seemed to be really "with it."

Snowdon was amazed when he had the opportunity to look at her brain. It was riddled with Alzheimer's and literally fell apart when he began his work on it. Judging from her behavior, no one would have ever guessed that she had this disease. It appeared that aging well was associated with living a healthy lifestyle and keeping the brain active. Snowdon's study offers insight into what can hold off or mask the symptoms of the disease. Things like college education and an active intellectual life create an overabundance of connections that allows for the loss of some without marked changes in behavior.

As your brain ages, areas that aren't in use begin to atrophy, in other words, waste away. This is particularly true in those who have not kept their brains active. Atrophy also tends to happen earlier for males. For this reason new learning is very important to continue to keep your brain active throughout your life. The more connections you have, the more you can lose before symptoms of dementia or Alzheimer's manifest themselves. In other words, the more paths you have to a destination, the more options you have when there are detours.

Brain science tells us that we can design our own brains. The fact that the choices you make affect your brain's structure and function puts a great deal of responsibility on you. (However, you can't control everything, and certainly not cognitive problems arising from stroke or disease.) Not only are you responsible for your own brain, but you may also be responsible for the brains of others. Are you providing stimulation for your employees? You want them to have good brains. Productivity and success hinge on the brains in your organization being at their optimal levels.

Three Brains in One: How Your Brain Combines its Tasks

Imagine a fragile gelatinous mass of tissue filled with brain cells, blood, oxygen, and nutrients determining your future. This collection of brain matter, which makes you who you are, can be divided into three parts with separate structures and functions that together comprise one brain.

The survival brain

The most primitive part of the brain includes several structures that serve the purpose of keeping you alive. Some literature simply refers to this brain area as the *brain stem,* but you may also read about it as the *lower brain,* the *survival brain,* or even the *reptilian brain.* (Take a look at the brain stem and other brain structures in Figure 2-2.) These nicknames may have arisen because the survival brain doesn't think; it responds in a reflexive manner. Nor does this brain feel; the emotional brain is connected to the brain stem but not part of it.

Some researchers suggest that the brain stem and the amygdala in the limbic brain are really the decision-makers of the brain even though both are primitive structures. The survival brain meets the basic needs of the body. Below are the definitions of several structures that make up the survival brain:

- ✔ The **pons** regulates respiration and relays sensory information between lower levels and upper levels of the brain.
- ✔ The **medulla oblongata** regulates heart rate and blood pressure
- ✔ The **reticular formation** or reticular activating system is brain's first filter and alerts the brain to changes in the environment.

This primal structure, the RAS, receives all of the sensory input from your world. And as the brain's first filter, the decision is made by this structure whether information reaches higher levels in your brain.

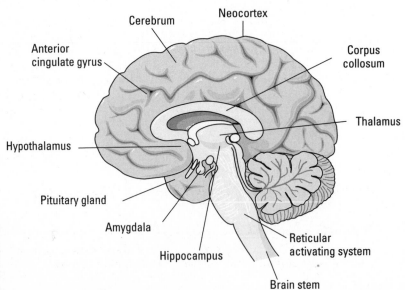

Figure 2-2:
Structures
of the brain

The reticular activating system: Your brain's decider

Some researchers believe that hundreds of billions of bits of information are available to the senses every second. The brain can process only a few thousand of those bits, and so the reticular activating system (RAS) decides what your brain attends to. This survival brain structure makes these decisions based on your needs and desires. If you're sitting at the airport waiting for your delayed flight, you find the area noisy as passengers mill around waiting for their flights. Perhaps you pull out a book to read while you wait. As you open *The Leadership Brain For Dummies,* you feel that your attempt at concentration will be futile as the noise level continues to increase with each plane that is delayed. Amazingly though, after five or ten minutes you're totally engrossed in your book and don't even realize where you are until you hear your flight called. Your RAS has filtered out the extraneous noise. That sound of the flight number and destination are wired into your survival brain because you really want to get to your destination. Your amazing reticular activating system allows only this information to enter your brain and change your focus. Had the loud speaker called your name, you would have responded just as quickly.

As sensory information enters the brain in the form of sight, sound, taste, smell, and touch, the reticular activating system, or RAS, filters out unnecessary information. For instance, you don't notice how your feet feel inside your shoes unless they hurt. The reticular activating system can't absorb all of the incoming sensory information; it also won't pay attention to input that doesn't affect survival, isn't novel, or is just plain boring. This filter is why getting through to others is not always easy.

Your reticular activating system is programmable. You sometimes program it unconsciously. Think about that car you fall in love with on the showroom floor when you take your old car in for service. It's a beauty — shiny, red, great mileage, beautiful black leather interior. You want that car! As you drive around the city for the next several days, you keep seeing "your" bright red car. You have programmed your RAS to notice that car. You never realized how many people own your dream car. One of two things can now occur:

✔ You get so tired of seeing that red car that your brain habituates and the car blends in with all of the other cars; it's not so special because there are so many of them.

✔ The excitement builds each time you see the car, and you want it even more!

Eventually, your higher level brain gets involved, and you weigh the practical side of the matter. Perhaps you can afford the car and buy it, or you see that the time is not right for a new car and let go of the desire.

The survival brain's reticular activating system has the following functions:

- ✔ Regulating wakefulness and sleep.

- ✔ Constantly scanning the environment for change. If incoming information appears to be threatening, the brain stem releases molecules of the neurotransmitter norepinephrine to prepare the brain for the stress response.

- ✔ Keeping you sane. (It tries, anyway.) If you didn't have this filter, you would be bombarded with sensory input that would eventually make you crazy.

The emotional brain

The Tin Man in *The Wizard of Oz* lamented that he needed a heart. The seat of emotions, however, is located in the middle part of the brain called the *limbic system.* The limbic system, or limbic brain, is often called the emotional brain, but it does much more than deal with emotions. This brain includes the following important structures (see Figure 2-2):

- ✔ The *amygdala* is an almond-shaped structure that is the brain's second filter. It helps store emotional memories. The memories themselves are stored elsewhere in the brain at higher levels, but the amygdala is said to catalog those emotional memories.

- ✔ The **hippocampus,** a seahorse-shaped structure, helps form long-term factual memories. Both *semantic* (or word-based) memories and *episodic* (event or autobiographical) memories are cataloged in this structure.

- ✔ The **thalamus** is the relay station for various kinds of memories. The thalamus sends visual memories to the visual part of the brain and auditory memories to the auditory section. It is sometimes described as the brain structure in charge of external information.

- ✔ The **hypothalamus** is in charge of internal information; it helps regulate temperature, hunger, thirst, sex drive, and so on.

- ✔ **Basal ganglia** are a group of structures that partially surround the thalamus; the basal ganglia, regulate, initiate, and terminate voluntary movement and emotion.

Because the brain has two hemispheres, each of these structures found deep in the brain (except for the basal ganglia) has a twin. One resides in the right hemisphere and one resides in the left hemisphere.

The hippocampus and the amygdala are directly related to memory. Because they're right next to each other in the brain, storing emotional content that is also factual in long-term memory is easy for them.

The amygdala is so connected in the brain that when it receives a strong emotion, it sends out chemical signals throughout the brain — in a sense saying, "This is important information that must be remembered for survival." The hippocampus gets this information at almost the same time that the amygdala does.

The hippocampus remembers factual information, and the amygdala remembers emotional information. So the hippocampus knows who your best customer is, and your amygdala knows whether you like her or not.

Information that has been accepted through the reticular activating system's filter must pass through the amygdala, which is often thought of as the center of the limbic system or *limbic brain*. This is the second of the three brains, sometimes referred to as the gatekeeper, because it connects the lower and upper brain.

The amygdala is very responsive to fear and threat and will start a stress response under any threatening condition. The stress response was originally set up in the brain to respond to very real physical threats like lions and tigers and bears. (Oh, my!) In the 21st century, however, one person's stressor may be another person's pleasure. Your very dear friend may be thrilled at the prospect of climbing Mt. Everest while your heart races at the very thought of taking an elevator to the top floor of a building.

The stress response includes a rise in heart rate, rapid respiration, pupil dilation, dry mouth, and upset stomach. The stress response can be brutal and damaging to brain and body. As your brain prepares for the stressor, your heart rate increases to get blood pumping to the correct areas: to your hands to fight or to your legs to flee. Your stomach upset is due to digestion coming to a screeching halt. The blood you needed to digest your food is sent to the extremities, as well. (Why digest breakfast if you may *be* breakfast?) Your heavy breathing gets oxygen where your body needs it. Hope that your immune system isn't fighting any infections or disease because that process is going to stop as well. No need to worry about disease if you aren't going to make it anyway! And your reproductive system may not be functioning at full potential either. Can't worry about reproduction at a time like this.

The emotional brain filters and makes some decisions based strictly on emotional input and prior emotional experiences. Sometimes it takes the low road and causes chaos when it may not be necessary. The emotional brain is powerful and helpful, but it's not always wise.

Caught in the rough

Jim's best client has been bugging him to golf at the country club. Jim likes to golf and has gone with Ralph on several occasions, but this Saturday Jim had planned to golf with the old gang from the technology department. Jim knew if he told Ralph he was golfing with someone else that he would sulk until Jim invited him along. But this time Jim begged off by telling Ralph he simply had some things he needed to get done and they would go to the club another time. Jim arranged with the tech guys to go to a golf course about twenty miles away in a small community and set the tee time for 7 a.m. Ralph would be sleeping in for sure. And Jim was right. Ralph slept in. Jim forgot about Ralph's wife, Stella. She played in a nine-hole league that traveled around to play at different courses.

Jim didn't even think about the possibility of running into Stella until he was on the ninth hole and heard some females speed by on their way to the clubhouse. A blonde woman waved to Jim and said hello while the brunette next to her stared straight ahead. Can that be Stella? Jim's mind raced to remember exactly what she looked like. "Oh, boy, am I in trouble," he thought. "She must know Ralph wanted to golf with me because she sure gave me the cold shoulder." Jim's heart started racing just as his brain started searching for a way out of this mess. "Maybe she didn't see me or recognize me and that's why she didn't look at me," he thought. "She wouldn't expect to see me here."

As he walked up to tee off, his mouth was dry and his hands were unsteady. He swung his club and missed the ball. His buddies chuckled. His second attempt got the ball in the fairway, but Jim's mind was scrambling. He had to find out whether he had really seen Stella, and if she had really seen him. Jim's next swing hooked to the right and he ended up in the rough. It took him two shots to get out and he ended up chipping his ball into a water hazard. His foursome was shocked. Jim finally made up an excuse that he didn't feel well and left his foursome and went home. On the drive he tried to come up with excuses for Ralph. The entire weekend he played over and over in his head how the next meeting with Ralph would go.

Monday morning rolled around and Jim had a standing appointment at Ralph's place of business. Sheepishly, Jim walked in to Ralph's office ready for whatever grief Ralph would dish out and hoping that an excuse that the in-laws came to town and he had to take them golfing may smooth things over. Ralph smiled when Jim entered, stood up, and shook his hand. "I had a great weekend, Jim. I'm glad we decided not to play golf. Stella convinced me that we needed some time away, and took a quick trip to Vegas for the weekend. I won $1,000!" Jim grinned and heaved a sigh of relief. He realized that he had ruined his golf game and his whole weekend over something that had never really happened.

The amygdala is sometimes called the affective filter. It can keep the brain from thinking at high levels. Information stops in the emotional brain if incoming data is too emotional or if the brain already is in an overemotional state. Emotions are double-edged: Too little emotion finds the brain dropping some factual information because of boredom or insignificance, but too much emotion and the brain can't send information up to the higher level.

The thinking brain

When looking at the thinking brain, you can see its lobes, their locations, and their functions. (See Figure 2-3.) The topmost layer of the brain is called the *neocortex,* or gray matter. It is about one-quarter to one-eighth inch thick and consists of the neurons' cell bodies. The neocortex is about the size of a large dinner napkin and so is folded in the skull. Beneath it is the white matter, also part of the thinking brain, it consists of those myelin-coated axons that send and receive messages from the top down and bottom up of the brain.

The two sets of four lobes of the brain have different functions:

- ✔ **Occipital lobe:** Located in the back of the brain behind the parietal and temporal lobes, this lobe is responsible for receiving and processing visual information.

- ✔ **Parietal lobe:** Located at the back of the top of your head, this lobe processes sensory information as well as spatial awareness and perception.

- ✔ **Temporal lobe:** Located on the sides of your head above your ears, this lobe processes some speech, hearing, and memory.

- ✔ **Frontal lobe:** Located at the front of the top of your head, this lobe is responsible for decision-making, planning, judgment, and creativity.

As long-term memories form, parts of each memory are stored in various lobes. Visual memory is stored in the occipital lobe, auditory memories in the temporal lobe, and so on. Where the temporal and parietal lobes meet in the left hemisphere is a structure called *Wernicke's area.* This is the brain's mental lexicon filled with all of the words and definitions that you know. The frontal lobe holds another speech center called *Broca's area.* Here your brain puts sentences together and activates the motor cortex, a strip on the top of your head that controls movements involved in articulate speech. A pathway connects the two structures.

Notice in the figure the small structure at the bottom of the brain, beneath the occipital lobe. This is the *cerebellum,* which coordinates movement. Research is discovering that the cerebellum is a navigator of sorts for muscle movement and assists in navigating thought processes.

The frontal lobe is the last area of the brain to develop. It may keep maturing through your mid-twenties, which means that you may not acquire some higher-level skills until then, either. The frontal lobe is the only structure in the brain that can control emotions. It acts as a damper for the more primitive emotions of the amygdala.

The frontal lobe also contains a composition of neurons called the *prefrontal cortex.* Here is the true executive of the brain. It is probably the most interconnected structure in the brain as it must receive information from all other areas and send out commands to them, just as a leader needs to communicate with all of her subordinates.

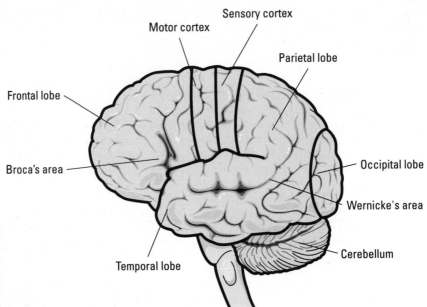

Figure 2-3:
The parts of
the thinking
brain.

Thinking through three levels

Information entering the brain moves through its three levels as follows:

1. **New information enters the survival brain through the senses, which include sight, smell, touch, taste, and sound.**

2. **The information is received in the brain stem and must pass through the reticular activating system, the first filter in the brain.**

3. **If the brain stem sends the information higher in the brain, it enters the limbic system, or the emotional brain.**

4. **The thalamus begins to relay the sensory information, and the amygdala filters the information for emotional content and for emotional memories.**

5. **Non-emotional information enters the hippocampus, which sends the information to the prefrontal lobe storage areas and other executive function locales (the thinking brain) to be examined for connections to prior knowledge.**

   If the brain has prior knowledge of the new information, the brain sends it back to the hippocampus, where new and old information are related.

6. **Finally, the new memory formed from combining the new information and the old information is sent back to storage areas in the neocortex.**

The thinking brain is what separates us from other animals. The ability to plan ahead, make decisions, organize, and control our impulses is at the core of human brain development.

Thinking about thinking

Being able to stop, reflect, and think about how you're thinking is a remarkable gift that enables the brain to monitor how it is doing and then change according to its needs. As a leader, you use this strategy most of the time. When you encounter problems anywhere within your organization, you must think about what's happening and make changes.

Your job is to not only take care of existing business, current employees, and present practices, your job is also to create. Creativity is part of the function of the prefrontal cortex. This is the area of the frontal lobe located right behind your forehead.

Perhaps your creativity led you to your leadership position. Possibly you have made changes in your business to create more business or better products that benefit your community, your society, or your world. Some scientists believe that by exercising your prefrontal lobe you open yourself to more creativity. One of the ways to exercise this area is to learn new things. Take some of your business ideas and apply them in another way or to another field. Keeping your brain active and connected keeps it open to new ideas and original concepts.

Two Brain Hemispheres, Two Ways of Working

The specialization of the brain's two hemispheres plays an important role in information processing. Although the hemispheres have separate functions, if you were born with only one hemisphere or had to have a hemisphere removed at a young age, the remaining hemisphere would take over most of the functions of the other.

Your two hemispheres are connected by a band of fibers called the *corpus callosum.* This large structure consists of axons that are coated with myelin and send information from one side of the brain to the other. Between 200 million and 250 million fibers connect the two hemispheres.

When novel challenges arise in your business, you and your leadership team process the information and create answers by using your right-hemisphere functions. This doesn't mean that you won't be using your left hemisphere as well; humans are whole-brained. In the same fashion, your left hemisphere responds to familiar challenges. Leaders also lead with their left hemisphere when confronted with challenges for which they've already established responses.

Some people naturally use more right- or left-hemisphere-directed thinking when approaching their lives.

Leading with your right: Novel challenges

To deal with novelty, your brain

- ✔ Thinks about the information holistically
- ✔ Focuses on the big picture
- ✔ Considers both pleasant and unpleasant aspects
- ✔ Considers gut feelings
- ✔ Synthesizes the information
- ✔ Uses its interconnectivity to gather information from other areas through its white matter

In addition, when receiving information from others, your brain notes the prosody and tone of the speaker, and it reads body language and gestures.

Intuition is said to be part of the function of the right hemisphere. As it interprets information it deals with the bigger picture — the forest rather than the trees.

If your leadership style uses more right-hemisphere-directed approaches, you most likely do some of the following:

- ✔ Present your vision in a graphic manner
- ✔ Use and respond to body language
- ✔ Gesture when you speak
- ✔ Speak metaphorically
- ✔ Prefer the picture rather than the thousand words

Leading with your left: Familiar challenges

Your left hemisphere has different functions from your right. Because it responds to familiar challenges and responds with routines that have previously been established, it will

- ✔ Function in a logical manner
- ✔ Check for details

✔ Analyze the information

✔ Review the sequence of the routine

✔ Use its gray matter to choose the appropriate routine

Left-hemisphere oriented leaders listen to facts, numbers, and other data. They listen more to the words others say rather than their tone of voice or body language.

If your leadership style lends itself more toward left-hemisphere-directed approaches you may

✔ Present information to employees and clients in a logical, sequential manner

✔ Share your vision in words

✔ Include a lot of data

✔ Analyze information and share that in written reports or prepared presentations

✔ Prefer the thousand words rather than the picture

How the hemispheres join forces

The way the hemispheres work is a good metaphor for how leaders plot a course for their organizations. The corpus callosum enables everyone to use both hemispheres, and most of what the brain does requires both even though one hemisphere may be more active than the other. A good leader has employees with different responsibilities, and together they work toward common goals. Like the left hemisphere, the leader makes some employees responsible for keeping the status quo by responding to situations in established ways. Other employees are led to respond more like the right hemisphere when they tackle new situations and create methods of dealing with those.

As novel challenges become more commonplace in the brain, the left hemisphere fine-tunes the process created by the right hemisphere. In reality, they both receive the information simultaneously, but because the left hemisphere has no immediate answer it awaits instruction from the right.

The brain moves you through time and space. The right hemisphere gives you the ability to think about where you are and where you want to be. The left hemisphere examines what occurred in the past, what is happening right now, and how it will affect the future.

The right person for the job

Edgar is the leader of his organization. He is a visionary. Edgar speaks in metaphors and paints wonderful verbal pictures for his workforce to help them better understand the goals of their company. Some of his employees say his words are like a melody and his presence usually indicates that exciting things are happening.

One of the nearby universities approached Edgar about becoming a mentor for one of their leadership development students. Edgar thought it was a fine idea, and Tyra was sent to learn from Edgar. With notebook in hand, Tyra arrived ready to write down every move Edgar made. She had heard that his company was productive and successful, and she wanted to learn from the best. When Edgar spoke to his employees, Tyra wrote down his words, and when she had a few minutes alone with her boss, she questioned everything he said. Whenever he or his employees generated new ideas, Tyra wanted to know what made them good. She asked for data to share with her class. The more comfortable she became at the company, the more she questioned motives, rewards, and innovations. She began to drive Edgar crazy. Her body language clearly showed him that she didn't approve of his leadership style. Rather than send her back to her professor, Edgar decided she needed a day as leader. He gave her full rein, and for one day she ran the company. Tyra arrived that day with memos for each employee. Included in the memo was their job description, and she asked that no one deviate from the description. She then asked for reports detailing their productivity from each employee at the end of the day. Tyra spent time in each department detailing system and procedural changes. She thought she was doing a

magnificent job. At the end of the day she met with Edgar.

Edgar wanted to paint Tyra a picture of what she was doing, but he knew that wouldn't sink in to her brain. She's a lefty, he thought to himself. So he approached her with the facts in a logical, sequential manner. He showed her the daily productivity for each person and each department for every day that month. He had that information because he had people just like Tyra taking care of details for him. But they worked covertly. Every employee knew that the reports were made daily from the computer programs, but it wasn't discussed unless it became necessary. When Tyra compared her leadership day's reports to Edgar's, she was astonished. Productivity was down. Innovation had halted. And from comments that were sent to Edgar, motivation was down. After looking over all of the facts, Edgar explained to her that she was trying to run a very tight ship. She was using her left hemisphere functions and not allowing her right hemisphere to get involved. He then had her list the traits that she was working with and compare them to his style. Edgar told her that she may be a great leader one day if she worked on a whole-brain approach. For now, he said, she was managing people and trying to control them with data and procedures. Tyra left that day knowing she was not the "right" person for this leadership position. She knew that she needed to learn more and balance herself more. The left/right hemisphere discussion she had with Edgar was a metaphor for leadership. She realized that Edgar cared more about his workers than he did about the details, which didn't mean he cared any less about the bottom line. In fact, his style was all about success and productivity for everyone.

Chapter 3

Discovering the Elements of Learning and Memory

Current brain research is making the way the brain learns clearer. Knowing how the brain processes information, searches for meaning, seeks novelty, and pays attention offers leaders, trainers, and educators the tools to enhance their own and others' learning.

Ask yourself how business and leadership have changed in the past 50 years. For a shorter list, ask yourself what *hasn't* changed. Change is inevitable, and knowing how the brain learns makes changes faster and easier to process.

This chapter looks at the basic principles of learning. Based on studies, anecdotal evidence, and brain imaging, learning can be easy and should be fun! When it's time for you to learn new skills to keep up with competitors and keep up with your workforce, will you be ready? After you read this chapter, I hope you can answer with an enthusiastic "Yes!"

The Brain Learns through Patterning

The brain seeks patterns that have been previously stored in long-term memory. As you train employees and work with customers, they search for patterns in what you say or experiences they can relate your message to.

As you try to persuade, convince, or simply present information to them, their brains search. You can't convince a customer to buy a hybrid car, for example, if he has no idea what a hybrid is. First, you explain how a car normally runs. As you do, your customer draws on his car experience to understand what you're talking about. As you explain the difference between the normal car and the hybrid, he works from the pattern he just established.

You must help your employee or client find established patterns. You most effectively give them new information by adding to those patterns.

Patterns and schema

As you take a look at Figure 3-1, your brain immediately tries to find a pattern so that you can understand what you see. If I ask you what you see, some of you may say "Pac-Man" because the shapes bring to mind the pattern you have stored of the Pac-Man game icon. If this figure does not bring Pac-Man to mind or if I ask what else you see, you probably say a square or a four-sided object. Is it really there? No. But as your brain tries to make sense of what it sees, invisible lines between the shapes appear in your mind.

A *schema* is an organized unit of information that your brain stores. Patterns form schema. Some people compare brains to filing cabinets. Using that metaphor, a schema is information stored in a file. Within that file is everything you know about something. You have a schema for your organization. In that file you have stored your mission, vision, goals, employees, productivity data, information about your working space, prior experiences at work, and anything else connected to your work.

Figure 3-1:
The brain
seeks
patterns.

Because neuroscience knows a lot about how the brain stores information, imagining that all of this information is stored in one file in your brain is an oversimplification. Each unit of a schema may be stored in a different part of your brain.

For example, as you recall a meeting with an employee, you picture that person's face and body. These units of information are held by networks of neurons. One network holds the image of her face and another her body. You might also have a network that retains what she was wearing. These pictures are stored in the visual cortex at the back of your brain. When you remember what she said, you activate units in the auditory cortex. The conversation during that meeting is stored in yet another area of your brain, and you may have emotional memories of this meeting and other experiences with this employee that are stored in the emotional area of the brain. The networks in each brain area form patterns, and all of these patterns link together when you associate them by recalling the memory.

Neurons that work together form networks. Networks that interact form patterns, and patterns combine to form schema. If you look at a painting, the big picture — the whole of the painting — constitutes a schema; the objects or people in the picture make up patterns, and the patterns are made up of tiny dots networked together.

As you encounter your world, your brain searches for patterns that fit into your schema, your particular view of the many situations you encounter. The different types of schema help you make your way in the world.

Your social schema determines how you behave around people in certain situations. If you receive an invitation to a black-tie dinner in honor of your chairman of the board, your brain immediately brings forth the social schema for this type of occasion. You would arrive on time, dressed in a tux, and behave in a formal manner. If an invitation arrives inviting you to a backyard barbeque, not only would your clothing be different, but your conversations and interactions would be less formal.

You may be creating your leadership schema as you read this book. If you're already a leader, you have a schema embedded in your brain, but by reading, learning, and asking questions, you may change some of the patterns there. As you watched other leaders on your way to this role, you may have adopted patterns that you liked and changed others that you observed did not work well. For instance, if you observed a leader yelling at an employee in front of others, you may have stored that in your brain as a pattern not to include in your own schema. But if you were listened to and viewed as a valuable part of an organization, you probably decided this was a behavior you want to imitate.

Sylvia in two worlds: The family schema

Sylvia is the CFO of an architectural firm that employs over 500 people. When Sylvia walks into a room, people feel her presence. She is charming, warm, and a power to be reckoned with. Under her financial leadership the company has doubled its revenue in the past four years, acquired two other firms, and opened three new offices. Sylvia is currently working on taking the organization overseas and creating a mentoring program for new hires.

Recently Sylvia went back to her hometown to visit her family. At home, you wouldn't recognize the successful, motivated, hardworking woman. She reverted to the "Sylly" that she had always been at her parents' home. In essence, she became a child again. This regression is not at all unusual. Sylvia's role in the family is one who is taken care of, who relies on others, and who gets to relax.

People tend to become the person they need to be for the environment they're in and for those people in the environment.

Making connections

Neuroscience explains that knowledge grows when new neural connections align with those previously stored in memory. Information that relates to your previously stored patterns is easy to connect to the pattern.

The brain likes to think in stories, because the story form helps you fill in gaps. Your brain understands the pattern for stories — they have a beginning, a middle, and an end.

Dreaming gives a good example of your brain creating patterns. You have remnants of a crazy dream, little snippets: grandma in the bathtub, the phone ringing, yourself at work, the family dog barking. As you tell your dream to someone, it often becomes a story: "I was at work when my phone rang. It was my grandma. She was taking a bath and couldn't get the dog to stop barking. I don't know what she expected me to do from work!"

Procedures are a kind of pattern. Perhaps your workday pattern looks like this:

8:15	Arrive at work
8:20	Pick up messages and mail from assistant
8:25	Grab a cup of coffee
8:30	Return e-mail messages
9:00	Meet with team leaders
9:30	Check sales reports from previous day
10:00	Begin day's appointments

Until 10 a.m., you don't have to check your schedule; it is solidly stored as a pattern in your brain. Some patterns are procedures, and human capacity for procedures is strong. If your production team asks for a meeting time with you on Monday mornings, your pattern on Mondays is interrupted. Now you have to add this meeting to your pattern. You may have to rearrange your pattern to fit the production team into your schedule, or you may just change the Monday routine and begin the day's appointments a bit later, say 10:30 or 11. Adding to a pattern on a temporary basis isn't going to change your brain, but because this is a permanent change for Mondays, your brain needs some time to change to the new procedure and store it.

A more major change is on the horizon if, for example, you have to change how you do business. The market is changing. Younger people are interested in your products. You decide to go global. Your marketing is going to be Internet-based. You have to hire tech people who know about advertising and your product. They must be part of the 'Net Generation, young and very tech savvy.

As you look at your business, you may see that your vision, your goals, and perhaps future products from research and development are components that help you create your schema. These help guide you as you redirect your business.

Such a major change requires a whole new way of thinking, which Figure 3-2 illustrates. Your advertising schema consists of print advertising in newspapers and magazines. But your ads aren't paying off. You have a Web site that offers a modest overview of your product, but the site needs an overhaul. Your Web site and print advertising are part of your business schema, and now you begin to connect them more. Any print ads refer customers to your Web site, and your Web site provides links to online print information about the company. You begin to lay down new patterns as you add the Internet ideas that your new global marketing team creates. As you can see from your business schema, you have developed some new connections.

Even if your brain needs to connect opposites, the process works. In fact, the brain likes differences; they provide another way of sorting and organizing information. Knife and fork are stored in your brain under the category "eating utensils." But their differences stand out more than their similarities. One researcher puts it this way: Your brain stores by similarities, but it retrieves by differences. In your schema, you have items that you can sit on — a couch, a chair, a pillow, a bench — and each is stored in a generic group by what it's used for. To recognize one of those items, your brain looks at the item and differentiates it from the others.

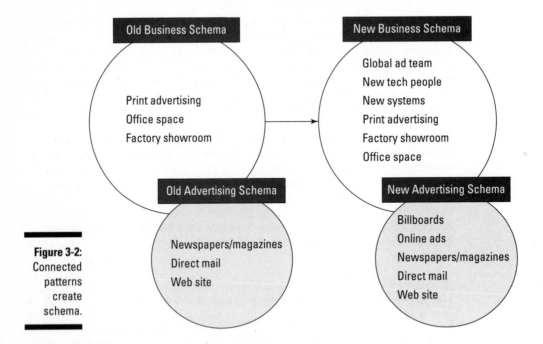

Figure 3-2:
Connected
patterns
create
schema.

The Brain Needs Predictability

Put simply, predictability is knowing what's going to happen next or expecting certain things to occur. Inquiring brains want to know. The brain handles novelty and actually seeks it when it has a framework of predictability. In other words, if your brain is less stressed because you can count on certain predictable events, you can better handle the novel events that may cause some stress. Many schemas begin with expectations. The brain expects certain things to occur; when they don't, the result can be interest — and often is stress.

Making it into the gene pool

If not for the survival skills of our ancestors, you wouldn't be here today. They had to be smart. They had to be strong. They had to know when they were being threatened. In those days there were just two states of being related to predictability: You were being threatened or you weren't. Even if you weren't but thought you were, you reacted as though there were a threat. You responded as though your life depended on it.

Life today is not so different. Your brain reacts quickly to threat. Your amygdala responds first, and your anterior cingulate cortex and your frontal lobe jump in to help. (Turn to Chapter 2 for more about the parts of the brain.) If they get the chance. Sometimes your amygdala is too quick, too scared. You want your amygdala to respond quickly to keep you from danger. If a fast-moving truck rounds the corner as you cross the street, you want your amygdala to act reflexively and make you jump back onto the curb. If you were interested in the color, style, and make of the truck, you would have to wait longer for your reflective frontal lobe and anterior cingulate to provide you with that detailed information. By then, it would be too late to get out of the way.

Even though the threats you face today are different from your ancestors', they still call for decisive responses. All of your experiences provide you with information to best make decisions that keep you alive. Staying in the gene pool relies on your brain's ability to recognize dangers via your amygdala, and make a quick response.

For survival purposes, your brain looks for opportunities to enrich your life. Perhaps becoming a leader is one of those!

Inquiring brains need to know

Stress is a situation, real or imagined, in which the body or brain is overwhelmed. Stress interferes with learning, relating to others, and getting work done. Although the unknown is sometimes exciting, our brains want security. Have you ever attended a meeting without an agenda? Although some meetings can be fun, most are considered obstacles to getting real work done. But without an agenda, how do you know when it's going to be over? How can you plan for the immediate future? These are questions that prey on the brain of anyone who needs predictability.

I was recently part of a training program in Fairbanks, Alaska. It was a wonderful program with a terrific training manual. The week's agenda was placed at the beginning of the manual, but the trainer in charge of the planning forgot to pass out the daily agenda until midmorning. At the end of the day, the trainees had to submit exit cards stating one thing they had learned, one question they had, and one comment. Over 25 percent of the comments were, "The agenda should have been given out at the beginning." The brain needs predictability. You may think that a missing agenda is no cause for alarm; however, new employees and trainees probably enter a training feeling somewhat stressed. Any confusion or irritation compounds that stress.

What happens when the brain doesn't know what's going to happen next? It feels threatened. No lions or tigers or bears here; no real need to feel threatened if you're using your prefrontal cortex and looking at a situation in a logical, thoughtful manner. But when your emotional center (the amygdala and the rest of the limbic system) begins to imagine what horrible things could happen, the stress response kicks in. What do attendees focus on then? Worrying about what is going to happen rather than the content of the meeting or training.

Anytime you can provide an outline, agenda, or other framework for your employees, you lower their stress levels. Knowing what the procedure is going to be gives the brain a feeling of control. Late meetings can be stressful for workers who need to get home to families or have personal plans. An overview of the meeting with a projected ending time can help people focus and contribute more.

The Brain Seeks Meaning

The brain more effectively remembers information and makes connections when an experience is meaningful — when it has clear relevance to your own life. Learning takes place either by connecting new information to old or by having a brand-new experience. Because new real-life experiences are sometimes hard to come by, making meaning through prior knowledge is easier. Your new employees and your veterans can't connect on the same level because the new ones experience more novelty. As a leader, you therefore need to know how to present meaningful information to employees, investors, and customers. This section shows you how to make sure that you powerfully present your vision and mission.

Linking meaning and memory

Making meaning and making sense don't always provide the same response. If I tell you that I'm traveling from a town in West Virginia to a town in Virginia that is only two-and-a-half hours away and I am going to drive the distance rather than fly, that may make sense to you. But is it meaningful? Because the situation doesn't concern you, you probably don't care enough about it to save it in your memory. If information is going to be stored for the long-term, sense is not always enough.

Three levels of understanding exist in the brain:

- ✔ **Sense:** Understood, but not relevant or necessary
- ✔ **Meaning:** Understood and related to something else you know
- ✔ **Personal meaning:** Understood and related to a personal experience

Like the drive to Virginia, making sense isn't always memorable. Imagine yourself walking through the supermarket looking for toilet paper. The first brand you see is called "Toilet Paper." That makes sense. The second brand you see is "Two-Ply Toilet Paper." There may be some meaning there for you because you have found that single-ply is used up too quickly. The next brand, however, hits home. "Soft, Strong Two-Ply Toilet Paper" reminds you that your spouse complained about the toilet paper feeling like sandpaper, and this personal connection may make it the perfect brand for you.

Metaphors and similes are effective tools for injecting meaning. *Metaphors* compare two dissimilar things: She is the rising star in our organization; he plows through his work. *Similes* are comparisons using *like* or *as:* She was as bright as the sun. The beauty of using a metaphor or simile is that it gets to the point and avoids useless or boring information. Your short-term memory can hold only five to seven bits of information at one time, and then for only thirty seconds. Comparing information to something else provides an immediate connection to another pattern and therefore sticks in your brain. The metaphor drives home an idea for your employee or customer to remember, enabling you to strike a note with your listener.

The brain drops any information or experience that isn't meaningful. Some research suggests that the brain forgets or doesn't even pay attention to almost 99 percent of incoming information. You're competing to be part of the 1 percent that your customers' and employees' brains take in!

Sense and senselessness

If experiences aren't meaningful and don't make sense, not only are they easily forgotten, but they can also cause frustration and stress.

Imagine, for example, that Bob goes to his local lawn-equipment store to purchase his first riding lawnmower. As he checks out all the different models, Scott, a young salesman who just attended a two-day sales training on riding lawnmowers asks if he can assist. Bob tells Scott that he's interested in a rider and knows very little about them. Scott unleashes a 30-minute detailed description, telling Bob about hydrostatic drive, PTO, pneumatic deck glide, and individually clutched drive wheels. (This approach is sometimes called the *show-up and throw-up* method of selling.)

Naturally, Bob becomes overwhelmed and is embarrassed to admit he understood only a third of what Scott was saying. Bob thanks Scott for the information and is about to escape when the store owner, who caught the last part of Scott unloading on Bob, steps in to try to save the sale. The owner, Tony, starts by asking Bob about his lawn — how large it is, how many trees and bushes are on it, and whether he gardens. Tony explained to Bob how the hydrostatic drive makes the mower easier to drive forward and backward, how the PTO operates a garden tiller, how the pneumatic deck glide cuts more evenly, and individually clutched drive wheels make trimming around trees a snap. Tony asks whether Bob has any questions or is unclear about any of the features. Tony answers all of Bob's questions and writes up the salvaged sale.

Bob couldn't make sense of Scott's speech about the lawnmower. It might as well have been in a foreign language. Employees need to know when to offer detailed information to customers. Looking for a universal language that all understand is the first priority. Then, if a customer requests technical details, knowing your stuff may make a great deal of difference in making a sale.

The Brain Responds to Novelty

Some researchers describe a *novelty center* in the brain that responds to unusual or surprising circumstances. Initially, information moves to the hippocampus, which helps you form long-term memories. The hippocampus tries to connect the information to a pattern that was previously stored as a long-term memory. When it can't find one, it releases dopamine, the neurotransmitter of pleasure, and causes the amygdala, your primitive emotional center, to react and enhance the memory. Because of the dopamine release that accompanies it, novelty motivates.

The first time the 1984 "Where's the beef?" television commercial aired, viewers were captivated by the little old ladies peering into a giant hamburger bun and grumbling about its meager contents. The second time people viewed the commercial, they stopped to watch and listen. But eventually the novelty wore off; their brains were not as intrigued.

The brain must attend to unusual information because it may be related to your survival. Incoming data spurs the brain to rapidly ask questions like the following:

- Have I seen this before?
- Can I eat it?
- Will it eat me?
- Do I need it?
- Do I want it?
- Can I mate with it?

The answers to those questions determine an action or behavior. (If it's going to eat me, I'm leaving. If I'm going to eat it, let's fire up the grill!) The brain uses prediction to enhance survival. When a pattern enters the brain, the brain calculates what the effect or outcome will be. If the prediction doesn't match, the brain becomes very active and attentive. In other words, the pattern or the schema failed, and the brain wants to know what's going to happen and why. Because the amygdala and the hippocampus are excited, the novel situation has a better chance of being remembered well.

If the brain likes predictability, how can it also like novelty? The brain attends to novelty but doesn't always like it. However, attending to novelty is part of the brain's job. Novelty engages the brain and makes experiences interesting and memorable. Because the brain wants to be engaged, it scans its environment for novel things. Predictability actually has to come first: If you're in a conventional environment, novelty is more tolerable. Stress levels are lower when predictability is in place.

Unexpected behavior stresses employees

Chuck is in a leadership position at a big-box store. He gets along well with everyone. He knows every employee's kids' names, what's going on in their lives, and when they took their last vacation. He really cares about his people and shows it. Everyone in the store appreciates Chuck's interest, and so they generally grant him a little leeway if he isn't always the most organized boss. Because Chuck is so casual and also a very random thinker, he isn't always prepared for his meetings. But he warms everyone up by asking them questions about their personal lives, always has a big grin on his face, and charms them all. They feel safe and secure.

At one of the weekly Monday morning meetings, Chuck walks in silently. No smile. No "Hello, how are you? How are the kids?" This was a Chuck no one had ever seen. He walks to the front of the room where he usually hopped up on the desk and started speaking in his random way. But today he sits behind the desk. The employees are concerned. "Hey, Chuck, whatsamatter?" George asks. "Somebody die?"

Chuck looks up with an evil glance at George, and turns to his audience. He blurts out, "Our sales are so low, we might be closed! What is wrong with you people? Don't you know we have quotas? Don't you know you're not meeting yours? Aren't I good to you?"

When he stops, the entire room is silent. Although some of the employees want to yell back at Chuck, they're trying to figure out why they're being attacked by the boss who is so easygoing. Rather than even thinking about what Chuck has said, they go into a fight-or-flight mode where logical thinking doesn't take place.

Janice is the first to speak. "I thought our meetings were to boost morale. You never gave us quotas. We didn't have any idea sales were down. Our meetings were always about solving little problems, changing schedules, and new hires. Why didn't you tell us?"

The predictable store leader surprised his employees with uncharacteristic behavior. Because he didn't begin his meeting in the usual way and instead began to attack his people, they became defensive. The novel behavior caused them more stress than necessary. If Chuck explains the seriousness of the situation without throwing out unexpected and hurtful questions, he's going to get the behavior from his employees that he needs rather than defensive looks and thoughts.

The Brain Needs Repetition

The fortunate part of speaking about the brain to audiences is that if you repeat yourself and realize it, you simply follow it with "Repetition is good for the brain!" And that is so true. And that is so true.

If you want to store information for the short-term, like a phone number, you repeat it until you can write it down or get it programmed into your phone. Long-term memory requires more repetition and connections to other information already in your brain. Repetition sounds boring, but it doesn't have to be.

Learning to remember

The brain is better at forgetting than remembering. In fact, some researchers say that the brain is programmed to forget. It lets go of trivial or no longer relevant information to make space for more important information.

Temporary memory is divided into two types:

- ✔ **Sensory/immediate memory** is the shortest and allows only seconds for recognition of incoming sensory information. If sensory memory acknowledges the receipt of the information, then the immediate memory process begins. Immediate memory allows you about 30 seconds to hang on to the fragile memory. You can do so by repeating the information to yourself (verbal memory) or you may create a picture of it (visual memory). If the information then can be attached to some previously stored patterns, the working memory process takes over.

- ✔ **Working memory,** a short-term memory process, takes information from sensory memory and can hold onto it for hours, days, and even months. But working memory, as its name suggests, requires work. The brain must engage with the information. For example, if you have just received the new commission rate for selling your product, you might do some calculating to find out how much you can make on each unit sold. Calculating is a working memory process. After you work this formula repeatedly, it becomes a long-term memory.

You form long-term memories through repetition. Rote repetition, just repeating things over and over in the same way, is not a good way to get most information into long-term memory. Elaborating on the information and repeating it in various formats makes storing the information in your brain much easier and more enjoyable.

Rehearsing to retain information

Consolidation describes the conversion of short-term memory to long-term memory. This process takes time and rehearsals of the information. Unless you have a strong emotional attachment to the memory, you need numerous rehearsals to store it.

Short-term memories become long-term memories that are easily accessible if the rehearsals involve many of the senses. For example, talking about the information, creating graphics, and role playing — which is especially effective if the memory is a process or procedure — are effective practice methods for learning a new computer program or a new sales approach.

How many repetitions are enough? Educational research shows that learning a new concept or skill might take a few dozen rehearsals. Your brain cells need time to go through the changes that convert a short-term memory into a long-term memory. Every time the neurons connect, cellular changes occur to ensure that the next connection happens quicker and easier.

The first time you drive to work you may go slower as you look for road signs and landmarks. Each day you get better at remembering the streets and other familiar sights. By the end of the first week, you're a pro at getting to work. The mental map you have created becomes very powerful and even when you don't have to go to work, you may find your car driving you there!

Repeated experience is what wires and rewires the brain. Although rote repetition has its place in learning, elaborate rehearsal usually does a better job of creating strong, lasting memories. Strategies for elaborative rehearsal include categorizing, classifying, and forming auditory or visual images.

Vision is a more effective rehearsal tool than the other senses. Anytime you create a mental picture or even draw one that represents what you're learning, you more easily remember it. Using mnemonic devices for visualization helps you rehearse information into long-term memory when the information is not easily associated with other material or easily connected.

Remembering names is difficult for most people. As a leader, a salesperson, or as anyone else who deals with new people often, using a visual strategy to help you remember is a good idea. People are more responsive when you use their names in conversation, and so remembering names is an important business skill. Many individuals have trouble remembering names, and names have no synonyms — you can't replace a person's name with another word while you talk to them.

In one episode of the television sitcom *The Office,* Michael shares his mnemonic strategy for remembering names. Michael goes around the room, sharing the trick he uses for remembering each person's name. He points to one person and says "baldy," to the next person and says, "mole"; "sugar boobs" is the next person (a young lady with large breasts and a low-cut blouse).

"Baldy" is the guy with no hair, of course. His head is shiny, and Michael can see his reflection in it. Mirrors reflect; the word mirror starts with M, as does the man's name — Mark. This is a long way to go to get to the name, but his strategy works for him.

Finding something significant about a person's face and using it to help you visualize his name can be powerful. If Bill has bushy eyebrows, picture a dollar bill buried in those brows. If Lucy has large teeth, look at her teeth and imagine that one is loose. (Loose = Lucy.) Choose a visual that works for you. You may find it helpful the next time you meet shareholders or potential clients. Just don't share your strategy, like Michael did.

Making money by making memories

Have you ever thought of becoming a memory expert? You can compete in the U.S. Memory Championship or even the World Memory Championship. If you have a lot of time on your hands to practice the strategies (one champion learned the skills in jail), you might find a new career. Many audiences find this entertaining and pay you for your time.

The world-class memory champions memorize several decks of playing cards after an outsider has shuffled them. Their memorization often is a very short process that takes about five minutes. They accomplish it by using mnemonics or memory strategies. The strategies are so well

rehearsed that the *mnemonist* (memory expert) simply attaches each card to a visual he has stored, such as an object in his home. These mnemonists often have five to ten objects in each room of their house that serve as their house files. As the cards are turned, the mnemonist works around the first room attaching cards to each object, and then he moves on to the next room. After all of the cards have been turned, the expert tells the cards to the judges or audience in whatever order they want them — first to last, last to first, or just answering a question like "What's the 77th card?"

The Brain Learns through Feedback

Do you remember playing the "Hot and Cold" game as a child? Someone hid an object in a room while you waited in the hall. Then you were called in and started looking for the object. When you were close to it, you were told you were getting warmer; when you strayed away from the object, you were told you were getting colder. If you got very close to the object and still hadn't found it, you were told you were hot or red hot. That game is a great example of getting feedback to let you know how you're doing. Feedback is even more important in the leadership game.

Feedback works on the emotional system in the brain. Knowing whether you are hot or cold at your job brings out an emotional connection. And it activates more than the raw emotional center, it enables the brain to use higher-level thinking skills to decide how to continue doing good work, make the good work better, or make changes to garner more positive responses and work harder toward company goals. Your leadership skills rely heavily on your ability to give and receive feedback.

Feedback is sometimes divided into two types: motivational and informational. Both types of feedback need to be timely — offered within a short time after the event at the heart of the feedback — to really make a difference. You can't overrate the importance of timely feedback.

Feedback helps the brain stay focused on its target. Motivational feedback keeps up morale, and informational feedback enables employees to keep track of their accomplishments.

Feedback works in both directions. You want your employees to provide feedback to you, too. I talk about his kind of feedback in Chapter 5.

Giving timely feedback

Timely feedback is often immediate: You see something you like, and you let your employee know. You want to comment while the task is still in the mind of the employee. Doing so is of particular importance if you're working toward a specific goal and you want to keep the momentum going.

If you see some improvement, even in small increments, you provide verbal and maybe written feedback on the progress. New goals or time-consuming goals require intermittent feedback. People need to know how they're doing, where you think they are in a process, and whether you're looking for something in particular.

Specific feedback more effectively corrects or reinforces certain behaviors, enabling the brain to focus on something concrete, which it does do not from an "Atta boy!" type of reinforcement. The brain likes celebrations, so be sure to celebrate each success. If you decide to congratulate employees as a group, be sure to talk to each one personally as well. You find more information about giving employees feedback in Chapter 20.

Making feedback motivational

A high-performing team usually is made up of individuals who are self-motivating. But for some employees, motivation doesn't come so easily from within. Therefore, once in awhile you need to either provide a "pat on the back" of some sort, or in some cases a "kick in the pants" in a subtle and supportive way.

The more time you spend as a visible leader walking around and observing, the more likely you are to catch someone doing something right. If you know your employees, this can prompt you to provide that pat on the back in the format most effective for the employee. For instance, if you know your employee likes to hear praise and be praised in front of others, you would say something loud and clear like, "Great job, Vickie, you're responding to those customers in a manner that keeps them coming back!" Other employees may not like a public "atta boy" and prefer that you literally pat them on the back as you pass by.

A swift "kick in the pants" is something you do only on a face-to-face basis, in private.

Occasionally you have a very visual employee who responds best when information is spelled out, literally, in a note with step-by-step feedback that tells him how to improve. This type of written feedback is a little different from the informational feedback I describe in the next section. Informational feedback is usually written, but it keeps a running score of how the employee is doing.

Offering informational feedback

Besides giving your employees motivational feedback, you need to give them hard data. This informational feedback should be graphic. A picture is worth a thousand words. In an instant, employees can see their progress — or lack thereof. Along with the graphic, include specific suggestions for improvement and acknowledgment of jobs well done.

Goals help the brain focus. Using informational feedback based on goal attainment is fair and may be as encouraging as motivational feedback. Timeliness is as important for informational feedback as it is for motivational feedback. The process is more involved because it definitely involves graphics and writing.

Some employers want to encourage competition, and so they ensure that the entire organization or department sees how everyone is doing. For example, in the customer service department, they post informational charts with the number of service calls and satisfied customers for each customer service representative. A quick glance at the ongoing status of each representative may inspire those not living up to the goal of service and satisfaction.

The Brain is Social

Our ancestors had to rely on each other to survive. Going out hunting for prey by oneself wasn't a wise thing to do. In groups, hunters had eyes in all directions to help protect themselves and find more food. At home, the families stayed together for protection, comfort, and sharing. This social system resulted in brains accustomed to working and living with other brains.

Social gain or brain pain

Social status affects the brain in different ways depending on whether one is going up or down the social ladder. Studies suggest that the brain responds positively to the possibility of social gain at work. That status is based on work, productivity, and sometimes personality. Social hierarchies develop in all species, and the brain's need to find a place in its environment overcomes even the most valiant attempt at eliminating hierarchies and treating everyone equally.

In any organization, you find someone at the top of the ladder who produces more, has more energy, and gets along well with others. This outward appearance of social rank leads other brains to believe that someone is at the bottom of the ladder.

Brain scans have shown that those who believe they're on top or on their way up in the social strata show activation in the emotional center of the brain, the amygdala, and in the frontal lobes, where planning takes place. A brain that feels inferior may become motivated and focus more attention on productivity. Others may feel the situation is hopeless and activate the emotional pain areas in their brains.

Brains place great importance on hierarchies. Although not all relationships are hierarchical, knowing who's in charge and who isn't is a priority at work. The more stable the environment, the less likely problems such as lack of motivation are to occur. If all stakeholders see the possibility of a positive change in social status, the environment becomes more stable.

Social success or stress?

Leading the social brain requires a knowledge of oneself, an empathic brain, and an understanding of stress. The social brain seeks social success in every aspect of life. Because most of one's day is devoted to work, being accepted, admired, and well-liked is especially important to workers. Protecting your employees from social stress is impossible, but dealing with it is necessary.

Feeling successful in social situations at work causes the release of feel-good chemicals. But even an employee at the top of the social ladder may lose his footing. The brain responds in a negative way when challenging work experiences make an employee feel as though he looks bad to others.

How serious can stress at work become? Stress at work can cause health problems. Anytime stress levels are chronically high, the immune system can be affected. This can cause mental health problems, such as depression and anxiety, or physical problems. Physical health issues as common as the cold may be a result of a fragile immune system. Health issues lead to lower productivity due to absences or an inability to focus. Workers who are persistently missing work due to illness often return to a situation feeling out of sync in regards to expectations and what has been missed. This can cause more stress and continue the cycle.

Feeling like the underdog causes the brain stress, and the brain directs that stress elsewhere. Often, the brain interrupts whatever is taking place that makes it feel stressed. Feeling comfortable again with the content of a meeting or project, reduces stress and enables an employee to become a team player again.

A disgruntled team member may unconsciously delay work on a project. Doing so reduces his stress about not knowing what he is doing, not being accepted by others, or being afraid to speak up about a personal conflict with the project.

Social stress may be alleviated by some of the following:

- ✔ Reviewing the way decisions are made, work responsibilities, and how conflict can be resolved
- ✔ Taking the team out of the office for a social lunch to help everyone feel included
- ✔ Creating a support group in the company in which anyone can participate
- ✔ Immediately meeting with any team member who is slowing down progress to discuss any problems
- ✔ Making sure team members get recognition for their contributions
- ✔ Providing a suggestion box in which employees place thoughts anonymously

Remember that team leaders are often trying to lead their peers. Doing so is no easy task, and so checking in with these leaders to see how they are coping with their own social stress is a good practice.

Chapter 4

Leaders Are Made, Not Born

In This Chapter

▶ Discussing nature and nurture

▶ Recognizing leadership attributes

▶ Fostering success throughout your business

▶ Communicating your vision

*W*hat happens in the brain to make someone a leader? The debate has been ongoing and the results are becoming clearer. Researchers assert that your brain can learn anything. The brain's plasticity enables it to keep changing no matter your age.

Many leaders emerge later in life. Some people find their passion when they're young, but for others, finding that passion takes half a lifetime. (Maybe a midlife crisis is really no crisis at all.)

Leadership doesn't necessarily extend to all areas of your life. Most leaders direct their passion to one or two aspects and follow in others. The knowledge required, the time demanded, and the amount of stress embedded in leadership limits the desire to lead.

In this chapter, you find out how leaders are made, how to take action, and how to share your vision. To be a leader or to remain a leader, you need to continuously develop your skills, goals, and relationships. To become a leader, you have to have followers. To have followers, you have to instill a dream and the opportunity to be part of that dream.

Considering a Leadership Gene

Whether human DNA includes a leadership gene is a topic for great debate. (No such gene turned up through the Human Genome Project.) Are you born with leadership ability or is it learned? Most leadership and brain experts agree that the brain is malleable and under the right conditions can develop leadership skills.

Nature versus nurture

Have you become who you are because of what you inherited genetically from your parents or because of how your parents raised you? Whether you have blue, green, or brown eyes is a product of genetics. Your height is determined by nature; so is your hair color (and whether you keep your hair or go bald).

The genetic influence might not end at physical factors; some noted scientists believe that genetics play a role in behavior and personality traits. But this is where the connection between nature and nurture begins. A child born with a trait called shyness can be nurtured into becoming a less shy or even outgoing individual. That is, the genetic component can be changed or compensated for. The child's environment and how the child is mentored by her primary caregivers makes all the difference. The brain's *neuroplasticity,* its ability to change through experiences, enables the child to overcome shyness.

For example, you're genetically programmed for language. At birth, you have the ability to learn any of the 6,000 languages spoken on Earth. The language that you hear is the language you learn. If you were fortunate enough to be raised in a multilingual environment, you may be proficient in more than one language. The bottom line is that nature (the ability to learn a language) and nurture (learning the language of those in your environment) combine and form your language abilities.

And so it goes with leadership. If a leadership gene is eventually discovered as the scientists study the 30,000 genes in the human genome, it will be only a starting point for the discovery of how a person becomes a good leader. All of the factors that affect the brain would be involved in whether that gene is *expressed,* or actively used. Certain genes are turned on and turned off throughout our lives. Some genes remain inactive until an experience creates a need for them — kind of like library books just sitting on a shelf until you crack one open to find the information you need. Lifestyle, nutrition, environment, experiences, and relationships are only some of the factors that affect that process.

Born to lead

You have probably heard someone called a "born leader." According to the research, such a person may not exist. Everyone knows of motivating, inspiring, knowledgeable people with visions that have others willing to do anything to follow them. Think about some of those leaders who charismatically created a large following: Barack Obama, John Fitzgerald Kennedy, Mahatma Gandhi, and Golda Meir. Although you may not agree with the visions of all of these leaders, they did, indeed, lead many people to their way of thinking. But were they born to lead? Most people believe that leadership is learned from others or through experience. If you're willing to learn to interact with others on an emotional level, you can get others to see things the way you see them. You can also learn to express empathy when dealing with others' personal and professional situations. With these skills, you're on your way to leading.

Educators often say of their classes, "If I could only pick their parents!" Birthright creates many people who *get* to be leaders. Some are born into royal families with titles bestowed upon them, but that good fortune doesn't necessarily make them leaders — especially if the leaders who came before them did not model good leadership skills. Their genes allow them the right to take over the organization, but do they have credentials beyond family connections?

Leadership skills aren't hereditary. The desire to lead may be instilled by your role models, but the characteristics of good leaders are learned.

Leading opportunities

Your genes change and respond to your environment. They can't work without the amazing effects of your brain's differing levels of neurotransmitters, hormones, oxygen, water, and nutrients. These levels are affected by the foods you eat, the culture you live in, your stress levels, and the amount of sleep you get — to name just a few.

If someone inherited a potential for great leadership but never got the opportunity to lead, his potential would never be reached. Some business experts believe that everyone has leadership potential and with the right situation, opportunity, and passion for an idea, can effectively lead.

Leadership is learned, but sometimes the people around you teach you in an unconscious way. From their backgrounds and their passions, some employees have an ability to connect with others, and their observation skills enable them to rise to the occasion when a leader is needed.

Our nature is to nurture

Nurturing seems to be hard-wired into human brains. The release of the brain chemical oxytocin occurs in the brains of parents when their babies are born. This bonding chemical encourages the brain to nurture the new life. Survival necessitates relying on others and being relied upon in return. Taking care of others not only helps perpetuate the species but is vital to personal growth. As you nurture relationships in your life, you create relationships that provide emotional and professional support.

See Art lead

Art has a plan: Go to the best school, get the best internships, work for a good company, and look for the possibility of getting in on the ground floor of a start-up business. From there, he wants to learn from leaders, work with leaders, and if a leadership opportunity presents itself, jump at the chance. His plan works better than he expected. Art has never been much of a leader in school or in organizations that he belonged to; he just knows that this is what he wants. The "ground floor" of the new business is literally the ground floor. The first floor of an older building a bit off the beaten business path provides the shell of this new computer consulting start-up. Art begins as one of the worker bees, but he wants to always keep his eye on the prize. So he watches the CEO and the CFO, listens to their decisions, and makes mental notes of their actions.

Not wanting to tell his peers what to do, Art builds good relationships with his peers so he can offer suggestions without sounding like a know-it-all. With humor and enthusiasm, he creates an environment in which he can use his prior knowledge to help his peers. All the time, though, his eyes are watching and his ears are hearing what the leaders say and do.

Soon enough, his colleagues are working well together and accomplishing the goals they have set. Art has them working like an orchestra, and he conducts less and less as they all begin to do their jobs well and he offers to participate in other projects not related to his team.

What Art doesn't know is that while he is observing the leaders, they are watching him. Because they themselves are exceptional leaders, they have been keenly observing every employee as they look for leaders. They know Art has taught the newbies a lot, has set them up for independence, and not only does his own work but works on other projects sometimes moonlighting to do so. The CEO approaches Art, tells him what a great job he is doing, and offers him a project of his own. Art thanks him and tells him how he appreciates the chance to prove himself as a leader. The CEO smiles. He knows what Art doesn't yet. That he has already proven himself as a leader, and now he is moving on to a much bigger leadership opportunity.

Outlining Leadership Attributes

Wanted: Person or persons with perfect decision-making skills; the ability to communicate flawlessly with superiors, subordinates, board members, and clients; and listening skills so superior that you understand what is being said as well as what isn't being said. Must be calm in the face of adversity and able to inspire others. If you're interested in bringing out the best in others and in yourself, inquire within. Unqualified persons need not apply unless willing to learn all of the above and more.

Don't worry. You can develop all of these skills. The upcoming sections get you started.

Taking the actions that make the leader

The list of leadership attributes is endless, but if I were going to create an inventory of traits that no leader can be without — attributes that would please the brains of most employees — it would include those in the upcoming sections.

Be in touch

Let your employees know that you're with them, which gives them a sense of security and calms the emotional area of the brain. When emotions are calm, you're less likely to initiate the stress response, and instead your brain is open to new information and responds better to others. In our global society it is easy to be in touch as a leader. You can tweet your way into the lives of your employees on a daily basis. By using the social network Twitter, you can send messages to every employee, letting them know where you are and what you're doing. You can call a meeting in a matter of seconds, and send short important messages.

Be visible

You want to be certain that employees see you on a regular basis. One senior leader makes certain that she visits each team every day. She may give only a quick greeting and ask whether they need anything, but she's there for them to see.

Visibility is advantageous for three reasons. First, it provides your employees with the knowledge that you care and are approachable. Second, it enables you to always know what is going on. Take every opportunity to work among your employees, greet them, and treat them with respect. Third, it lets employees know that you are ready to join in and help if needed.

Hone your communication skills

Your brain is hardwired for language. Individuals with good communication skills get promoted more often and rise to higher levels in organizations. Communication is a two-way street; to be an effective communicator, you have to be a good listener as well as a good speaker. Whether communicating face to face, via the Internet, or through text messages and cell phones, make sure you relay your message at the level of understanding of the persons receiving it and listen carefully to responses. Workers who feel that information is shared with them stay in their jobs longer and are more motivated — maybe because communication activates both the language centers and the emotional centers in the brain.

Keep your emotions in check

Make sure that you can lead yourself before you begin leading others. Keep a handle on your emotions. Use them to help you make decisions, but don't let them use you. Decide who's in control. Your brain is easily overwhelmed with emotion unless you have learned to use your prefrontal cortex, the executive of your brain, to temper those raw emotions. Doing so requires that you practice emotional intelligence skills I describe in Chapter 8, such as the ability to recognize your emotions. As you begin to recognize them, you can also determine the best way to handle them.

Inspire teams

You can't be a leader if you don't have any followers. Be the type of leader who walks with your teams, not in front of them. You may turn around one day and find that you are alone.

The brain is social and gregarious. Offer yourself, your hopes, and your goals to the teams making things happen for you. You inspire by being able to explain complex issues in a way that your followers understand.

Your self-confidence that the job can be done or the goal can be reached inspires them to work. Show them that although you make mistakes, you pick yourself up and try again. These kinds of inspiring behavior stimulate the brain's emotional centers.

Sharpen your decision-making skills

As you see in Chapter 9, knowing how to make rational decisions and snap decisions is part of leading others. To sharpen those skills try the following:

- ✔ Practice identifying problems and presenting them simply.
- ✔ Invite brainstorming to create as many possible solutions as you can.
- ✔ Determine consequences for each possible solution.
- ✔ Activate your decisions and follow their outcomes.

You instill a sense of safety and security in your employees when they can count on your good decision-making skills.

Know your people

People need to feel connected to others. The leader who gets to know his employees both professionally and personally has an easier time motivating them and getting them to make changes, and those employees who feel connected to their superiors like their jobs better.

I ask every executive that I come into contact with what they do to get to know their staff. Most have individual meetings with each employee to find out what they like or dislike about work. They also find out about their personal goals and desires. This is effective for most leaders, but it's not nearly as much fun as the parties that other leaders have. Parties, retreats, and games may sound like child's play, but the brain loves to play and learns through play as well. Give your employees the opportunity to let their hair down and really talk to you and to their colleagues.

The brain is social; interaction provides a feeling of importance and self-confidence found in the limbic system and frontal lobe.

Place others' needs above your own

When you talk to your employees ask them what they want from their jobs, what their future goals might be, and what needs they have that have not been met. Helping your employees achieve their best and expand their careers helps your company in the long run. If your workers believe that you will help them, they will be more willing to help you meet your organizational goals. Your interest provides a feeling of belonging and increases the release of feel-good neurotransmitters including dopamine and serotonin.

Lead people where they want to go

If they want to go, why don't they just go? Fear — the same fear that keeps many people from becoming leaders. Your inspiration and the fear that you conquered give your followers the courage to walk with you. As their fear subsides, their levels of the stress hormone cortisol fall as the levels of dopamine, the reward chemical, rises. Find those who share your vision, who want to make things happen, and who want to make a difference.

Keeping expectations high

High expectations tend to support high productivity. Employees live up to what you expect of them. Setting clear expectations defines the boundaries. Within those parameters, you may expect creativity and new ideas. What you don't want is everyone in your organization doing their own thing or doing the same old thing.

Expectations provide predictability, which lowers stress and allows your employees' brains the freedom to create change in the form of new ideas, new products, and new processes.

A fair lady

All people tend to live up (or down) to expectations that others have of them. The George Bernard Shaw play *Pygmalion* has an extraordinary line in it. The play is about Professor Higgins, who claims he can take an ordinary flower girl, Eliza Doolittle, and pass her off as a lady — and does just that. After Higgins's training, Doolittle says, "The difference between a flower girl and a lady is not in how she behaves, but rather in how she is treated." Her point, which has become known as the Pygmalion Effect, has been seen in schools in which teachers are assigned students and are told that the students are gifted when in reality they have had little success in school. The teachers treat them as though they are gifted, and the students rise to the expectations and do very well.

The Pygmalion Effect and other studies show that you get what you expect. High expectations along with proper training encourage employee growth and increase productivity.

Do your employees know what your expectations are? If an outsider were to come into your company and ask any employee to name his department's goals for the month, could he answer? When you hire a new employee, she knows her job description, but job descriptions change, and you need to keep employees up to date about job descriptions and expectations.

Keep expectations clear, and track employees' progress by doing the following:

✔ Meet with all who report directly to you and find out whether they know

- The expectations you have of them.
- The expectations of everyone who reports to them.
- The job descriptions of all who report to them.

✔ Meet with your direct reports on a regular basis to discuss how their work is affecting the goals and expectations of the company.

✔ Post your expectations throughout your building, offices, factories, and so on.

✔ Treat your employees as if they can meet all expectations.

✔ Accept nothing less than what you expect; make time for revisions.

✔ When time is at a premium and revisions aren't possible, keep a watchful eye on progress.

✔ Motivate your workers regularly; become a cheerleader.

Expecting (and embodying) integrity

One of the most important characteristics of an effective leader is integrity. The leader who is honest, respects herself and her employees, and holds herself accountable for her actions is the leader to follow.

You learn integrity through life experiences. Just as you learned integrity from the significant others in your life, your employees can learn it from you.

Your thoughts, feelings, and actions must align in every aspect of your life. If you don't match your actions or behaviors to your values, you come across to your employees as untrustworthy. Each experience in which you exhibit or practice integrity makes it more likely you can continue that pattern.

Your morals and values are found in the frontal lobe of your healthy brain. You judge yourself and others in this brain area. You know when you're about to do something wrong, and the feelings associated with this knowledge keep you from doing it. You can see the consequences of such actions and you know they can make you feel awful, so you take the high road.

With the dishonesty of leaders making the news, trusting leadership is very difficult for employees and customers. One Enron makes it harder for numerous leaders to lead — and the ripple effect of distrust goes on for years. Run your business as the perfect role model, and whenever corporations are exposed as frauds, show your employees in yet another way the integrity of your business.

Developing emotional intelligence

I devote an entire chapter (Chapter 8) to the discussion of emotional intelligence, but the topic deserves mention here, too, because understanding yourself and others is key to leadership.

Dealing with employees' and clients' emotions has typically been considered a *soft skill* — one that directly relates to people's feelings rather than business. But 21st century leaders must use more than their cognitive skills, they must be able to lead others using their emotions and emotional intelligence competencies.

Leaders are under an enormous amount of pressure. Pressure causes the brain to operate at a lower, more instinctive and reflexive level. Old habits and patterns begin to appear, and the stress and frustration spread throughout the organization. You may begin to seethe or micromanage in order to get control. As one very wise (and very brave) member of my team said to me, "What's out of control in your life that you're trying to control mine?" She was right on the money with that question. It caused me to pause and reflect. Given time, I discovered where my issues were and set about fixing those, instead of trying to fix her work (which didn't need it at all).

Walking the walk

Integrity boils down to the saying, "Walk the walk, don't just talk the talk." Honest people want to work for, be close to, and emulate honest people. Gandhi was famous for his integrity. As one story goes, a mother traveled many miles to take her young son to meet with the leader. She asked Gandhi to tell her son to stop eating sugar because it wasn't good for his health and would rot his teeth. Gandhi listened to her request and told her to come back in a month. Disappointed and angry the woman took her son and left, but did return a month later. When the boy approached the leader, Gandhi took his hands and said, "Do not eat sugar. It is bad for your health." The mother looked at Gandhi and asked why he had not warned the boy at their first visit. Gandhi looked at her and said, "Because, Mom, I was eating a lot of sugar myself, then."

You are bombarded with information, requests, denials, and problems 24/7. Understanding your emotional responses helps you deal with the challenges you face, and taking into consideration the emotions of others makes you a leader with powerful influence.

You need more than your rational brain when dealing with others. Your gut feelings tell you whether you're making the right choices and going down the right road. Acknowledging both your rational thoughts and your feelings is part of being an emotionally intelligent leader.

Comparing effective and ineffective leadership

The leadership attributes that I tell you about in the previous sections are undeniably important. But many of you have — or wish you had — other characteristics that make great leadership qualities.

I want to be like Mike. No, not Jordan. Mike Mercer was my first real leader. He didn't micromanage. He inspired. Using humor, creativity, hope, a sense of right and wrong, and his power in positive ways, Mike created a team that was unstoppable.

After that example of good leadership, here's an example of its opposite. I will call him John. John micromanaged everything. He wielded his power whenever possible. In the beginning, he kept professional development to a minimum. When desperation hit, he threw professional development at us. No choices, no input, no way. John is what I call the "What have you done for me lately?" boss. Make him look good or add to his bottom line and you can be his favorite employee. But mess something up or remain behind the scenes and you get little positive response or recognition.

And then there's Lucy Goosey. Here's a leader who has potential. She doesn't micromanage, but she has no organizational skills, either. Fly by the seat of her pants Lucy. She calls meetings at the last minute, and usually cancels prescheduled meetings. Lucy often leaves early, or she may come in late. As long as you know your job, you're okay — unless she doesn't like you. She's too nice to fire people, so Lucy ignores or somehow mistreats her employees until they get fed up and quit. Lucy's decision-making skills are almost nonexistent. She lets her indecision make the decision. Oops! It's too late to bid on that project! Oh, well, another will come along.

What kind of leader do you want to be? Take a close look at the characteristics of Mike, John, and Lucy in Table 4-1. Clearly, Mike is the best leader. If you have some of the traits of either of the other two "leaders," you might want to reevaluate your actions as well as your motives for becoming a leader.

Table 4-1	Comparing Leadership Characteristics	
Mike	*John*	*Lucy*
Honest	Dishonest	Who knew?
Humorous	Mean	Laughable
High expectations	Secret expectations	Low
High emotional intelligence	Low emotional intelligence	Moderate
Clear vision	Strict competition	Whatever
Clear communication	Unclear	Little or none
Good decision-maker	Makes decisions based on his needs	Wishy-washy
Knows employees	Knows employees by skills	Knows little
Leads	Micromanages	No leading or management

Encouraging Success through Leadership

A leader's success depends on the success of his employees. Bringing out the best in others is what flourishing leaders do. In this section I share several ways that you can help others succeed.

Imagine employees' possibilities

Your bottom line is getting the results you want. Your employees help you get there. To use the greatest attributes or talents of each individual makes sense, and many leaders do just this. Don't stop there. Let them stretch themselves and work on their weaknesses.

Where do you begin? The following are starting points:

- ✔ **Take a look.** Observe your employees as they perform their duties. Keep track of how they interact, at what speed they work, and what they seem very good at.

- ✔ **Take some time.** Discuss with each employee the strengths that you see. Then discuss what you and they see as a weakness. Find out how interested they are in working on areas in which they're less proficient.

- ✔ **Offer help.** Send them for trainings in areas of weakness if you believe building a particular skill is important.

- ✔ **Try it out.** Give them the opportunity to build up those weak points. Let them know that you don't expect perfection. Failure is disappointing, but you learn from trial and error.

Let your employees know what value they have to the company. If they share your vision, acknowledge how much more valuable they can be if their weaknesses turn into strengths.

Provide useful feedback

Whether you have one employee or thousands, staying connected through useful feedback is not only possible but critical. Even if you're new to the digital game, connecting to your workforce is valuable; not connecting is wasting a lot of time and potential interaction.

Personal meetings are not always appropriate or easy to schedule. Of course your direct reports can provide feedback to many of your employees, and other team leaders can be doing so, as well. But how can you reach them all? How can they know you're watching, supporting, and that you care?

Remember that providing feedback is one of the most important attributes of a leader. Find ways to provide feedback individually and to the organization as a whole. Try some of the following:

- ✔ **Online newsletter:** Post a weekly or bimonthly newsletter that shares recent progress, achieved goals, personal victories, and new projects or customers.

✔ **Twitter:** Tweet employees whenever something new is happening, something good has happened, or something is about to happen.

Look into using Yammer, which is a communications tool like Twitter, but that provides security, so that only employees with a company e-mail address can use it.

✔ **Video conferencing:** Video Web conferencing makes a large organization smaller. The Internet enables you to have face-to-face contact with employees in your building or on the other side of the world.

Mentor and coach

A mentoring or coaching program may be just what your organization needs. Assisting new hires in adjusting to their new surroundings is just one aspect of mentoring. Large corporations, like Microsoft, use mentoring programs to sustain high-performing employees and prepare some for leadership positions. High-performance athletes use coaches in the same way as businesses use them: for encouragement, motivation, teaching, and maintaining success.

Make sure your business is in a position to handle a coaching program before you proceed. The time is right if

✔ You and your employees have time to meet.

✔ Several employees are interested in having or being a mentor.

✔ The office climate is healthy, and business is going well enough that this program won't be a burden. (You don't want to lay someone off in the middle of this program!)

Before you can match up mentors and mentees, you need to establish clear goals. The following are possible goals for the program:

✔ Making sure that you have the right person in the right position

✔ Helping new employees adjust to the work environment

✔ Encouraging leadership roles

✔ Reinforcing strengths, assisting with weaknesses

✔ Modeling acceptable work habits

✔ Clarifying work expectations

✔ Working as a team

A successful mentoring program hinges on crafting productive matches among employees. Just as Yenta, the matchmaker in *Fiddler on the Roof* often had trouble finding perfect matches, creating a mentor/mentee team that works is likely to be a challenge for you.

Take into consideration the following kinds of compatibilities:

- ✔ **Match the novice and veteran employees.** The veteran may be able to share information about the position, the environment, and successful approaches to the job.

- ✔ **Pair an employee who has a particular weakness with an employee who is strong in that area.** If the employee is interested in developing her weakness, the other employee can model the strengths and explain how to improve.

- ✔ **Compare professional goals and match those with the same goals.** Employees who value the same purpose may have a lot of other commonalities.

- ✔ **Match employees who have common interests.** Developing relationships at work is easier when common ground exists.

- ✔ **Pair employees according to the type of intelligence they share.** (Chapter 7 outlines multiple intelligences.) Those with the same intelligence strengths may approach issues similarly and be able to share ideas in a format that is easy for the other to understand.

One corporation used a speed dating approach to match mentors and mentees. Each mentee spent ten minutes talking to a mentor, and then a bell rang and the mentees moved on to the next mentor. The group actually thought this was quite fun and released a lot of tension. After all the "dates" were done, employees and mentors asked to selected three people with whom they felt they could work. In many cases, the selections matched and the program began. Those few who had no exact matches tried a few more "dates," and eventually everyone was partnered up.

After the matches are made, your mentor/mentee pairs may spend time together in informal settings like lunch or coffee dates, or you may want to set up mentoring meetings in which all pairs get together to share experiences, build relationships, and improve the program through suggestions and comments.

Coaching or mentoring doesn't work without clear expectations for all stakeholders. Someone may be wonderful at his job but unable to explain exactly what he does to someone else. Your coaches or mentors may need to be coached themselves!

You must be certain that your coaches are prepared to coach. First and foremost, your coaches or mentors must have emotional self control and empathy. Their job is to build rapport with a potentially valuable member of your team — someone who someday may be a leader in your organization.

Sharing Your Vision

Sometimes you look at your business as a whole — the big picture. Your right hemisphere dominates your thoughts, and the business becomes a living, breathing organism. All of the parts work together to make the whole — to meet the requirements of your vision, your dream.

At other times, you may see what your left hemisphere sees: the details. The individual cogs in the wheel. When you see these pieces and parts, you can see each employee and each job description that makes up the guts of the business.

Employees usually are focused on the left-hemisphere vision: They're stuck in their individual cubicles, sections, or teams unable to see where their part fits into the whole. Often every one of us gets so caught up in the nuances of our own responsibility that it's difficult to see beyond that. When employees get mired in details, your job is to bring them back to the big picture.

Your vision statement may use words, but it needs to inspire through story, metaphor, or even song, and it must be believable and achievable to the stakeholders you share it with.

You start with the future. Where do you want to go? How long will it take you to get there? You don't have to outline yet how you will get there. In fact, the people you share your vision with may have a great part in the design of the process.

Look at Microsoft's vision statement. In earlier days it was "A PC on every desk and in every home." But mission statements and vision statements change with the times. Today their statement is to "help people and businesses throughout the world reach their full potential." Their recent statement is a bit more abstract than their initial vision. You can visualize a PC on every desk, but it's a little more difficult to get a concrete picture of potential. However, both statements are inspiring and emotional. Therefore they are easier to get across.

When organizing your vision statement, ask the important questions:

- **Who** is going to do this?
- **What** are you going to do?
- **Where** is it going to happen?
- **When** will the action take place?

It looks like you will write a newspaper article, but these are the questions that need to be addressed in a vision statement. Save the *how* for your mission statement. The stakeholders you share your vision statement with may be helpful in constructing and streamlining your mission statement.

Probably one of the most emotional and dynamic vision statements comes from the famous I have a dream speech by Martin Luther King, Jr. His vision was easy to picture and carry in your mind with statements like, "I have a dream that one day on the red hills of Georgia the sons of former slaves and the sons of former slave owners will be able to sit down together at the table of brotherhood." And his repetition of the statement, "I have a dream" in a voice that carried confidence, passion, and compassion made it easy to remember.

What is your dream? As a leader, you need to share your vision. King could have shared his statements with pure fact and no emotion, but the result just wouldn't have been the same.

If you're passionate about your leadership vision, share it with every employee, every stakeholder, and anyone who will listen. Make it visible throughout your organization, your offices, and your building:

- ✔ Include it at the top or bottom of each e-mail or memo.
- ✔ Hang a framed copy in the reception area.
- ✔ Post it in every cubicle or office.
- ✔ Include it on your letterhead.
- ✔ Make it part of your logo.
- ✔ Heck, hang that sucker in the restrooms.

Chapter 5

Linking Leadership and the Brain

*N*ot too long ago, leaders were chosen for their IQ scores, grade point averages, and general knowledge of business. But the times, they are a-changin'. Many board chairmen were surprised to find out that the exemplary student with a high intelligence quotient wasn't quite cutting it. The then-typical leader (whom you find in many corporations today), was a business person rather than a people person. When psychologists and neuroscientists began looking at the brain, the job description of leader began to change.

In today's successful companies, leaders are doing more than using their heads; they're using their brains. The cognitive skills that helped them remember business law and technical knowledge were hard at work. But their people skills were lacking. You can become a stronger leader by understanding your own brain. You can then use that information to guide your leadership role and your entire organization. You can offer employees stimulating opportunities, or you can keep them in a rut. You have the power.

In this chapter, you find out about the ideal leader's brain, how to work with different brains, and how to attract the best brains. Great leaders bring out the full potential of those they lead by working with the brain instead of against it.

Glimpsing the Ideal Leader's Brain

Great leaders have good heads on their shoulders. (You can quote me on that.) The effective leader of today has the opportunity to have a solid understanding of how the brain works and can recognize where his thoughts and behaviors are coming from. This leader influences how his own brain works from acknowledging what he's paying attention to, what his emotional brain is up to, and how well his thinking brain is, well, thinking!

I know it! I'll think of it! Give me a minute!

How many times have you had that "tip of the tongue" experience? You know the one. Someone asks the name of the actor who was in that movie with Nicole Kidman. They were in Australia and life was really hard. You know, don't you? And yet you can't think of it; neither can your friend. You asked your brain to retrieve information, and it cannot. Usually this is a case where your working memory is so busy that your brain has no time or space for retrieval of the tidbit you want. Later, when your working memory is less busy, the answer simply pops into your head. You may also run across the name of that actor in another film or in an article that you're reading. Your brain says, "Aha! I've got the answer." Your brain notes the name because you programmed your RAS to attend to this information when it became available.

Getting your RAS in gear

The *reticular activating system* (RAS; I describe it in Chapter 2) is the portal through which nearly all information enters the brain. (Smells are the exception; they go directly into your brain's emotional area.) The RAS filters the incoming information and affects what you pay attention to, how aroused you are, and what is not going to get access to all three pounds of your brain.

For survival's sake, your RAS responds to your name, anything that threatens your survival, and information that you need immediately. For instance, if you're looking for a file that you're sure you placed on your desk, your RAS alerts your brain to search for the name of the file — Andrews vs. State of Illinois, say — or focus on one word in the file name to help you find it.

The RAS also responds to novelty. You notice anything new and different. For leadership purposes, this includes anything out of the ordinary in day-to-day activities within your organization, attending to changes in your employees relative to production, mood, and interactions with others.

Your RAS is a great leadership tool. It is your radar detector. As long as you don't bog it down with your own personal issues, it will work for you. Program your thoughts each morning by doing the following:

✔ **Take care of your personal issues.** If you're concerned about your child's behavior, for example, devise a plan to deal with it. Make sure your plan includes an appropriate time that you can put your plan into action. And then put the issue on the back burner until you can act on it.

✔ **Read over your long-term goals.** Make sure they're still pertinent to your vision. Change, delete, or add goals as necessary.

✔ **Read or create your short-term goals.** Determine the timeline for each. Change them according to current needs, trends, and modifications in your mission or vision.

Make sure that the last list you look at is your list of short-term goals; your RAS helps you keep them in mind. Even when you don't realize you're thinking about these goals, your brain knows that they're important and makes note of anything that might relate to them.

Leading with your limbic system

The best leaders incorporate the emotional intelligence skills that I outline in Chapter 8. Your limbic system houses your amygdala, the almond-shaped primitive emotional structure that can run your life and your organization. (Chapter 2 tells you more about the brain's structure.) Whether you will be the master of your limbic brain or its slave is the first decision you need to make as a leader.

Should you become the slave of the limbic system and the emotions it generates, you may see one of two scenarios. *Limbic denial* occurs when you ignore your own and others' emotions, and *limbic overflow* comes about when you can't ignore or control any of your own emotions. Table 5-1 compares the two.

Should you choose to master the competencies of leadership — that is, build your emotional intelligence as described in Chapter 8 — your situation changes dramatically. As a leader who has the ability to control her emotions and handle the emotions of others, you begin to lead more through managing relationships, empathizing with employees, and using emotion to guide your decisions. I call this *limbic leadership,* because it draws on the emotional skills of self-confidence, emotional self-management, empathy, and feedback.

You likely create an environment where employees feel safe to share their feelings. When you master your emotions, you see patterns similar to those in Table 5-2.

Table 5-1	Comparing Limbic Denial and Overflow
Limbic denial	**Limbic overflow**
Your decisions are based totally on hard data with no intuitive influence.	You really can't make a decision; sometimes you feel very strongly that something should be done, and the next minute you don't think it's such a good idea.
You greet employees with a brusque hello and/or questions related to their job, customers, or hard data.	Your meetings with your team leaders are taken over by whichever one talks the loudest and has a lot to say. Your presence is all but ignored.
Your relationships with your subordinates disintegrate because you don't nurture relationships or put their needs above yours.	Those who report directly to you don't look forward to meeting with you as you tend to not give any specifics. You're not sure they are heading in the right direction, so you continually have them change their approaches.
Your clients either choose to speak with one of your subordinates rather than you, or your customers find another company to do business with where they can find compassion and empathy.	Organizational meetings that include all employees are a joke. You are like a bad seventh-grade teacher spending all of your time trying to gain control. No one respects your authority.
You are a hard-nosed son of a gun who cares little for other's feelings and can't build any new relationships. If your business is successful, leadership responsibilities have been taken on by top-level executives who appear to care about others.	You spend so much time trying to make up your mind that you have little time for anything else.

Within the limbic system, the hippocampus is located next to the amygdala. The hippocampus helps you form long-term memories and responds to incoming information by checking for a pattern that has been previously stored. Seeking a pattern and not finding it is a surprise to the hippocampus and calls for special attention to the situation.

Because of the proximity of the amygdala and the hippocampus, emotional information is easy to remember. When you control and use your emotions, you also provide a greater opportunity for long-term memory storage. Your emotions don't get in the way.

Flip the emotion coin and you find a different approach to emotion and memory. Add some emotion to the information you want to share and have remembered, and you get a stronger memory. (But watch out for too much emotion, which can cloud the memory process.)

Table 5-2	Benefits of Limbic Leadership
Master of self-awareness	*Master of handling others*
Your decisions are based on emotional and cognitive information.	You consider the emotional needs of employees, clients, and customers.
You excuse yourself from meetings when your emotional state is not helpful to the situation.	When emotions are strong, you offer your staff the opportunity to reflect and to vent in order for them and you to come to terms with their feelings.
You are aware of emotional contagion and shield yourself from negativity.	You use emotional contagion when you are feeling positive, passionate, and excited about work-related issues. You "spread the news."
You work your own feelings into planning and responding to others. Individuals with whom you interact know that you're a feeling, caring person.	You consider other's feelings when making decisions and work your understanding of those feelings into your responses.
You "roll with the punches" when it comes to changes within your organization and between your organization and others. You control and use your feelings so you are flexible.	You work with others to adjust to change. You help others understand their feelings and encourage them toward change and flexibility.

Promoting your frontal lobes: The brain's CEO

The frontal lobes are sometimes referred to as the brain's CEO. All executive decision-making takes place in this area of the brain. It works most efficiently when information is not waylaid by other structures. As the emotional system filters incoming information, it either passes it along to the CEO, or if the information is alarming, delays information processing. Blocking information may mean that your brain is in survival mode and the information will be sent to the automatic, reflexive brain, where you react without rational thought.

Frontal lobes do the following for leaders:

✔ Help identify goals

✔ Plan to reach goals

✔ Organize time and manpower to follow the plan

✔ Project future consequences of poor implementation

✔ Project future results of proper implementation

✔ Come up with alternatives

✔ Enable creativity

✔ Provide freedom to imagine

✔ Judge and interpret data

✔ Connect new ideas to previous experiences

✔ Juggle ideas

✔ Control impulses

Bright lights, big mistake:
When emotions steal the show

Chuck finds out about interfering emotions the hard way. He sends a top technician, Justin, to Las Vegas for a training of trainers session for a new product that Chuck's company plans to carry. His plan is that Justin can return to the company after the training and pass on his knowledge of the new product line to the rest of the employees.

Justin has never been to Las Vegas, and so is very excited. He arrives on Sunday for the two-day training. That evening he gets a phone call from his mother that his father has had a mild heart attack. She reassures Justin that Dad is doing well. He is sitting up in bed joking with the nurses. Although Justin is relieved that his father is okay, he can't stop thinking about the fact that he wasn't there to see him or support his mother. When the training begins the next morning, Justin tries to concentrate on the new product, but everything reminds him of his dad. For one thing, the trainer is an older guy who is balding just like his dad. Justin continually refocuses on the training and finally gets into the flow of things. At the end of the first training day, he feels like he has a pretty good understanding of what's going on.

Justin calls and speaks with his father that evening and feels reassured. When the next day's training begins, Justin is completely focused and very optimistic about the new product and is getting a handle on how to train the rest of the company when he gets home. Mid-morning Justin's cell phone rings. His sister, Julia, is calling to tell him that his dad had yet another heart attack. This one not as mild and the doctors are going to perform open-heart surgery. Because Justin is returning home later in the day, Julia tells him not to worry. They won't be starting the surgery until after Justin arrives.

The rest of the day, Justin can't concentrate on any of the training. He can think only of his dad. He is sad that he is not with him. He tries to get an earlier flight and just leave the training, but no flights are available. So he stays at the training, but his emotions overwhelm him and even though the trainer is doing a great job, Justin can't get himself to absorb any of the information.

Chuck is, of course, sympathetic about Justin's problems, but he has spent a lot of money for the training that was unsuccessful. Justin's emotions were out of his control, and although he tried to control them, his fear and concern for his father were more than he could handle.

The frontal lobes work with the *insula,* a structure deep within the brain. This piece of brain geography is aware of all of your physical responses. In other words, that feeling in the pit of your stomach when you know you've said something you shouldn't have or forgotten an important event comes from the insula. The insula helps you decide whether to head to the refrigerator when you're hungry. It's involved with social interactions, guilt, and lust. The insula interacts with the frontal lobe to respond to those gut feelings.

The ability of your insula to translate your unconscious emotions into conscious feelings provides you with information to help you make a decision. Attending to your feelings assists the CEO of your brain in problem-solving and decision-making. For example, you have to decide which manager should take over some newly acquired territory. Hank has the smallest territory of all of the managers, but every time you consider him, you find a reason to pass him over. Something about Hank bothers you. In fact, you get irritated when you look at his name on the list. This irritation comes from your insula and relates to a previous experience in which Hank neglected someone in his territory, and you had to soothe the disgruntled customer. Even though it happened long ago, it affects whether you give Hank more customers.

You combine the information from your insula with the data you have on your managers to help you make a decision. Deciding whether to trust Hank with a larger territory depends on your feelings as well as his recent sales record. If his sales are low, you go with your feeling to not expand his sales territory; however, if he's producing, you may find yourself giving him the opportunity to try out the larger territory. As a leader, regarding your feelings can help you make better decisions.

Examining the Leader from Hell

An old and jokey bit of wisdom advises that if you can't be a good example you should at least serve as a terrible warning. In this section you find the terrible warning — the problems that can be created when the leader's brain is not functioning well. Everything you say and do is a result of your emotional and cognitive responses to the current situation. Not taking care of your brain can put you in a leadership category that you want to avoid. You don't want to ruin the relationships you have.

Prefrontal cortex in overdrive

The prefrontal cortex has needs. Rest is one of them. It needs some quiet time. The brain is never completely at rest, but when any area of the brain is overworked, important brain chemicals are depleted. As a result, you have trouble focusing, creating, and controlling the emotional center in the brain.

In other words, some of your impulse control vanishes if you overwork your prefrontal cortex.

Overworking the prefrontal cortex may give you an overall feeling that something is wrong. You may feel anxious and unable to focus and make good decisions. In this state of stress, lower levels of the brain may take over and cause you to fall back on old habits that are familiar to you. This shift in the brain appears to be a defense mechanism or an attempt at survival.

When your prefrontal cortex is overworked, you make decisions without using your brain's executive functions. For example, maybe you have worked to become a better listener, to communicate clearly and in a kind way, and you take others' emotions into consideration when making decisions. But 18-hour workdays, eating on the run, and inadequate sleep take a toll on your body and raise your stress levels. When a project fails, you forget all of your training and begin yelling at your subordinates, refusing to listen to their concerns, and alienating everyone in the company. Your overstressed, overworked prefrontal cortex can't control your impulses, and as a result you revert to old, bad habits. You have, indeed, become the leader from hell.

A prefrontal cortex without rest may become obsessed with a need to control and even punish. If you become the leader who needs to micromanage, you may have an overactive prefrontal cortex to blame. Worry and anxiety may be causing your behavior. Follow the advice for taking care of your brain in Chapter 17.

Prefrontal cortex stalls

An underactive prefrontal cortex often leads to attention difficulty. Attention deficit disorder probably arises from underactivity of the prefrontal cortex and its lowered ability to use or access the chemical dopamine, which helps calm other brain areas and enables the brain to focus on one thing at a time.

Someone with an underactive prefrontal cortex may notice a decreased ability to express himself or his emotions, which may lead to problems in all areas of life. Shortened attention span, distractibility, disorganization, poor judgment, and short-term-memory problems may result.

A prefrontal cortex that shows little activity has also been associated with some forms of depression. If your prefrontal cortex can't communicate well with the rest of your brain, incoming messages are examined only on an emotional level. If you have just heard that the chairman of the board wants to meet with you, for example, and you think that means you're going to lose your job, you may dwell on this idea. Given the opportunity, your prefrontal cortex would look at the meeting request from many logical angles — perhaps you're being considered for a bigger position or are being commended on a job well done. But because these rational thoughts aren't at your disposal, you remain entrenched in the negative.

Staying ahead by using his head

Jay has his brain linked to his leadership position. He is an entrepreneur with several businesses under his ownership and leadership. In enterprises from alcohol to art, he must masterfully lead many kinds of people. Now in his fifties, Jay began the pattern of working with his RAS at the beginning of each day long ago.

Jay organizes his personal life and deals first with the most important people in his world, his family. Each morning in his office he reaches for legal pads with his goals on them. Every day for each of his businesses he looks first at his long-term goals and then his short-term goals.

Jay rarely changes his long-term goals, but he might change his short-term goals in response to the economy, production, new employees, and any other factors that could change his way of doing business. Jay continues his day with his brain primed for those short-term goals. He has meetings with his managers throughout the day — in person and by video conference. He begins each meeting with some personal conversations. Keeping up with the families and activities of his managers is a priority for Jay. He likes to keep up to the minute, and so

his recommendations, requests, and questions take into consideration the emotional states of the people he has put in charge to keep his businesses productive and profitable.

Each of these conferences includes discussion of problems and next steps. Jay knows that he needs his people for future planning and problem solving. He makes sure that he considers all suggestions from his subordinates; they're free to share any problems and concerns, and to disagree with Jay without feeling their jobs are in jeopardy. Jay physically makes appearances at each site monthly.

As a CEO, Jay uses the CEO of his brain — his frontal lobes. He has trained his brain to be aware of what is important to keep his businesses running smoothly. He is aware of his own feelings and the feelings of his employees, and he uses the information to create and keep good relationships. As a result of his brain's ability to stay on task and keep his emotions in check, he utilizes the executive functions of his brain with ease. He focuses on the future, reaches his goals, and keeps his employees happy.

A person with an underactive prefrontal cortex may behave immaturely. When the executive functions are not actively involved in decision-making, poor judgment often results. This leader may get into sexual harassment trouble because he is acting or speaking inappropriately or may even cheat on a business deal.

To keep your prefrontal cortex active, do interesting and exciting things in your life and at work. If you find yourself unfocused or feeling depressed, choose a part of your work that you really like and concentrate on just that for a while. Get others, like those on your senior team, to take care of the more mundane work until you feel better and your behavior changes.

Gage in a rage: A tale of prefrontal lobe damage

"Gage in a rage" sounds like a Dr. Seuss book, but it refers to the story of Phineas Gage, whose prefrontal lobe damage changed his personality and his ability to lead. Phineas was a railroad worker in the in Vermont. He was foreman of a group that used explosives to remove debris so track could be laid. Coworkers described him as a likeable man who worked well with his peers and did a fine job of overseeing the work that was so important to the railroad.

One day in 1848, however, Gage suffered a terrible accident. An unintended blast sent an iron rod up through Gage's left cheekbone and out through the middle of his forehead.

Amazingly enough, Gage stood up after the blast and spoke to his workers, who immediately loaded him on a cart and took him to a doctor. After several months of recuperation, Phineas went back to work. His personality, however, had changed dramatically. From the popular foreman with a head (no pun intended) for business, a good friend, and a loveable character, Gage became nasty, obstinate, fitful, and profane. He made inappropriate remarks and sexual gestures. He was fired, and eventually his wife left him. He lived another 12 years.

Decades later his body was exhumed as doctors realized that his story held valuable information about the brain and personality. The damage to his frontal lobes changed him and his ability to deal with his emotions and with others, and it certainly damaged his leadership ability.

Faulty emotional thermostat

A good leader takes the emotional temperature of the organization on a regular basis. But sometimes leaders are clueless: They may have thermostats that don't work or not even know there's a thermostat! The leader from hell may let her emotions run the organization and disregard the feelings of others, or she may have a faulty connection between her emotional brain and her logical brain that causes her to run the business in an unfeeling, simply logical manner.

If you can't take your own emotional temperature, you'll have trouble determining whether things are heating up at work. If the leader's thermostat's broken you might experience the following:

- ✔ Mood changes
- ✔ Negativity
- ✔ No respect for others
- ✔ A "winning is everything" attitude

- ✔ Failure to share or exhibit good values
- ✔ Taking things personally
- ✔ Inability to acknowledge others' feelings

To adjust your emotional thermostat, try the following:

- ✔ Be vigilant. Observe your feelings as they creep up, but don't necessarily act on them.
- ✔ Take note of employees' and customers' responses to you.
- ✔ Make yourself take the time to listen to others, no matter how difficult that seems.
- ✔ Exercise.
- ✔ Eat high-protein foods to increase neurotransmitters like serotonin.

The brain's emotional center has many more pathways to the prefrontal cortex than the prefrontal cortex has to the emotional center, which means that you feel faster than you think. The executive brain evolved from the emotional brain, and the emotional brain is designed to keep you from danger. Lions and tigers and bears taught the amygdala to respond by running, but unfairness is a more likely threat today, and our primitive brain needs the executive to ponder situations such as fairness or jealousy or the many other situations facing leaders today.

Basal ganglia bottoms out

Basal ganglia refers to several structures located deep in the brain. Still being studied, the basal ganglia are responsible for helping you perform simple procedures. In contact with the prefrontal cortex, the basal ganglia can help you change by storing new messages that may become new habits. That's all well and good. But the basal ganglia sometimes seem to have a mind of its own. Because basal ganglia store our habits and habits are hard to break, you may follow old leadership habits, especially in times of stress. What worked in the past doesn't necessarily work today. And if you have gone out of your way to provide safety, security, and predictability for your workforce, a surprising change can cause distress and loss of productivity.

The most promising way to avoid falling back on old habits is to be sure that your new habits are properly ingrained in your brain — practice, practice, and more practice. If you understand why the new habits are helpful and feel the importance of creating a successful atmosphere, you're much more likely to change.

Meeting the Brain's Needs

Chapter 3 details several of the brain's requirements — basics that the brain needs in all environments. As a leader, how do you encourage employees to meet these needs in their own brains? You need to know what makes those brains get up in the morning and want to come to work for you. The following sections outline some ways you can make that happen.

Predictability

Because all information enters the brain through the brain stem, and the brain stem is in charge of survival, your employees must feel physically and emotionally safe. Providing predictability for them helps them meet this need.

A predictable atmosphere and a schedule help the brain relax and feel free to use higher level thinking to get the job done. Knowing what you need to do frees working memory for imagination and creativity.

You need organizational and planning skills to create a predictable work environment. Subordinates need to know the plan or the agenda. They need to know your vision and the goal of the organization. They need clear targets.

Challenge

Brains explore, test, and challenge. Adult brains can change and grow and make new connections. The brain is born wanting to learn. By providing challenging experiences to your employees, you help keep their brains active and young.

How does challenge fit in with predictability? Very well, actually. When the brain can count on the framework of its environment, it's primed for challenge.

Make sure that any challenge you issue is appropriate for the worker's experience and education. For instance, if all John has ever done for you is work on the assembly line, you wouldn't throw him into a position in research and development. At least, not without coaching.

And appropriate challenge is key. Challenge should be just a level above the brain's comfort level. Taking someone out of her comfort zone is great, as long as she knows what is expected of her and coached through the new or more challenging experience.

You can provide challenge for your workers in endless ways. The following is a list of suggestions:

- ✔ In small groups or in their teams, ask employees to come up with a better way to accomplish this or that task.

- ✔ Ask an employee to cover for another worker doing a job that is slightly different.

- ✔ Ask employees to think of ways to improve their current duties.

- ✔ Challenge your teams to increase production in a certain area in a specified amount of time, but make it low stress.

- ✔ Challenge your employees to think of a problem at work, and to come up with the solution.

- ✔ Challenge your employees to have conversations about issues at work and include conflict in those conversations.

Through challenge your employees become energized. If you challenge them and train them, the learning opportunities may help you retain them. The brain prefers to be challenged!

Feedback

Imaging of the brain reveals that areas associated with motivation show more activity when someone is learning a task and receiving feedback compared to others not receiving feedback but learning the same task. Feedback feeds the brain. Just as it needs blood, oxygen, and nutrients, the brain needs to learn and receive comments about how it's doing. (Chapter 3 tells you more about the brain's love affair with feedback.)

As a leader who provides your employees with what they need, choosing how you give and receive feedback is essential.

Lack of feedback can actually cause the brain to be stressed. Studies have shown that negative feedback may be less stressful to the brain than no feedback at all.

Some of today's young people are satisfied with yearly reviews. Some of the largest companies give feedback only when it is requested. Interviewing some employees from these companies shows that they didn't seem concerned. They figured as long as they were doing a good job, it didn't really matter if they had formal feedback on a regular basis. But they *are* getting a lot of informal feedback. "No news is good news," and so employees may interpret not getting negative feedback as a message that they're doing well.

Memos, e-mails, and text messages are not good ways to give and receive feedback. Print or digital messages are easily misinterpreted. (Chapter 15 talks further about communication.) Face-to-face feedback is best.

Feed employees' brains by trying some of the following:

- **Be specific and timely.** When you match the message to the event and deliver it on time, information reaches the prefrontal cortex, where new ways of getting things done can be generated. Take care of problems when they occur. Doing so prevents employees from getting habits formed that are incorrect.

- **Connect your feedback to company goals.** Make your employee feel that her contributions are valued and create a positive emotion with the feedback.

- **Set up a schedule for follow-up conversations.**

- **Put your message in writing as well as delivering it verbally.** Graphics have impact.

- **Build on employees' strengths when giving negative feedback.** By beginning with the strengths, you involve the prefrontal cortex right away. If you begin with negativity, the information may never reach the frontal lobe; it may get stuck in the primitive emotional areas and put the employee in survival mode. Always give suggestions for improvement.

- **Feedback is a two-way street.** Ask for feedback from your employees on your own performance and on company policies.

Connecting feedback and stress

At a biochemical lab, three teams worked on a faster way to determine water quality for residents living on small lakes in a Midwestern state. After the teams worked for a week on the project, the administrator came around to see how things were progressing. He walked around the lab observing each team at work. He stopped at Team 1's work table and told them that he believed they were headed in the right direction and to keep up the good work. Team 2 was having some disagreements. The administrator stopped and told them that they weren't quite on the right track. He thought Team 2 was working on a test too similar to ones they already had and would end up nowhere if they didn't change

their focus. He didn't say a word to Team 3. He stopped and looked, and then left the room.

If the stress levels of these three teams had been tested after this visit, the results would have been very interesting. According to some studies, Team 1's levels of stress hormones would be quite low. Good neurotransmitters would have been released in their brains from the positive feedback. Team 2's stress levels would be high. After all, they had to go back to the drawing board and find another approach to their work. But Team 3's stress levels would be highest of all. They hadn't received any feedback and had been treated as though they didn't really exist. No one deserves to feel extinct.

Creating a Brain-to-Brain Link

Understanding where your employees are coming from — which areas of their brains are active when you communicate with them — will make your relationships stronger. This brain-to-brain link is the ultimate way to build rapport, express empathy, and increase confidence in you and your company.

When your prefrontal cortex is working well, you can use your RAS, your emotional brain (amygdala), and your higher-level thinking and decision-making skills in every endeavor. With this high-performing leadership brain, you can link yourself to other brains. You understand whether you're communicating with an employee or customer who is operating from her survival brain, her emotional brain, or her executive brain, and then you can meet her at that level, and help her utilize higher levels.

Imagine, for example, that you have a meeting set up with an employee who isn't meeting his portion of the goals for the team. He will probably be in survival mode. The employee's RAS isn't going to be responsive to your detailed dialogue.

To figure out his mind state, take some time to observe actions and reactions before you start a dialogue. You may clearly see anger, frustration, sadness, or fear on his face. His mode may also show up in his words, tone, and gestures. Harsh movements or even gloominess can be signs that he's in survival mode.

What do you do? In the survival mode everything is about the "I" in the person, not about the "we" in the organization. Begin by reaching out to that "I." Instead of beginning with the factual information in your executive brain, first ask how he's feeling. Present the problem from his perspective. For example, "John, I'm sure you aren't happy about not meeting your goals. What can I do to help you?" This approach takes away some of the threat that he feels. He can reach up to the emotional part of his brain and begin to tell you how he feels. You've linked to his brain and already he is moving closer to executive function.

After he explains how he feels and what he thinks is causing those feelings, ask him what he thinks he can do about it. Now you're considering those feelings in his emotional brain. He feels like you understand him. Asking him for suggestions accesses his executive functions. He can explore what he's done before and he can create a new procedure.

Relaxing the emotional brain and letting an employee feel that he is not alone enables him to involve his executive brain, which begins to suppress the emotions and think logically about the situation. When he meets you on your executive level where solutions to the problem lie, you can lead him toward making wise choices and solving his problem and yours.

Helping an employee move out of survival mode

Linda owns her own real estate company. She has a total of 50 people working for her, including — 30 realtors and 20 assistants and support-staff members. Linda receives hard data on listings, sales, rentals, and showings each day. When sales are down because of the economy, construction, or school crises, she makes sure to speak with each of her agents to determine whether they're stuck in survival mode. When Linda approaches Richard, one of her top agents, she finds him preoccupied.

"How's it going, Rich?" she asks. "Just fine, Linda. But I'm really busy," he says as he tries to blow her off.

Linda sees from his tone of voice and attempt to avoid her that Rich is in survival mode. He hasn't made any sales in two months, he has a daughter going away to college soon, and he recently bought an expensive car to impress his clients.

"Oh, I'll just keep you a minute," Linda says. "I had a couple of calls this week from former clients. I think they're looking for something in the new developments on the outskirts of town."

With this Rich directs his attention to her, but he's a little cautious. Linda continues: "Well, I don't have the time or the energy for these clients right now. I'm working on the merger with Blew Realty, and I have my hands full. Do you think you could show these people around?"

Rich smiles and nods. Linda can see his stress levels lower as he relaxes in his chair. "Can you e-mail me their information? I'll squeeze them into my schedule."

This smart leader knows that her best agent is in a rough spot. By checking with him and recognizing his fight-or-flight response, she saw that he needed her help. By offering him a few of her clients, she changed his emotional state. She used the planning and empathy skills of her prefrontal cortex and her limbic system to move him out of survival mode. He could now use his emotional skills and organizational skills to do a good job for both of them.

Part II

Tapping Into the Brain of a Leader

The 5th Wave — By Rich Tennant

@RICHTENNANT

"Bob, I want to tap into that part of your brain that wants to lead, that wants to inspire, that wants to stop leaning against my desk..."

In this part . . .

Leadership doesn't come in just one flavor, and in this part you find out about traits that go into leading well and the various leadership styles you might draw from. I tell you about the many ways in which individuals may be intelligent and how you can increase your own emotional intelligence quotient. Finally, I share how the brain functions during the decision-making process under various conditions to help you make the best leadership choices.

Chapter 6

Becoming the Leader You Want to Be

So, you want to be a leader. Or you are already a leader. Do you know what kind of leadership style you're using? Perhaps you have worked for leaders with different styles and you know what kind of leader you *don't* want to be.

Some leaders find their style and stick with it no matter what, but different situations may call for different leadership styles. You may find yourself in a leadership position that calls for one approach, but as the business changes or new employees come on board, you might adopt a different style.

In this chapter, you find out about different leadership styles. I include a tool for assessing your leadership style and show you how changing styles may make sense to you and your brain.

Running Down Classic Leadership Styles

The most common leadership styles — authoritarian, democratic, and delegative — refer to the types of decision-making that commonly go on in an organization. The upcoming sections give you details about each of these styles.

Authoritarian

Authoritarian leaders know exactly what they want done, who is to do it, and when it should be completed. Although these leaders don't offer much wiggle room, they often get the job done, and they make their expectations obvious.

Many authoritarian leaders

- ✔ Fail to seek questions or comments
- ✔ Make decisions with little or no input from employees
- ✔ Are characterized as bossy and compared to dictators

If you're the leader of a small organization and your employees are untrained and need a lot of management as well as leadership, you may need to adopt this style to get things done.

Some employees thrive under authoritarian leadership. The traditionalist generation (probably the oldest group of workers you have; I talk more about them in Chapter 15), has few problems with this leadership style; employees from that era respect authority and don't question decisions made by bosses, supervisors, managers, or leaders. The younger generations, those employees in their mid-30s or younger, don't easily offer their respect to authority figures until those figures have proven themselves, therefore they don't do well under the authoritarian style. Older baby boomers may like this style but younger ones often prefer more input into decision-making.

The authoritarian style can elicit a stress response in employees' brains. If employees feel they're constantly being watched, aren't trusted, and have no control over their lives, stress hormones may be circulating in their brains and bodies. Chronic stress can interfere with work and with higher cognitive functions. Health problems may occur as a result of chronic stress, as well. The employee who isn't comfortable with authoritarian leadership may feel he has to leave his job to protect himself. Chapter 2 tells you more about the stress response.

Democratic

The *democratic* style is also called *participatory leadership* and encourages employees and stakeholders to participate in decision-making. With an experienced workforce, the democratic style can be a positive experience for all stakeholders. Because everyone is included in making decisions, the decision makers need to be knowledgeable about the business, the process, the product, and the vision statement.

In general, participatory leadership requires more time to get things done. Because a democratic leader intends to honor the thoughts, feelings, and needs of the employees, discussions may be lengthy. (And the larger the group, the longer the discussion may continue.) If the employees need more information to make their comments and assist with decisions, the process takes even longer.

The democratic leader usually has motivated and inspired workers, and more motivation means more work gets done. When problems need to be solved, employees are encouraged to help and often have excellent suggestions. All employees are kept up to date with the inner workings and outer interactions of the business.

The democratic leadership style is great for those brains that need to have input and a feeling of control. When someone is listened to and understood, the brain releases feel-good neurotransmitters. This reaction contributes to motivation, focus, and attention, and it increases the brain's ability to think on a higher cognitive level.

Who's the boss?

When Maya accepted the job as department head for the small research section of the pharmaceutical lab, she was excited. As head of the department she assumed she would have a lot of say over the research projects, how funds would be allocated, and which employees worked on each project. Although the president of the company had been a little scary, Maya assumed that because she wouldn't be reporting directly to him that she had no worries. He seemed kind of strict, like her grandfather had been, but she loved grandpa and thought she might get used to this guy. She planned to stay with this job for one or two years, and then she would be off to California and hoped to have an online research position so she could stay home with her future children.

Maya had her speech prepared for the researchers she would be overseeing. She couldn't wait to meet them and share her ideas as well as listen to theirs. When she entered the small research lab, she was shocked to see the president at the front of the room. All of the researchers walked into the lab quietly and sat before him. No one even glanced her way. Maya swallowed her surprise and walked straight to the front of the room.

"Good morning, Mr. Ross," Maya said in her friendliest voice.

"Have a seat with the others, Miss Taylor," Mr. Ross responded. He sort of smiled, but his eyes didn't look happy.

Mr. Ross began, "People, I want to introduce you to your new department head, Miss Maya Taylor. She will be reporting directly to me. Nothing will change here. Your current projects will remain the same with the same deadlines. I don't want newcomers causing any kinks in the timeline that we have. Miss Taylor will be using the regular assessment tools and report forms. I assume she will have no trouble following the format. It is too bad that Mr. Newcomer, your previous department head, left for another opportunity. He wrote excellent reports. You have a lot to live up to, Miss Taylor. That's it, people. Get to work."

With that, he placed several files in Maya's hands and walked out. The researchers headed to their project tables without even a hello.

"Well," Maya thought, "There go all my ideas. Either this guy loosens up or I'm out of here."

Maya's generation doesn't show the loyalty to a company that older generations usually do. Therefore, Maya has no problem leaving a company if she feels she has no input. Let your interviewees know what style of leadership you use and tell them about your expectations of employee responsibility and behavior.

I think I can, I think I can — or can I?

François is good at his job. He has the unique ability to match the seller of a small business with small business buyers in such a way that everyone leaves the deal happy. He just joined a new business brokerage firm that allows him total autonomy over his work. François works on commission of 12 percent per transaction. His boss offered him his first deal for the company, saying only, "Take care of this one. The seller is having some trouble with the buyer. Seller thinks his business is his baby and wants to find the right people to take it over. Handle it any way you want. Just get it done. With your reputation, I don't expect to hear from you until the contracts are signed, sealed, and delivered."

François smiled and thought this would all be a piece of cake. Every seller has trouble separating from his business — especially the Baby Boomers who don't really want to quit working but think it's time to retire. François met with the seller that afternoon. Tom Kuntz and his wife, Jennifer, were interested in selling their stained glass business and moving to the Midwest to be closer to their children and grandchildren. They were sincere, motivated, and had thought they were ready to move on. Until now. François questioned them about their feelings about the current offer that was on the table from the buyer. They responded that the price was too low. The offer was only $5,000 less than the asking price! François had heard others talk about seller's remorse where the sellers decide they can't give up the family business, but he had never had the problem.

François excused himself and called his boss. "I think these people are experiencing seller's remorse. What can I do?"

His boss bristled, "You handle it. That's why I hired you. Are they using brinkmanship?"

François had no idea what brinkmanship was. "What do you mean?" he asked.

"You know, are they threatening to pull out? Are they raising the price?" his boss responded gruffly.

"I don't think so," François replied. "They seem like really nice folks."

"Listen, kid, this is your job. Don't blow this. These people want to sell. Remind them how much they want to sell!" With that, his boss hung up.

Somehow François convinced the Kuntzes to go through with the deal. They weren't happy when they left. François wasn't happy, either. He had never felt so out of control of a situation. And François's boss was very, very unhappy. He had been disturbed in the middle of a business deal. He couldn't afford to have someone like François conducting his business. He was just too wet behind the ears. François went back to selling cars.

You may need to change your decision-making style in order to train and help out new employees. If François had truly been ready to make all of his own decisions and understood the business completely, he wouldn't have phoned his boss with a common problem in this business. Delegative leadership works well only if the staff is highly skilled.

Delegative

Trust and confidence are hallmarks of the *delegative* leadership style, which is sometimes called *laissez faire leadership* because of its minimal interference in employees' efforts. Under a delegative leader, employees have free rein to make decisions and get their jobs done. This style works very well with an educated and experienced workforce.

Some employees love the freedom of this style and thrive as they themselves become leaders. Those who are good decision-makers and don't require guidance benefit from this style. If you're especially interested in molding leaders to use for other acquisitions or expanding your business, delegative leadership provides on-the-job training that works. It increases employees' pride and motivation. (But those who are insecure, afraid of making mistakes, or have difficulty communicating with others have difficulty operating under this leadership style.)

Younger generations, who prefer to work on their own, find the delegative style especially appealing. These employees don't require a lot of face time with colleagues, and so do well with digitally based work.

If you have employees who need more direction, the delegative style can cause stress. The uncertainty of getting the job done well and the lack of guidance may be overwhelming. Even if employees who prefer direction are working in a team, the team members who are confident in their work may make those less confident feel inferior, which can cause chronic stress. The circumstances for delegative leadership may be limited to situations in which every employee is well-versed in her role, feels in control of the situation, and loves her work.

Assessing Your Leadership Style

Chances are good that you have more than one style of leading. That's not unusual. Most people copy traits from others and combine styles. Under certain circumstances you may have to change styles. As long as you don't compromise your values or let the change affect your vision or goals, it will probably work out for you.

The upcoming assessment gives you a good idea of your strengths. Knowing your leadership style may help you understand why you lead the way you do, whether changing your style will be easy, and what kind of people you need to hire to compensate for some areas of weakness.

On a scale of 1 to 5, with 1 being *never* and 5 being *always,* use Table 6-1 to rate yourself on the following statements:

    1. I like power and control.

    2. I listen to others, but I like to have the final word.

    3. I am not an expert in all areas of my business.

4. I don't care what others think; I do what is best for me.

5. I like shared decision-making.

6. I prefer control to be with my followers.

7. I micromanage.

8. I like to recognize achievement.

9. Group members should create their own goals.

10. I do not trust my employees.

11. I like to encourage collaboration.

12. I allow group members to solve their own problems.

13. Employees do only what they're told.

14. I want my business to run through teams.

15. I am not good at following up with employees.

16. I decide how to fix problems.

17. I like to help my employees grow and learn.

18. I give very little input because my employees know their jobs better than I do.

19. I don't want to make time for employee input.

20. I like to hear the opinions of my employees.

21. Employees have the right to create their own objectives.

22. I like being in charge.

23. I want input from my employees.

24. I like my employees to make decisions on their own.

25. I tell my employees what to do, when to do it, and how to do it.

26. I want my employees to fulfill their potential.

27. I don't want more authority than others in my organization.

28. Mistakes are not acceptable.

29. When things go wrong, I ask for advice from team members.

30. Power belongs to the entire organization.

The column with the highest total is the style you use most often. One high score with two low scores indicates a strong preference for that leadership style.

Table 6-1		Scoring Your Leadership Assessment			
Item	**Score**	**Item**	**Score**	**Item**	**Score**
1		2		3	
4		5		6	
7		8		9	
10		11		12	
13		14		15	
16		17		18	
19		20		21	
22		23		24	
25		26		27	
28		29		30	
Authoritarian total		Democratic total		Delegative total	

Adapting Your Leadership Style

Leadership styles change according to situations, needs, and the business environment. During a turnover in staff, for example, delegative leadership may not be best. In this section you find out what necessitates changes in leadership style and what leadership techniques and responsibilities are possible.

Changing styles

Leadership style affects employee motivation and, consequently, productivity. You need to be aware of your dominant style and be ready to change your style for different situations. The wise leader knows that his style may be good for some employees but not for others. (Recognizing what employees respond to is dependent on a leader's emotional self-awareness. Chapter 8 delves into emotional intelligence.)

Circumstances may force you to change your leadership style. Some examples include

✔ Big changes in the business leave little time for training employees and call for authoritative leadership.

✔ When an organization reaches a point at which all employees are well-trained and attuned to the vision of the company, a more delegative style is appropriate.

✔ If your company hires a large group of Generation X and Y workers who need freedom and input for their jobs, you might want to try a more democratic leadership style.

✔ A big project with a short deadline that allows no time to ask for group decision-making calls for slightly authoritarian leadership.

✔ When the economy is down, stock prices have tanked, the company must pull together and work only on products that produce revenue. In order to save employees' jobs, some must change current duties and take on new ones. You need an authoritarian approach.

Leadership style is a choice. Circumstances can cause you to change your style; certain departments or teams require a different kind of leadership than the rest of your business. The smart leader is ready to modify her leadership to meet the needs of all employees.

Noting further leadership techniques and responsibilities

As circumstances present themselves, you may have to make some changes in how you lead by adding some influential approaches to working with subordinates. You have a responsibility to your employees to lead using whatever strategies work best for the good of your workers and your organization. The situational leader diagnoses problems and responds in appropriate ways to change the circumstances or make them fit into the vision of the organization.

The charismatic leader

You may think immediately of a world leader like John Fitzgerald Kennedy when the word *charisma* is associated with leadership. A leader needs to be charismatic or to find someone in the organization who can take that role. There are times when the one sharing the company vision must be captivating and convincing. Often the leader herself can do this because the vision is so personal as well as professional — the leader feels this vision within her soul. But there are leaders who have difficulty expressing themselves, and a leader cannot be all things to all people.

The charismatic leader

✔ Is extremely self-confident

✔ Is an inspirational speaker

✔ Has high emotional intelligence

✔ Stimulates questions

✔ Energizes the environment

Short-term projects and projects that require energy and motivation need charismatic leadership. One of the problems with charisma is that an organization's success may rest on a leader's charisma, and so productivity suffers when the leader is gone.

The transformational leader

Transformational leaders charge toward change. You might take on this role as the new leader of an organization or the current leader who knows that without change the organization can become obsolete. The transformational responsibility includes a new vision, a map for that vision, and inspiration for others to follow.

Transformational leaders do the following:

✔ Challenge the status quo

✔ Offer intellectual stimulation

✔ Use influence rather than authority

Companies that are stagnant and require change need transformational leadership.

The visionary leader

Visionary leaders look into the future and share with stakeholders what lies ahead. Stating the vision, defining the vision, and creating the big picture of the organization in the minds of every employee and all stakeholders is the primary responsibility of every leader.

Visionary leaders

✔ Know exactly what they want

✔ Share the big picture for all to see

✔ Win people over

✔ Speak about and act on their vision

Visionaries are often motivating. Seeing and sharing long-term goals, they often see the best for all involved in the organization.

The reflective leader

Reflecting on the state of your organization — its successes, failures, opportunities, and so on — is an opportunity to reassess the direction you're taking. The brain shows great activity during reflection time, and reflection offers an opportunity to place more information into long-term memory. Reflection is not a luxury; it is a responsibility.

Reflective leadership characteristics include

✔ Emotional intelligence skills

✔ Ability to admit weaknesses

✔ Knowing when actions conflict with the values of the organization

Some reflective leaders keep journals in order to record information that may help the entire organization. All leaders need to take time for reflection to provide more insight as they encounter decisions that can impact the organization.

The collaborative leader

Every leader must maintain relationships within the organization. Great leaders manage to work well with teams and individuals to keep their vision and sight and fulfill the organization's mission.

Collaborators tend to

✔ Build trust with employees

✔ Include everyone

✔ Ensure fairness and openness

Collaboration helps build environments in which new and creative ideas are generated. Being collaborative can promote the development of plans to increase productivity.

The analytic leader

Leaders need to make the important things measurable instead of making measurable details important. Analyzing figures and looking at bottom lines are important. But analyzing and problem-solving do not involve only looking at data that has been gathered; leaders need to examine that data and form questions whose answers can take the organizations to higher productivity levels.

Analytic leaders do the following:

✔ Look at hard data

✔ Base decisions on facts

✔ Control their emotions

Analyzing data is an important component of good leadership. In good times or bad, you must know the bottom line to reach your goals. Following the data often leads to decision-making, but this leaves out the feelings and opinions of others. As you analyze, keep your emotional intelligence skills in mind and include your own feelings and the feelings of others who are affected by the decision.

Chapter 7

Harnessing Multiple Intelligences

. . . .

In This Chapter

▶ Getting a grip on general intelligence

▶ Introducing multiple intelligences

▶ Using different intelligences at work

▶ Assessing multiple intelligences

. . . .

*N*umbers are important in the world of business. The data you collect on products sold, the number of your employees, and the bottom line on your profit and loss statement are reliable and useful. Numbers indicating someone's intelligence may be less than reliable. In the 21st century, the important measure may not be how intelligent you are, but how you are intelligent.

A neuroscientist might tell you that your intelligence lies in the top layer of your brain, the *neocortex,* because judgment, decision-making, and future planning all reside in this area. Albert Einstein may be the person you think of as the smartest person who ever lived. But his entire neocortex was not larger than average; rather, it was found to be thinner than others. Some specific areas of his brain showed marked differences that many believe were the source of his genius.

Intelligence in Einstein's brain may be different from the intelligence that you possess. Scientific research suggests something unheard of even 15 years ago — intelligence isn't fixed. In other words, you can increase your intelligence throughout your life.

This chapter introduces you to various definitions of intelligence from the conventional to the nontraditional and shows you that how you are smart may be more important than you think. The information you find here may affect your hiring practices, the makeup of your teams, how you delegate work, and which tasks you do yourself.

Machiavelli said, "The first method for estimating the intelligence of a ruler is to look at the men he has around him." As a leader, your success depends on the men and women you employ and place in the correct positions.

Grasping General Intelligence

Researchers used to think that people were born with a brain that was a blank slate, one that could be taught just about anything that was presented in the appropriate way. Others believed that DNA was destiny. You could either blame your educators for not filling your brain with what you needed to know, or blame Mom and Dad for any failures — they didn't provide the genetic combinations to make you smart.

Testing intelligence

Some call intelligence *G* for general intelligence, others call it *IQ* or *intelligence quotient* — the number derived by dividing your mental age (determined by a test) by your chronological age and then multiplying that figure by 100. Intelligence tests, which you can find on the Internet, face looming questions about validity.

Alfred Binet is credited with the first intelligence test. Designed to discover children with special needs, the test was based on comparisons with children of the same age. It included items such as naming parts of the body, counting, vocabulary, and filling in missing words in sentences.

The intelligence tests used today are designed to predict academic success. Intelligence testing shows little correlation with your career success; your IQ score may have little effect on what you accomplish in life.

The stuff you learn: Crystal intelligence

When you learned the states and their capitals, your multiplication tables, and how to write an essay, you added to your *crystal intelligence* — learned intelligence that includes the knowledge you've accumulated and the experiences you've had. Your crystal intelligence is measured by the standardized tests you took at school. Researchers believe that your crystal intelligence increases throughout most of your life.

Thinking outside the box: Fluid intelligence

Fluid intelligence is the ability to look at things from a different angle, use abstract reasoning, and problem-solve. This kind of intelligence is independent of learned knowledge. So those states and capitals that added to your crystal intelligence did nothing for your fluid intelligence. Researchers think that fluid intelligence peaks during young adulthood and then declines throughout your life.

Those who are capable of changing strategies easily when dealing with new and different problems are said to have a high degree of fluid intelligence. Most intelligence tests measure crystal and fluid intelligence. But much of the new thinking about intelligence and its measurement is changing the need for IQ tests.

Discovering Multiple Intelligences

When it comes to discovering *how* you are intelligent, a psychologist named Howard Gardner came up with some great ideas. In 1972, Gardner was co-director of Project Zero, a research group at Harvard University that was established in 1967. Project Zero's mission is investigating how organizations, adults, and children develop learning processes. Gardner questioned the singularity of intelligence and searched for evidence that there was more than one way of being intelligent, of knowing.

Gardner proposed a theory of multiple intelligences in 1983. At that time, he anticipated seven intelligences. Later he added an eighth and finally a ninth. The following are the nine intelligences defined by Gardner that I address in this chapter:

- ✔ Verbal/linguistic
- ✔ Mathematical/logical
- ✔ Musical/rhythmic
- ✔ Visual/spatial
- ✔ Bodily kinesthetic
- ✔ Naturalist
- ✔ Interpersonal
- ✔ Intrapersonal
- ✔ Philosophical/moral/ethical

 Understanding and using multiple intelligences in the workplace can help you see the gifts that your employees bring to the table and assist you in predicting how employees will work together well (and determining why they don't). It can help you see your own intelligences and understand why you have the people you have around you as well as whom you might need.

You can look at employees' IQ scores, their grades from high school and college, and their class ranks, but none of that information tells you the whole story.

The Temporal Intelligences

Language, music, and mathematics relate to either sequencing or timing. Each of these *temporal* ways of knowing relies on the ability to rapidly sequence digits, letters, or notes in a way that shows comprehension and the ability to manipulate these sequences.

The capability to insert meaning into such sequences as numerals, letters, and musical notes are basic to our human existence. Frank Sinatra's ability to sing "Chicago, Chicago, that toddling town" provides us with information in an emotional tone that has taken musical notes and sequenced and timed them to be pleasing to the ear. Verbal/linguistic information from the visitor's bureau in Chicago would instead be presented in logical, informational, and even geographic format.

Verbal/linguistic intelligence

She was in your leadership class. She took great notes. She wrote the most comprehensive business plan the professor had ever seen. Effortlessly, she took words and created beautiful pictures that everyone understood. You wanted to hate her. But you couldn't. She talked you right out of it. She listened to you, spoke poetically, and helped you write your business plan. Such are the qualities of the verbal/linguistically intelligent person. She could have been a he, by the way. Although (as you see in Chapter 12) females have a brain edge when it comes to language, many men have this intelligence.

The upcoming sections detail the traits that define this kind of intelligence.

Telling it like it is

Networks of neurons in the temporal and frontal lobe of the brain are strong and plentiful. One of these networks, called *Wernicke's area,* is located in the left sensory lobe and contains a mental lexicon of words that flow beautifully through speech or writing. *Broca's area,* found in the left frontal lobe, offers the gift of grammar that puts together sentences that summarize, paraphrase, and translate information as this brain solves problems, tells stories, and sometimes makes you laugh.

People with a high level of linguistic ability succeed at most of the following:

✔ Writing reports

✔ Analyzing written and verbal information

✔ Understanding written and verbal language

✔ Telling stories

✔ Listening to stories and remembering them

✔ Adding humor when they speak

✔ Telling jokes

✔ Using language that suits the audience

✔ Organizing written and verbal information

Communicating at work

Every organization requires the skills of verbal/linguistic intelligence. Perhaps you have those skills and your organization is small enough that you have it all covered. If you're working in a larger company, you need others to take on various verbal/linguistic tasks. Table 7-1 shows ways you might put verbal/linguistic intelligence to work.

Table 7-1	Verbal/linguistic Intelligence at Work	
Position	**Job description**	**Verbal/linguistic skills**
Complaint department	Handling customer problems; keeping customers happy	Understands and solves problems; makes customers confident in your business
Receptionist	Answering phones; greeting clients	Speaks clearly; listens carefully; takes good notes
Human resources manager	Interviewing; promoting and demoting; creating manuals	Listens, communicates clearly, changes tone for situation; organizes
Production supervisor	Conducting individual oral and written reviews; goal-setting	Writes well; reviews with appropriate words; promotes goals; resets goals
Salesperson	Selling himself; presenting information; closing the deal	Creates rapport with words, speaks confidently, clearly, and appropriately; knows product and can explain information at different levels of understanding
Trainer	Motivating; communicating clearly; storytelling	Creates written materials; speaks clearly; keeps trainees alert and involved

Mathematical/logical intelligence

Even back in high school she was a killjoy. You know, the girl who always comes up with the reason why we can't do something fun, something risky. We'd all be hanging out and someone would say, "Let's hop in the convertible and go scoop the loop on Main Street Hill." Almost everyone would jump up and say, "Yes, let's do it!" And then there would be that voice of reason, the logical one in our group who would come up with every "what if" in the book. What if the cops are cruising Main Street and there are too many of us in the car? What about some of the undesirable guys who hang around Main Street? (Wasn't that why we were going?) What if our parents find out? If we got arrested, we'd never get into college. We'd have police records. Everyone would talk about us at school. And we'd get grounded. The logic was a killer. She had it all figured out. We never scooped the loop.

Mathematical/logical intelligence is much more than math. Solving problems in a logical way and being able to communicate that logic, dealing with scientific and technical information, and fixing faulty machinery or products are talents of a person who has this gift. The ability to use logic to perform tasks in a sequential manner and unravel mysteries following a pattern of sequences are additional traits of this temporal intelligence.

Grasping more than numbers

Mathematical/logical people may be political. Politics involves organizing people and laws in a logical manner. The mythical detective Sherlock Holmes had a logical intelligence. Clue-gathering and intuitive reasoning are characteristics of this brainpower.

Even if you don't think you're a math person, you were born with some propensity for math. The ability to see abstract patterns, to comprehend logical and mathematical formulas and concepts is a right hemisphere function. Your parietal lobe is where your brain problem solves.

People high in mathematical/logical intelligence do well with these tasks:

- ✔ Calculating
- ✔ Estimating
- ✔ Measuring
- ✔ Remaining unbiased
- ✔ Using logic
- ✔ Grouping
- ✔ Scientific reasoning
- ✔ Organizing or ordering

✔ Testing hypotheses

✔ Reasoning

Doing a number at work

Even if you aren't number smart, you may be logical or scientific. Not everyone with a strong preference for an intelligence exhibits all of the characteristics associated with it. For example, some people balance their checkbooks to the penny but have no ability to remember card sequences and so have difficulty with games such as bridge or rummy.

Mathematical/logical aptitudes may be important in your organization in several areas. Table 7-2 proposes some possible job descriptions for this intelligence.

Table 7-2	Mathematical/logical Intelligence at Work	
Position	*Job description*	*Mathematical/logical skills*
Accountant	Interprets profit/loss statement; handles accounts payable and receivable; settles accounts; advises manager	Understands the numbers; logically figures out where problem lies; devises a plan
Receptionist	Organizing calendar and appointments; receiving money; giving receipts	Logically sets up schedules; tracks receivables
Human resources manager	Interviewing; promoting and demoting; creating manuals	Figures benefits for employees; problem-solves promotions and movement of employees within organization
Production supervisor	Goal setting; trouble-shooting	Logically plans goal achievement; solves problems on assembly lines
Salesperson	Promoting financial aspects of products; figuring discounts; adjusting quantities	Checks and knows prices, pricing plans, figures discounts mentally; adjusts prices for quantities
Trainer	Organizing training logically; setting up teams	Creates written materials in a logical manner; organizing trainees
Technology coordinator	Ordering and organizing digital technology; setting up communication systems; solving technology problems	Plans for the types of technology needed; keeps technology working and updated

Musical/rhythmic intelligence

You may think he's crazy as you watch him through the glass walls in his office. And maybe he is. But it's good crazy. The way he pushes his chair on its wheels from one side of the office to the other is interesting enough. But he does it to a rhythm that you can't quite put your finger on. He moves from desk to desk, almost flying in that chair, as he hits the buttons on the computers and the video screens that keep the small television station up and running. He's his own television show. He watches the screen, pushes a key, swivels the chair so he can view the screen behind him, grabs the edge of the desk and with one mighty push and a twirl, he's at the other lineup of screens ready to type and to push off again.

This man has musical/rhythmic intelligence, and he's great at what he does. His ability to follow a sequence of steps and put them to his own personal rhythm reinforces his skill.

Tapping potential

The person with a talent for rhythm and music is an auditory learner. A listener as well as a tapper. Musical/rhythmic people hear the sounds of your equipment and know when a machine isn't running right. They hear what you say and remember it.

People with musical/rhythmic intelligence have the following attributes:

- Interpret changes in sound and pitch
- Work to a rhythm
- Remember what they hear
- Pick out appropriate music for any audience
- Notice changes in the buzz of conversation
- Can be easily distracted
- Pick up foreign languages easily
- Hear and repeat dialects
- Create interesting multi-media presentations

If you have this intelligence, you may find that you need to have background music for meetings and for work. You may find yourself overhearing conversations without intending to do so. Distracting sounds may make you irritable because they interrupt your thought processes.

The brain responds well to music. The novice musician experiences and enjoys music in the right hemisphere of the brain. A trained musician, however, uses the left hemisphere to critique the music and may show more activity in this hemisphere than the right.

Working to the beat

Unless your business is music-related, you're unlikely to have a specific job for the musical/rhythmic person. Not everyone can make a living from songwriting or becoming a disc jockey, and many people use intelligences other than their highest intelligence at work.

Placing a musical/rhythmic person under your leadership may include positions such as those in Table 7-3.

Table 7-3	Musical/rhythmic Intelligence at Work	
Job	_Job description_	_Musical/rhythmic skills_
Sound supervisor	Setting up microphones; music, sound effects	Sound discrimination
Composer	Creating music for your product; advertisements; jingles	Sound discrimination
Presenter	Present your product, company, ideas	Creates interesting multimedia presentations
Negotiator	Negotiate contracts, working condition, salaries	Notices changes in conversation
Interpreter	Translating	Picks up languages easily

The Spatial Intelligences

Three of the nine intelligences are processed in the right hemisphere and deal with spaces and places. Visual/spatial, bodily kinesthetic, and naturalist intelligence are all spatially oriented. The ability to determine where you are in space and where you are going is part of what makes us human. Every organization needs to have those members who excel at determining where the business is and whether it's heading in the right direction as it follows its vision and mission. A spatially intelligent brain can comprehend the dynamics of space (visual/spatial), successfully navigate within it (bodily kinesthetic), and differentiate among the objects that occupy space (naturalist).

Visual/spatial intelligence

He flies through the air with the greatest of ease. At least, you hope so. He has you 38,000 feet in the air, and you want him to land the plane safely. You want your pilot — and your surgeon, dentist, architect, and designer — to be high in visual/spatial intelligence. People expect artists, sculptors, and illustrators to have visual/spatial intelligence, but set designers, movie directors, and actors have it, too. Mountain climbers, skate boarders, and dancers all have a high degree of this talent, as well.

Getting the picture

In the movie *The Devil Wears Prada,* lowly assistant Andrea is picked on because she doesn't appreciate the number of people and the amount of time that went into the colors and design of the clothing that she bought off the rack. Not being a very visual or spatial person, Andi threw on her clothes and walked out the door. She was a journalist with obvious verbal/linguistic talents. As the story unfolds, Andrea changes by becoming more sensitive to color and design. By the end of the movie she appreciates the work done by her coworkers, but decides this life is not for her and returns to her journalistic goals.

Andrea had a stronger orientation toward verbal/linguistics. She obviously also showed some strength in visual spatial skills, which may not have emerged without her job opportunity at a fashion magazine. Sometimes gifts and talents don't manifest themselves without the proper opportunity. Every normal brain has functioning areas for each of the intelligences; therefore each brain has the possibility of functioning via each intelligence.

Just as clothing designers are responsible for what people wear, the DVD and CD cover designers influence what people buy and rent. It takes a high degree of skill to make a cover catch your eye and make you believe that what's inside is the most exciting or violent or scary movie that you've ever seen.

Visual/spatial intelligence lies mostly in the right hemisphere of the brain. The right parietal lobe enables the brain to visualize objects and move them around in the mind to discover the best arrangement for them, and the right occipital lobe stores visual information.

Characteristics of visual/spatial intelligence include the following:

- Sensitivity to color, form, and space
- Understanding and creating visual representations
- Reading graphs, charts, and so on
- Preference for things to be in place and pleasing to the eye
- Rotating objects in the mind

Finding a spot

Everyone wants to find a spot where his desires and goals are fulfilled. Some find it at work; others use their highest intelligence outside of work. Kathy is a highly paid administrative assistant at a large prestigious law firm. She has been with the firm for 30 years. She's efficient and full of energy. When she leaves work, she becomes a Martha Stewart clone. She walks through craft stores and flea markets where she buys scraps of material and bags of sand that become centerpieces for a wedding. With an extraordinary eye for color, she blends fresh flowers with tropical grasses, adds some wire, makes a bird's nest and *voila* — a serving table for a South African barbecue.

When Kathy retires, she wants to be a party and wedding planner. She has an intelligence that is waiting to be unleashed on a professional level. You may have on staff a Kathy or an Andrea ready for your leadership skills to place her where she can contribute to your organization in a more valuable way.

Visual/spatial opportunities in your business may include those in Table 7-4.

Table 7-4	Visual/spatial Intelligence at Work	
Position	*Job description*	*Visual/spatial skills*
Marketing	Creating ads that are well-placed in magazines and newspapers; design copy for print ads and commercials	Color sensitivity and discrimination; an appreciation of space and balance
Sales floor manager	Displaying products in an aesthetically pleasing way	Creates an environment that is pleasing to the eye using placement, tone, and color; manipulates space and objects to attract customers
Sales presentation assistant	Creating slide presentations and other visual representations	Uses visual clues to detect quality limitations; creates visuals with an understanding of color and tone
Data interpreter	Reading bar graphs, charts, photos, and other visual representations	Translates visuals into real-world applications; modifies and monitors designs
Research and development	Understanding research data and applying it to company needs; creating new ideas	Reads and interprets existing data; creates visual representations of current data
Architect or interior designer	Designing new buildings and rooms for efficiency, practicality, and beauty	Uses color, space, and layouts to create usable and aesthetically pleasing spaces

Bodily kinesthetic intelligence

Michael Jordan steals the ball, dribbles down the floor, and in a movement that looks like flying, lifts his body in the air and gracefully stuffs the ball into the basket — an extreme example of bodily kinesthetic intelligence.

For a decade most boys and some girls yearned to be "like Mike." According to Malcolm Gladwell in his book *Outliers,* becoming like Mike might take some time — about ten years or 10,000 hours of practice for such expertise. Had those starry-eyed children been told that information, some of them might have buckled down and done more work. Jordan certainly worked hard to develop his body and his skill. Genetics play a part in having the height for basketball, but developing the body and skill requires opportunity, practice, and desire.

Brain areas pertinent to this intelligence include the motor cortex, the basal ganglia, and the cerebellum. (Chapter 2 tells you more about these parts of the brain.) The motor cortex controls movement while the basal ganglia and cerebellum navigate movement.

The best job for the one

Because of her flexibility, endurance, agility, and speed, Ashlee's work at the shipping and receiving department of the corporation was superb. She was in good health, partly because she was constantly walking, running, or loading packages. Her pedometer usually read 15,000 steps by the end of her workday. Interestingly, her manager suggested a promotion for the loyal, hard worker. The position was supervisory and landed Ashlee at a desk. She hated her new job, but the $10,000 it tacked on to her yearly salary was too hard to pass up. Sitting at her desk day after day making schedules and doing other paperwork made her so unhappy that she begged her manager for a demotion back to her previous position. It took another six months before a job became available. Excited about her return, she eagerly pursued her previous record of speed and accuracy. The months away from her rigorous routine, however, left her in poorer physical shape than she had ever been. It took her months to regain her former level of work.

When Ashlee used her bodily-kinesthetic intelligence, she was happier and more productive. The *Peter Principle* states that every employee rises to her level of incompetence. So often employees are rewarded for doing a good job by being offered a higher-ranking job with a higher salary. Eventually, they may end up in a position that does not suit their capabilities. Ashlee could do the job, but she was miserable because the job didn't fit her intelligence strength.

Shaking things up

Bodily kinesthetic characteristics are not just about sports. They're about movement — fine motor and gross motor movement. They're about touch and feelings, and navigating your way through space — on a field, in a car, in design, and so on. The following list shows more characteristics of this kind of intelligence:

- Physical endurance
- Flexibility
- Muscle control
- Physical fitness and overall good health
- Fine and gross motor skills
- Agility and speed
- Excelling at physical demonstrations
- Navigating through projects and processes

Moving into position

The positions in Table 7-5 rely on bodily kinesthetic intelligence.

Table 7-5	Bodily Kinesthetic Intelligence at Work	
Position	*Job description*	*Bodily kinesthetic skills*
Service	Repairing, installing, and removing equipment	Physical endurance, agility, speed
Sales	Demonstrating products; traveling	Physical ease with body and machinery; desire to move
Packing, shipping, receiving	Packing and carrying shipments; unloading products	Strength, agility, speed, endurance
Technology	Keyboarding, working with digital media	Sensitivity to touch, fine motor skills
Efficiency expert	Determining better performance procedures	Physical speed and flexibility
Choreographer	Demonstrating and teaching physical movement	Sensitivity to movement and touch; gross motor skills; agility

Naturalist intelligence

"Roughing it" for Zack was staying at the Holiday Inn Express. Raised in the city, Zack was dragged to the zoo and the park when he really just wanted to be reading. He read about wildlife and had a rock collection, but he preferred the great indoors. To inspire team growth, the Fortune 500 company that Zack worked for decided to send several of the teams on an Outward Bound expedition. Zack didn't know whether to quit his job or call in sick. But he really liked his job and wanted to stay with this company for a few years, so off he went.

Much to Zack's surprise, his extensive reading came to life as he learned to start campfires, navigate the water, and observe weather changes. His naturalist intelligence blossomed through this experience, and he adapted to his new environment as quickly as his teammates who were used to living with nature.

The naturalist is a must-have intelligence in any organization that is trying to make the world a greener place. Sensitivity to nature and an understanding of what is happening to the environment is an intelligence that is gaining respect and admiration. But the naturalist is more. She relates to her surroundings and knows how she fits in — a natural skill for a leader or a follower.

The brain's left parietal lobe helps people discriminate between living and non-living things. The right hemisphere provides the big picture of where you are in your environment. The prefrontal cortex processes empathy and ethics. The naturalist intelligence involves the connections among these brain areas.

Classifying and then some

Classifying and categorizing things in nature have long been useful skills for working in museums, zoos, and state parks. Now major corporations are "going green" and need this talent to assist them in making many choices to preserve and serve the environment.

The naturalist may have the following gifts:

- Interest in nature
- Ability to classify and categorize things in nature
- Collecting natural objects
- Enhanced alertness to their environment
- Affinity for animals
- Keen sensory skills

  ✔ Sensitive to environmental changes

  ✔ Understanding of ecological systems

Nurturing the naturalist

The naturalist at work is going to be most comfortable in a natural setting, probably outdoors. Short of that, a room with plants, windows, and natural sunlight may suit this person best. The naturalist can add a lot to your organization whether you're in the green movement or not. Perhaps you're the "natural" leader for your business. Or perhaps you need one.

Table 7-6 shows you possibilities for positions for the naturalist.

Table 7-6	Naturalist Intelligence at Work	
Position	*Job description*	*Naturalist skills*
Recycling	Controlling waste	Interest in preserving the environment
Organic	Researching ways to grow and obtain organic foods	Interest in the environment, health, and wellness
Marketing	Letting the world know that your organization cares about the environment and the future for our children	Understands how things work in nature; knows how to preserve the environment
Health and wellness	Setting up programs to get employees into nature; eating right	Understands things in nature, interest in the environment
Photography	Taking nature photographs to display in your offices	Appreciates nature; knows the effects of nature on body and mind
Green-collar worker	Creating and administering plans to make the organization more eco-friendly	Understands nature — what hurts it and what helps it

The Personal and Social Intelligences

The entire brain takes part in the personal and social intelligences. The frontal lobes in both the right and left hemispheres are particularly involved in building and maintaining relationships, understanding yourself, and knowing right from wrong.

Interpersonal intelligence

She is the one everyone turns to in your organization. Sometimes called a "shadow leader," this woman has the ability to put others at ease, and employees feel comfortable asking her about processes, problems, and procedures. She listens carefully and treats others in a way that shows she understands them. Some of the team leaders envy her seemingly innate ability to communicate and build rapport with others. But everyone has interpersonal intelligence, and some work at it more than others. You wouldn't have others following you if you didn't have a high level of this intelligence. And if you follow the suggestions in Chapter 8, you can raise your level of this intelligence, as well.

The people in the workplace with high levels of this intelligence have winning personalities. As part of a team, they usually are the team leaders. When you need someone with good social skills, an awareness of and concern for others, and ability to relate to people in general, you call on someone with high interpersonal intelligence.

Building relationships

This people person reads others well. Recognizing others' moods, intentions, and motivations, interpersonal people are good negotiators and great friends. Among the characteristic they are known for are the following:

- ✔ Valuing relationships
- ✔ Collaboration ability
- ✔ Sharing their personal stories
- ✔ Natural leadership ability

The brain structures involved in creating this intelligence are the frontal lobe, the right temporal lobe, and the limbic system. These formations help you understand how others feel, get the gist of how those feelings relate to the current environment, and assist in building relationships.

Social graces in all the right places

Having the ability to negotiate, persuade, and affect the working life of others is one way the interpersonally intelligent brain operates. Mediation powers make this person a good negotiator, counselor, and salesperson.

Table 7-7 offers job descriptions for interpersonal intelligence.

Table 7-7	Interpersonal Intelligence at Work	
Position	*Job description*	*Interpersonal skills*
Sales	Selling product after selling themselves and the company	Relationship building, persuasion, motivation
Human resources	Finding the right position for others	Getting to know people; reading moods; providing empathy, nurturing, support
Team player; team leader	Collaborating to get work done	People skills, leadership skills, motivation
Marketing	Discovering what the target audience wants and presenting it in appealing ways	Reading people, powers of persuasion
Manager	Dealing with people in all areas of the organization	People skills, motivation, influence, persuasion, negotiation
Negotiator	Negotiating contracts	Persuasion, negotiation, influence
Receptionist	Greeting customers	Supportive, caring

Intrapersonal intelligence

Kendra's favorite book is one from childhood called *I Like Me,* and that title is her motto. She has become her own best friend. Kendra knows her flaws and works with her strengths. She has clear goals and every intention of reaching them. She makes decisions with her best interest in mind. That doesn't mean she neglects others' feelings or needs, but Kendra knows herself better than anyone else and has a strong sense of purpose. Everyone wants to be on Kendra's team because she helps make it a winning team — it's for her own good!

The person with this intelligence knows his or her own strengths and weaknesses. Having the ability to recognize when to remain in a situation and when to leave reveals a level of intelligence and maturity that belongs in every organization.

Knowing thyself

Evaluating yourself in relation to your position at work and in life can be a valuable tool for redirecting or reinventing oneself or one's career. Recognizing your own feelings and responding to them in a constructive way are attributes of intrapersonal intelligence.

The frontal lobe of the brain integrates your feelings from the limbic system and sensory information from the parietal lobe. These connections help people with this intelligence address their feelings in an appropriate way as they realize their needs and desires.

Some characteristics of this intelligence include

- ✔ Recognizing your own strengths and utilizing them
- ✔ Recognizing your own weaknesses and working on them
- ✔ Ability to work alone and enjoy it
- ✔ Understanding your own needs
- ✔ Knowing how to motivate yourself
- ✔ Accepting responsibility for own success and failures
- ✔ Using feedback to better yourself

To thine own self be true

In order to maintain a positive outlook as he deals with the introspection of his life, the intrapersonally intelligent person works on understanding his experiences and how they affect his life. You rarely find people who are guided more by their own values than by the values of others or of society, because so many people are taught to please others.

The ability to direct oneself is one reason a person of this intelligence may be very important to your organization. The second reason may be even more important for the 21st century: With jobs changing rapidly, a person who knows a lot about him or herself can be more easily trained and change position more easily. This can be the most important intelligence to have in the global business world.

Table 7-8 suggests positions that utilize intrapersonal intelligence.

Table 7-8	Intrapersonal Intelligence at Work	
Position	*Job description*	*Intrapersonal skills*
Human resources	Helping others discover information about themselves	Sharing self-questioning techniques with others; recognizing skills in others
Traveling salespeople	Working alone on the road	Self-motivation; accepting responsibility for successes and failures
Research and development	Working online and in laboratories	Ability to work alone; self-motivation
Leading from a distance	Global liaison with workers in other locations	Self-motivation; using feedback; utilizing strengths

Philosophical/moral/ethical intelligence

Two teams, two team leaders, one department. Holly knows the difference between right and wrong. She does the right thing at the right time for the right reason. Her team members have never seen her "borrow" supplies, favor a friend, or work against the company's best interest to put her team ahead.

Brad leads the other team. He sometimes tells little white lies to his superiors if his team isn't exactly up to par. Brad moved one of his best friends into the department and onto his team so they could spend more time together. Unfortunately, his friend isn't a very good team player, and the team is floundering. Brad asks Holly to help out his team. She said she would if she had full rein. Brad agreed. Holly immediately placed Brad's friend in a different department where he could be useful. She then suggested that Brad step down and turn over the team to someone who could model fairness, a strong work ethic, and responsibility for moving the company forward. Brad refused, took back his control, and — just to show Holly — brought his friend back on board.

As Holly's team raced ahead, reaching goals and moving the company forward, Brad's team members began to beg to move to Holly's team. The senior team leader evaluated the situation. Brad was moved to a different department where his talents could be used without harm to the company or to other employees. Holly took over the entire department.

Philosophical/moral/ethical intelligence is the heart of good leadership. Many seemingly strong businesses have fallen under the influence of leaders who lack moral and ethical intelligence. Having ethical leaders, managers, and employees is necessary for any business success.

A morally intelligent person has the following traits:

- Integrity
- Honesty
- Impartiality
- Fairness
- Adherence to ethical policies

Table 7-9 suggests positions in which moral/ethical/philosophical intelligence is needed.

Table 7-9	Philosophical/moral/ethical Intelligence at Work	
Position	*Job description*	*Skills*
Human resources	Putting the right person in the right job for the right reason	Knows what is best for the company
Team leaders	Modeling appropriate behaviors for team	Exhibits fairness, integrity, compassion
Senior leaders	Doing what is right regardless of personal gain	Makes the right choices to further business without hurting others
Employees	Working in department and treating others fairly	Chooses to help further others' careers; works for the good of the company

How Are You Smart? Self-Assessment

You may find that what you do at work and what you might like to do are somewhat different. But anything is possible when it comes to brains. You have the potential to develop every one of the intelligences. For instance, you may be very good at math but would rather spend your time using verbal/linguistic intelligence to communicate within the company and with clients. You may find that you are very visual, but graphs and charts aren't appealing to you, and you prefer to have someone else translate that data.

You have the power to pick the people with those intelligences you need on your team to fill in the gaps for you. The self assessment that follows can give you some ballpark ideas about yourself, and you may choose to use this assessment on your workers as well. I find that most people enjoy knowing more about themselves. You'll hear some say "Wow, I never knew I was so good at. . . ." Or, "I always thought I was musically talented, I'd like to try to fit that into the business in some way."

To determine your predominant intelligence, rank how often each of the following statements is true for you. Use a scale of 1 to 4, with 1 being *never,* 2 being *rarely,* 3 being *sometimes,* and 4 being *always.* Record your responses in Table 7-10.

1. I am good at analyzing information in written and verbal formats.

2. I am good at solving mysteries.

3. I learn foreign languages and accents easily.

4. I am good at reading graphs, charts, and so on.

5. I am physically fit.

6. I am good at classifying things in nature.

7. People see me as a leader.

8. I work best alone.

9. I am good at knowing right from wrong.

10. I am good at using stories to get points across to others.

11. I can analyze numbers quickly.

12. I easily remember what I hear.

13. I can move objects around in my mind.

14. I am agile and flexible.

15. I notice things that are out of place.

16. I am a negotiator.

17. I am self-motivating.

18. I value fairness.

19. I remember what I read and what people tell me.

20. I am good at using numerical data.

21. I am good at creating multimedia presentations.

22. I am sensitive to balance, color, form, and space.

23. I have physical endurance.

24. I am sensitive to changes in the natural environment.

25. I get energy from being around people.

26. I improve myself through feedback.

27. I am a compassionate leader.

28. Information in written and verbal form is easy for me to understand.

29. I am good at problem-solving.

30. I am good at interpreting changes in sound and pitch.

31. I excel at creating visual representations.

32. I am good at physical demonstrations.

33. I believe strongly in the green movement.

34. I am good at collaborating with others.

35. I am good at meeting my needs.

36. I live up to my values.

37. I am good at changing my language to fit my audience.

38. I excel at math.

39. I am an accomplished musician.

40. I am keenly aware of sounds, sights, smells, tastes, and touch.

41. Health and wellness are important to me.

42. I excel at adapting to natural environments.

43. I can easily persuade others to my way of thinking.

44. I know my strengths and weaknesses.

45. I have a strong moral compass.

Table 7-10		Finding Your Intelligences				
Intelligence	*Scores*					*Total*
Verbal/linguistic	1____	10____	19____	28____	37____	
Mathematical/logical	2____	11____	20____	29____	38____	
Musical/rhythmic	3____	12____	21____	30____	39____	
Visual/spatial	4____	13____	22____	31____	40____	
Bodily kinesthetic	5____	14____	23____	32____	41____	
Naturalist	6____	15____	24____	33____	42____	
Interpersonal	7____	16____	25____	34____	43____	
Intrapersonal	8____	17____	26____	35____	44____	
Moral/ethical	9____	18____	27____	36____	45____	

Total the numbers for each intelligence. The intelligences with the highest totals are your strengths. Remember that you have all eight intelligences at various levels.

This is not a scientific test, but it gives you a good idea about your strengths. Most people figure out their strong intelligences after reading the descriptions and characteristics.

Chapter 8

Assessing and Applying Your Emotional Intelligence

*W*hen Descartes said that the emotions and the intellect were separate, he was wrong. And neuroscientists continually prove that we cannot separate the mind, the body, and emotions.

Emotional intelligence (often referred to as EQ) is the ability to recognize and use your emotions wisely. It's vital for working with others, and it can be learned, nurtured, and enhanced. Your emotional intelligence and that of your workforce can make the difference between success and failure. Working with other emotionally intelligent people is more motivating and fun than working with those with low EQs and high cognitive ability.

Intrapersonal and interpersonal intelligences (see Chapter 7) are part of this intelligence, but emotional intelligence is a talent that everyone can and should develop. High EQ people can control and even change their emotions. Controlling your emotions helps you recognize the emotions of others, and that emotional detection enables you to handle someone else's emotions and lead others to your way of thinking. Through honest emotional relationships you work better with your employees, peers, and customers.

In professional situations, you must be able to handle yourself in order to communicate in an appropriate manner. Emotions sometimes reveal themselves quickly; having power over those emotions can be beneficial because it gives you time to think and respond logically as well as to understand the emotions of the person you're dealing with.

The rise of EQ

In 1995 science writer and psychologist Daniel Goleman wrote *Emotional Intelligence: Why It Can Matter More Than IQ*. This book caused a sensation and a keen interest in how important a role emotions play in our lives. Although some people thought emotional intelligence would fall by the wayside as trends tend to do, the research behind his book and the studies that have been done since have shown that emotionally intelligent people may be more valuable in the workplace and as leaders than those with high grades and impressive test scores.

Many schools have tried to incorporate emotional learning into their curriculums. Illinois is the first state to require that social emotional learning be taught in the classroom. Carefully written state standards guide the implementation of this curriculum.

Incidentally, a high EQ may be good for your career in yet another way: A recent study revealed that doctors with exceptional people skills make just as many mistakes as doctors who don't possess those skills. But the doctors who know how to talk to people and make them believe they care get sued less often.

Your emotions are part of who you are. Understand and use your emotions wisely, and you become a better communicator, leader, partner, parent, and friend. In this chapter, I show you the components of emotional intelligence, show you how to recognize others who are high in this intelligence, and give you tips for using emotional intelligence to your advantage.

Grasping the Role of Emotions

Cognitive scientists sometimes refer to our emotions as *emotional states*. An emotional state is a combination of thoughts, feelings, and physiology. These states arise from responses to environmental cues. You respond to these cues emotionally, and doing so creates your thoughts. Every thought you think is in response to some level of emotion. Emotions cause you to change your behavior in order to survive. Whether to save yourself physically or socially, your emotions react to the environment you're in.

Reacting to your environment

The fly is buzzing around your picnic table driving you crazy. You take the kung fu approach and try to catch the fly in your hand as it buzzes by. You fail. You roll up the nearest magazine and swat at the fly but miss. The fly returns, and he seems to be even quicker. That pesky fly has changed his behavior in order to survive. Why does he keep coming back if his life is in danger? Because he has to eat to survive. Instinctively, your fly reacts to the environment, darting and diving to get food and keep from getting squashed.

It seems like a tough life, but you react in similar ways every day. On a purely survival level, you sprint across the street to keep from getting hit by a truck. On a more cognitive level, you respond in conversation depending on whom you are speaking to: with a close friend, you can throw in some expletives, with your mother-in-law not so much, and with your superior, you may be very careful in your use of language, context, and tone. Every action and reaction is the result of an emotional state. The emotional state you're in as you dart out of the truck's path is based on your physiology (your racing heart and blood being pumped to your legs), your thoughts ("Oh, crud, I can't believe I didn't see this coming."), and your feelings ("I don't want to die!").

Social survival

Emotions save your life. You look both ways before crossing the street because you fear death. (Or because you have your mother's voice inside your head — not listening to Mom may mean certain death!)

Social death is another motivator. As a teenager, if I attended a party where alcohol was served and I had a drink, I would think, "Please, don't let me get in a car accident tonight or my dad will find out and kill me." My dad isn't a violent man; he wasn't going to physically end my life. But I would have been grounded, and that meant social death. Knowing I should not displease my dad kept me very cautious about getting caught and kept my grades up, as low grades would also have caused a social setback.

Your emotions often lie at a subconscious level. In every environment you learn the emotional and then cognitive responses that can help you survive and thrive under those particular circumstances. Some of these become so automatic that the reasons you react the way you do never enter your mind. Yet sometimes your purpose is clear, and you respond on a conscious level, using your emotional states as a basis for what is good for you at the time.

Becoming Self-Aware

Too much emotion at the wrong time isn't good for vote-getting. Senator Edmund Muskie broke down when talking about the media's attack on his wife in 1972. Many analysts say that misstep lost the election for him. Hillary Clinton, however, must have broken down at the right time. Her show of emotions about the travails of the campaign made some voters see her as more human. Her campaign became stronger for a short while.

Before you can identify and deal with emotions in others, you must begin to recognize and deal with your own emotions. Emotions are present in all relationships. Some emotions save lives and others can destroy. Although many people think high IQs are the determining factor for success in the business world, some studies show that emotional intelligence is a much stronger factor.

Noting your feelings

Sometimes emotions are elusive. You may not feel quite right, yet you're not sure if you're sad, depressed, or frustrated. One CEO used to answer the question, "How are you feeling?" with "What are my choices?" Although he was trying to be funny, he brings up an interesting question. Can you choose how you feel? Some psychologists believe that you can. First, you must be able to differentiate among emotions.

How well do you know yourself? If you can identify your emotions and determine what you think about that mood, you're on your way to truly becoming self-aware. For instance, if you feel yourself becoming angry over a situation and think you might lose control of your actions or behaviors, you can choose your next action to create a better outcome.

Your sense of well-being relies on the emotional balance in your life. An extreme amount of emotion may lead you to poor decision-making, poor relationships, and poor self-esteem. When asked to name their emotions, most people list the following in no particular order:

- ✔ Happiness
- ✔ Sadness
- ✔ Anger
- ✔ Frustration
- ✔ Disgust
- ✔ Fear

These six emotions are considered universal emotions. In other words, people around the world experience these emotions and show them with the same kind of facial expressions. Consider how these emotions affect your performance, relationships, and reactions at work. Can you identify your own strengths and weaknesses? Doing so makes a difference in how you react to situations and to feedback from your employees and your customers.

Your brain's prefrontal cortex is in charge of many executive functions, including attention. Self-awareness involves attending to your feelings — and that includes your physical responses. The prefrontal cortex interacts with areas in the brain related to bodily senses: heart rate, respiration, digestive system, and temperature, to name a few. Awareness that your heart is racing provides information for the prefrontal cortex to determine what you're feeling and how you're reacting to it on a physical level. Armed with this information, you can make some choices as to how you respond to or control the situation.

Other emotional intelligence skills are based on your self-awareness. You are a self-aware leader if the statements that follow are true of you:

✔ I recognize my emotions.

✔ I am in touch with my body and its responses.

✔ I know my strengths and weaknesses.

✔ I understand my goals, dreams, and hopes.

✔ I trust my instincts and usually make good decisions.

✔ My work and my values match.

✔ I am inspired or energized by my work.

✔ I take time to reflect.

If you feel that you aren't good at recognizing your own emotions, try the following:

✔ Make the time to reflect upon your feelings throughout the day. How did you respond to them?

✔ Keep a journal of your feelings.

✔ When someone asks "How are you?" try to give a precise answer related to your current feelings. Instead of the automatic "fine" response, identify your feelings without boring people to death — "I'm curious about this meeting."

✔ Keep a scorecard of your feelings over several weeks. Average those feelings to determine which emotions are most prevalent and how they may affect your relationships.

Using your emotions productively

After you know how to recognize your emotions, you can then work on handling them. Emotional intelligence is not the ability to hide your feelings but rather to use your emotions wisely. Expressing your feelings in a productive way can be the difference between forming lasting relationships and destroying them. The prefrontal cortex of the brain plays a large part in regulating our emotions. However, the prefrontal cortex can also deregulate emotions.

Taking charge of emotions

During one corporate meeting at which leadership, management, and workers were exploring an obvious failure of a plan that had been initiated to increase production, the leadership was put "on the block." Employees let their frustrations run the meeting; they were angry about the amount of time wasted for this project. It had been a top-down idea, and employees ranted and raved over their feeling that they knew better how to create a successful plan.

The CEO's stomach churned; his heart rate became rapid, and his mouth was dry as his brain took him down to survival level. He was in a full-blown fight-or-flight response and about to override the yelling. He imagined different negative scenarios. But he caught himself before he was about to let loose. He walked a short distance from the others and counted to ten. He took several deep breaths. As he approached the front of the meeting room he put his hand up for silence as he picked up the microphone.

"I accept my responsibility for this failure," he began. The room quieted down. He took another deep breath. "You are all correct in assuming we made a mistake by not including you in the planning. Sometimes I forget that I am not the only person who has the best interest of this company as a priority. You are the foundation of this entire organization. It is time to regroup. A planning committee will be formed with representatives from each department. If you are not on this planning committee, please realize that we need all of you to put forth your efforts and indeed, your passion, to keep production as high as possible until we iron this out. Please e-mail me or make an appointment to see me if you have ideas that will help with this plan. I cannot promise that all recommendations will be used; that will be up to the new committee. But I promise that all will be considered."

By the time he finished, his heart rate was back to normal and he smiled and nodded at this passionate group of people who were going to help turn this failure around. By recognizing his emotions and putting forth effort to change them, he was able to keep control of the situation. And by admitting his weaknesses, he received empathy and support from the crowd.

Imagine yourself at a leadership conference. You come upon one of your friendly competitors and begin a pleasant conversation. At one point your competitor mentions bidding on a contract that he assumes you also were invited to bid on; however, you were unaware of the opportunity. Suddenly, your mood changes. Your brain begins focusing on not only the fact that you did not get this rather large contract, but your company wasn't notified of the bidding prospect. As the conversation continues, your competitor mentions another opportunity, one that everyone will be notified about. Your mind shifts to this new possibility and you listen with interest, but something in the back of your mind is bothering you. As you participate in this dialogue, you know that you aren't as attentive as you should be. Your competitor feels somewhat rejected by your lack of interest and finds a reason to move on to speak with others.

That nagging feeling of anger and frustration, perhaps even some fear over losing possible business, has caused you to damage the relationship you had with your competition. In the future, she may not feel obliged to share any pertinent information with you on potential contracts. The lack of control over your emotions can be very damaging.

If you monitor reactions such as these, you can learn to change them. What caused you to lose the connection in the conversation? Was it anger over feeling left out of the competition? Was it fear of not being good enough to be included? How can you overcome these feelings?

After any instance wherein your emotions take over your focus, take some time to reflect on what was going on inside your head. That inner dialogue was saying something to you that changed your feelings and your mood. Recognizing the reactions helps you gain control over them in the future.

Your attention to a conversation takes place in your working memory. Working memory is the active process of taking incoming information and connecting it to knowledge that you already have stored. As you spoke with the friendly competitor, your working memory was filled with the trivial information in your conversation until she mentioned the contract that you never got to bid on. Then the fear or anger from your amygdala, the emotional center in your brain, filled your working memory with doubts about yourself and your business. It was so full of these feelings and the thoughts that emanated from them that you couldn't focus on the rest of the conversation. Even after your curiosity was piqued by new information, the nagging thoughts remained and left you feeling uncomfortable and looking disinterested.

Lack of emotional control can hinder success. Learning to control your emotions in life-threatening situations is difficult, and controlling your emotions under perceived threat may be even more complicated. Some leaders respond to small hurdles as though their survival depended on it. Discovering what you need to handle your emotions and your impulses is sometimes a matter of trial and error.

What steps can you take to uncover and handle your emotions? Try the following:

1. **As you scan your work environment, be aware of those people, situations, spaces, and so on, that trigger emotional responses in you.**

   You may find that small meetings held in a cubicle affect your need for space, for example. Suggest the meetings be held elsewhere.

2. **Examine those triggers and learn to recognize them.**

   If you find yourself feeling angry every day at a certain time and you don't know why, take the time to go over any encounters you've had thus far and see whether you can pinpoint the problem.

3. Determine the appropriate responses to each trigger.

As you become aware of repetitious responses, decide how you can control or change the emotional states that result from those environmental triggers.

4. Make a list of any extraordinary challenges you face.

If you find recognizing and responding more appropriately to some triggers but are unable to avoid those triggers, write down the encounters and try to figure out another approach when you are away from work and no longer emotional about the situation.

5. Experiment with coping strategies.

If you experience chronic stress from these challenges, choose some strategies that have helped you in the past and try each one until you discover what lowers your stress most. For example, exercise, meditation, or stopping by another colleague's office to chat may help you keep your stress levels low. Make time to institute your favorite strategy regularly.

Stress expert and neuroscientist Bruce McEwen refers to the body's adaptive responses to stress as *allostasis*. The body tries to adapt to the stress responses by maintaining balance or homeostasis. With just a little stress, the body produces hormones that improve your memory and help you store important information. Acute or chronic stress hinders these same processes.

If your allostatic load becomes too great, it affects your mood, emotions, and behaviors. For instance, perhaps someone in your personal or professional life suggests that you might be stressed. You don't believe them because you're so used to the load you're carrying that you aren't conscious of your stress level. You think this person is crazy, but when a second person suggests you might need a break, even though you want to "shoot the messenger" you realize that would just prove their point. You decide to give it a try.

You put on your Alfred E. Newman tee shirt with the "What, Me Worry?" slogan and take off for the weekend. After all, you don't want to miss work, you just want to appease these people in your life. You go on a golf weekend with your friends. The weather is great and you have a wonderful time. You think, "Maybe they were right! I do feel better. And now they will all leave me alone."

When you return to the office with a healthy glow, all goes well — for a little while. The same old stressors are still there. Although you believe you have returned with a zero stress load, you find yourself flaring up more easily. Before the day is over, you realize that you can feel the stress. Why can't you handle situations more easily? Why aren't your emotions under control?

Worth waiting for

You are four years old. You have just been offered a marshmallow — quite a treat for a child in the 1960s. But wait — if you don't eat the marshmallow right now and wait for the marshmallow giver to return from an errand, you can get a second marshmallow. One now or two later? What's a child to do?

Stanford University conducted the marshmallow test with four-year-olds and uncovered interesting information about impulse control. The initial impulse is to eat the marshmallow. It's there. It looks delicious. But some of those youngsters were able to wait for up to twenty minutes. They distracted themselves. Some sang. Some ran around the room. Some just sat and stared at the marshmallow and waited. Others ate the marshmallow before the experimenter could leave the room. They weren't waiting for anything.

These children were followed into adolescence where some striking differences showed up. Those who waited for the marshmallow were more socially adept, had more friends, and were more resilient, dependable, and goal-oriented than those who could not wait. The kids who waited scored an average of 200 more points on their SATs than the non-waiters. Delaying gratification and impulse control lead to better decision-making, the ability to get along with others, and controlling emotions in order to learn more.

The great news is that some of those four-year-olds who were unable to delay gratification in the 60s learned the skill somewhere along the way. As adults, they are able to control their impulses and delay gratification. This important life skill is learnable. The brain can change!

Your stress level before you take your weekend retreat is very high and has been for some time. After the weekend your stress levels are lower, but not even close to normal. So when the week begins and you have done nothing to manage the stressors at work or your responses to those stressors, you jump right back to where you were.

High stress levels endanger your health, your relationships with others, and your ability to maintain your vision and reach long-term goals. Stress changes your outlook from long-term to short-term. Getting through the day or through a project is as far-sighted as you can be. Stress keeps you in the moment.

Motivating Yourself to Move Toward Goals

Motivated people get things done. This emotional intelligence competency includes having both hope and optimism. In this section I show you how to motivate yourself and increase your hope and optimism, so that you may model these competencies and teach them to your employees.

The prefrontal cortex, with the assistance of other brain structures, is in charge of self-motivation. Motivation comes from one of two sources: desire or need. If you or your brain feels you need something for your survival, you are motivated to do something about it. If what you're doing has no survival value, then you must desire it.

Your goals, your dreams, and your vision motivate you. With an optimistic outlook, you provide hope for your followers. As your organization works toward your goals, you find yourself hopeful. All of this provides pleasure that activates the reward system in your brain. The neurotransmitter dopamine is released, and it feels good. Because you want to maintain those good feelings, you are motivated to continue. Working toward a goal often is more pleasurable than attaining the goal. By the time you reach the goal, the brain has experienced enough of a reward for that particular accomplishment, and you're on to the next goal with equal determination, drive, and dopamine!

Cultivating hope

Hope influences inspiration and motivation, which in turn move you toward your goals. You have hope when you look forward to attaining your goals. It gives you energy to get the job done. Your hope inspires you, and you inspire those around you.

As an emotionally intelligent person, hope keeps you from backing down in the face of diversity. Hope keeps you from being overcome by depression because of circumstances that affect your goals and vision. Hope keeps you trying. How do you remain hopeful? You *can* learn to motivate yourself. Follow these steps:

1. **Break your goals down into small chunks.**

2. **Focus on accomplishing one chunk until it's finished.**

3. **Celebrate when that chunk is accomplished.**

   Each accomplishment gives you hope that you can achieve more and accomplish not just the next chunk, but the entire goal.

Think about how you inspire yourself with hope. Then reflect on whether you use that hope to inspire others. Leaders with goals, visions, and hope are willing to reshape those goals, especially in times of turmoil and change. If you find that you're unable to achieve any part of a goal, revisit the entire goal, rewrite it, and try again.

Moving from pessimism to optimism

If you've been accused of looking at the world through rose-colored glasses or of always seeing the glass as half full, you're optimistic. Hope and optimism are related. Optimists are usually hopeful and those with hope are most often optimistic.

The good news is that optimism can be learned. According to optimism expert Martin Seligman, anyone can change pessimistic views to optimistic ones. Seligman explains that an optimist

 ✔ Views disappointments as temporary

 ✔ Sees adversity as situational and not personal or enduring

 ✔ Looks at external causes of problems rather than blaming herself entirely

Pessimists, on the other hand, look at their misfortune as

 ✔ Permanent: "I never do anything right."

 ✔ Pervasive: "Things go wrong in every part of my life."

 ✔ Personal: "I am so stupid!"

If you're a pessimist who wants to become an optimist, turn negative thoughts into positive ones:

 ✔ Remind yourself that you will have other opportunities to get things right.

 ✔ Realize that adversity does not spread throughout all aspects of your life. Sometimes things go well!

 ✔ Although not blaming yourself is difficult if your background includes others telling you that you're an idiot, you can unlearn the habit. Look at the accomplishments in your life and realize that everyone makes mistakes.

Recognizing Emotions in Others

When you become self-aware and can handle your own feelings and motivate yourself, you're ready to deal with the emotions of others. Timothy Leary famously advised people to "Turn on, tune in, drop out." When it comes to emotions, you need to turn on, tune in, and drop in: turn on your emotional radar, tune in to other's feelings, and drop in to their world.

Tuning in — with a little help from the mirror neurons

You can tune into others' emotions after you have your own feelings under control. Because the brain cannot multitask, you can't focus on your own feelings and pay attention to someone else's. Tuning in to what someone might be feeling and thinking is usually called *empathy*.

Some levels of empathy make others feel listened to and understood. When an individual thinks you understand her, her brain releases important chemicals. Those chemicals — dopamine, serotonin, and endorphins — cause the brain to feel pleasure and feel close to you. When you listen as well as you speak, collaboration with employees or customers becomes much easier. You can persuade people to see your point of view through these healthy collaborations.

Many believe that empathy is associated with mirror neurons. These groups of brain cells are located in the left hemisphere and connect when you watch someone perform a task. They connect to each other as though you're performing the task rather than watching. Mirror neurons may go beyond physical tasks and make connections through emotional observations. These neurons basically read minds, or at least intentions.

When you see someone walking toward a car, your mirror neurons tell you that he's going to open the door and get in. You would be shocked if the person smashed the window instead. In the same vein, if you observe someone upset over losing a loved one, you may get choked up; if you've been through a similar experience, you have a pattern for this kind of emotion stored in your brain. Those who have the most active mirror neuron systems tend to empathize more than those who do not.

Empathy and influence

Empathy enables you to feel what others are feeling. Using your empathic skills to help others feel listened to and understood offers you an opportunity to wield your influence. Leadership expert John C. Maxwell points out, "People don't care how much you know until they know how much you care." Getting in touch with others' feelings is the pathway to understanding their values, interests, desires, and needs.

Empathy enables leaders to make better decisions based not just on fact but on intuitive reasoning. You may believe you know what is best for those you lead, but without using your influence from the strong emotional connections you have made, you may be the only believer.

Empathy begins at home. Most babies respond to the cries in the nursery by crying themselves, an indication that they recognize emotions in others. Circuitry in the emotional brain combines information from facial expressions, voice recognition, and body movement to help keep you attuned to others' feelings.

Begin honing your empathy skills by observing facial expressions, tonality, and gestures or body language. Then compare what a person says to your observations to get an idea of what the person is feeling. This intense observation may cause you to have that same feeling or at least enable you to respond appropriately.

Leaders used to believe that they needed power and control, but they were wrong. Power comes from understanding relationships. Control belongs to every stakeholder. When you make others feel that they have some control over their lives and the power to make a difference, they follow your lead. The brain needs to feel in control, otherwise it would be constantly stressed.

Modeling the Emotion You Want to See

Emotions are contagious. Catch up with someone whose emotions are stronger than yours, spend some time with them, and *voila!* You feel the same way. It's not voodoo; it's real.

Educators are experts at setting an emotional tone. Walk into a classroom in a neutral state and what do you get? Kids who don't care. Walk in excited about your content, and you get students who can't wait to learn. The same result occurs at a meeting. Team meetings, organizational meetings, and even client lunches need to be led by the emotionally attuned individual.

Observe friends or colleagues in a casual situation; you can see that their bodies tend to mirror each other after several minutes of chatting.

You can make an impact with your feelings both positively and negatively. Deep emotions tend to make the greatest impact, and negative emotions are more powerful than positive.

Studies have traced the flow of emotion from leader to subordinate. Researches used vehicles such as movie clips to initiate positive or negative moods, and then tracked leaders as they met with employees. The leader's mood usually prevailed and spread. Before you step into your next meeting, check your crabbiness level.

Selling with empathy

Phillip arrived at the restaurant a few minutes early. He didn't want to seem too eager, but he also didn't want to keep Roger Reed waiting. Rog had a reputation for leaving a meeting if anyone was even a few minutes late. The deal in the works would make Phil's month if it went through. Practice makes perfect, and Phil had been practicing his pitch for days. He was ready!

You could have knocked Phil over with a feather when Roger walked in with his wife screeching in his ear. Holding the phone as close to his ear as he could to keep others from hearing, Roger attempted to calm her down. He said he was sorry for missing the golf luncheon at the club today. He had forgotten about it and had made this luncheon meeting with a prospective ad agency. Of course, he would never let this happen again. He begged for her forgiveness, hung up the phone, and turned with a glare toward Phil at the table.

Phil knew it was time to regroup. His pitch would have to be put aside until he got Roger in a better state of mind. Rog sat down with a growl, sat back, crossed his arms and stared at Phil. Phil slowly sat back, nodded at Rog, and said, "I had a dental appointment run late last week. My wife was freaking out because our daughter had a recital. Boy was I in trouble!" With that, Phil sighed and crossed his arms. Rog seemed to relax a bit at this confession.

"My wife is receiving an award for the Nine Hole Golf League. She wanted me to be there. It would be me and 75 women probably talking more about what they wear on the course than what clubs they use!" Rog laughed. He unfolded his arms and leaned forward. "What do you have for me, Phil?"

With this, Phil unfolded his arms, leaned forward, and began his pitch. He was successful at a process called mirroring. Seemingly unrelated to mirror neurons, *mirroring* another person's actions can put breathing rate, heart rate, and possibly brain waves in sync. After they're attuned in this way, people often feel they're with their soul mate, someone who truly understands them.

Consequences of spreading gloom or anger are easy to predict. Consider the following two scenarios.

- ✔ **The grinning leader:** You walk into your meeting with a smile from ear to ear. You greet others still flashing those pearly whites. What do your employees do? Smile right back at you. Viewing all of those smiles looking at you makes the happiness escalate. The meeting is bound to be good with everyone in a positive mood.

- ✔ **The glum leader:** Doom and gloom have overcome you. You just lost an account and are very unhappy. Your meeting is scheduled, so you storm in. Your face shows anger or disgust. You look out at your audience. Of course, your subordinates react to the look on your face. They smile to try to change your emotional state. But their smiles infuriate you. After all, what are they smiling about? You just lost an account.

You frown and their smiles fade. They're thinking, "What's wrong with him? What did I do? That son of a gun better not think I'm going to go out of my way for him." Getting your message across at the meeting becomes a steep uphill battle.

When you cannot spread good feelings, get someone else to do it for you. Intense emotions may lead to circumstances that produce only negativity, an emotional environment you probably want to avoid.

Dealing with Out-of-Control Emotions

Even if you are able to recognize and deal with your emotions and the emotions in those you live and work with and even if you're a pro at motivating yourself and others, you're going to have a few fluke moments. Sometimes, something happens and you discover that your emotions run away with you and from you.

The upcoming sections tell you about the way your brain reacts to these situations and what you can do to regain control.

When your emotional cool is hijacked

You're cool, calm, and collected. You know your working environment; you understand your emotional triggers. Life is good. But out of nowhere, it happens. When you least expect it, an emotional surge overwhelms your brain, and your frontal lobe has no chance of suppressing it. Daniel Goleman, author of many books on emotional intelligence, calls this surprising rush an emotional hijacking. Your primitive emotional center, the amygdala, is so inundated that it takes over your brain. It causes a loss of control so over the top that when you come down you usually don't remember what has happened. And you don't understand what came over you.

Emotional hijacking may occur under circumstances such as when you

- ✔ Have been treated unfairly
- ✔ Have been insulted or disgraced
- ✔ Suffer a blow to your dignity
- ✔ Feel that your self-esteem is threatened
- ✔ Experience frustration or difficulty reaching a goal

Watch out for the (emotional) flood

Although emotional hijacking is problematic, occasional outbursts might be forgiven. They may even be an avenue toward improving your emotional intelligence skills. Reflecting on the situation and creating more positive responses is certainly helpful.

Sometimes hijacking leads to *flooding* — one hijack after another. Your allostatic load is so great that you are flooded with emotion. Ever hypervigilant, your body is ready for the worst. Your heart rate is up, your respiration accelerates, and you feel you can't get out of the way of your emotions. Responses become inappropriate, working at all becomes difficult, and if another hijack situation doesn't arise, you simulate one of your own. You anticipate a situation before it occurs. You make the worst happen; you damage relationships, say things you might regret, and you lose the respect of your colleagues, coworkers, and employees.

Flooding is the worst-case scenario of not having a handle on your emotions. If you feel like you have been in control and things have been going smoothly, but suddenly you start to lose confidence, have difficulty being flexible, and feel stifled by indecision, examine what has happened in your life to cause these changes in you.

Rather than missing solutions to problems, losing the confidence of your employees, and feeling lousy for hours, remove yourself from any situation that causes a hijacking or flooding. Step back and see what in your environment has changed that causes such inappropriate emotional responses. Answer the following:

- ✔ Is your personal life under control? Although you think you have left your life at home, doing so is almost impossible. Check out what's wrong and fix it.

- ✔ What changes have occurred at work? Sometimes minor changes can put you on edge. Then when something goes wrong in a meeting or discussion, your already-stressed brain begins to overreact.

- ✔ Is someone higher up on the leadership ladder putting pressure on you? When your organization isn't producing to the satisfaction of your board or investors, you probably begin each day more stressed than usual. Create a plan to solve the problem and keep yourself focused on following it.

- ✔ Are you eating well and getting enough sleep? A lack of nutrients and/or sleep produces stress. Your emotions are harder to control when you don't properly care for your brain and body.

Chapter 9

Thinking Your Way to the Top: Decision-Making

In This Chapter

▶ Calling on brain and gut to make decisions

▶ Discovering the brain's methods for deciding

▶ Bulking up your working memory

Some days, decision-making comes easily; on others, making up your mind isn't just an effort but a seeming impossibility. Successful leadership doesn't allow you the luxury of procrastination. Certain crucial decisions require you to make up your mind on the spot. Of course, what your brain determines is crucial may not be to others, which presents another decision: Do you decide right away or take the time to gather more information?

You may urge yourself or others to "look rationally" at a decision. Guess what? The brain doesn't work that way. You don't make rational decisions unless you look at data, and I mean just the bottom line, and decide based solely on those numbers. The rest of your brain may be screaming for input, or quietly whispering something to you after you make the decision. Do you ignore that and leave your decision as is? That may be the best way for a leader to present herself as a confident, no-nonsense, and goal-oriented person in charge. But will your brain leave you alone?

Making good choices is a matter of gathering input from all areas of your brain. Let the executive brain mull things over with the emotional brain and choose based on the perceptions of both.

In this chapter you find out how to use cognition and emotions in decision-making. You find out about the importance of working memory for combining information from different areas of your brain including your right and left hemispheres, your prefrontal cortex, and your emotions.

One Head, One Heart, Better Decisions

Thinking about your thinking is called *metacognition,* and it's a uniquely human ability. Aristotle said that the rational mind had the responsibility of controlling the emotional mind so that it could be useful in the world. Considering your emotions may be key in making decisions.

Making choices: Got guts?

I have a gut feeling.
I know it in my heart.
I feel it in my bones.

Almost no one says anything like, "My brain is telling me . . ." or "I can feel it in my mind." Although other parts get the credit, the feeling that you're right originates in the emotional center of your brain.

Do you remember Data from *Star Trek: The Next Generation?* Just like Mr. Spock who preceded him, Data examined only the facts. Captain Kirk added the human touch, the emotional component. Data rattled off, well, data, and logically offered decisions. Having a Data on your team or inside your brain is good, and having Data work with Captain Kirk to form a combined rational/emotional choice is even better.

You make decisions all day long. You make a choice about what to wear, what to eat, when to work, and when to play. Most of these choices are easy. (It's casual Friday; I'll wear jeans. I'm on a diet; I'll eat a salad.) But when it comes to the tough choices, the ones you may not have a feeling for anywhere in your body, you have to make a choice about how to make the choice!

When you face a decision, your course of action may be one of the following:

- ✔ You don't know what to do and so do nothing.
- ✔ You need to think about it.
- ✔ You know instinctively what to do, and you do it.

The upcoming sections describe ways to address each of these situations.

When you don't know what to do

When you know what to do but don't do it, you're procrastinating. Doing nothing when you don't know what to do is different, but both of these situations end up with the same result. By not making a decision or not acting on one, you make a decision. Sometimes "deciding" by default can haunt you.

Can't make up your mind about the new campaign? You do nothing, and you stay with the old campaign. Decision made. Don't know whether to invest in that stock? Do nothing and you're doing something — not buying that stock.

A good leader gathers great people around her to assist in decisions. It's okay to sit back, give others some power, and see what happens. But you must be ready to step in if you feel their decisions won't benefit your organization.

Thinking it through: Two types of decisions

Two kinds of decision-making strategies exist:

- ✔ **Veridical decision-making** is based on fact only.
- ✔ **Adaptive decision-making** is based on facts plus prior experience or emotions.

Some of the knowledge you have stored in your long-term memory consists of veridical knowledge. When you decide whether to pay with cash or credit card, the decision is made from a single answer as to how much money is in your account. Veridical decisions get you through most concrete problems that you deal with on a daily basis.

But most problems are somewhat ambiguous. Approaching fuzzy problems in a veridical fashion is difficult at best. Most leadership decisions are more adaptive in nature, and leaders must look at these problems from many different angles. When you decide whether to look for another employee for your accounting department, you have many angles to consider. Can you afford another salary? Can your current staff get the job done in a timely manner? Do you need specific expertise that you currently do not have?

As you run your organization, adaptive decision-making affects your productivity and your success. When making this type of decision, you consider the following aspects:

- ✔ **Environment:** What are the expectations of your company; how can your decision affect its culture and climate?
- ✔ **Individuals:** Will others be directly affected and need some input?
- ✔ **Priorities:** Will this decision be beneficial based on your current priorities?
- ✔ **Consequences:** Brainstorm all possible consequences. If they occur, was the decision too risky? Or is the risk acceptable?

The brain's prefrontal cortex handles adaptive decision-making and executive functions like judgment. The prefrontal cortex can consider various aspects of a decision, look at the options, and make a choice. Most of this work occurs in an area of the prefrontal cortex called the *orbito-frontal cortex,* which is right behind the eyes. This structure combines emotions from the amygdala with rational thoughts about the problem. It also takes into consideration the survival brain. Much of the adaptive decision-making process occurs without conscious knowledge.

Snap to it: Making decisions on the spot

Using your decision-making in an instant is sometimes called *snap judgment,* and it's the focus of a lot of ongoing research. When you're walking down the sidewalk and you see a piano falling from a window right above you, you don't stop to think about your options. You just move quickly. That snap judgment works well for you.

Researchers are looking at where these decisions arise in the brain, and whether decisions that are made very quickly are as valid as decisions made using more time and analysis.

Dopamine is no dope

In Chapter 2, I show you how the neurotransmitter dopamine affects your reward system and attention system. Because it's released for these two functions, dopamine is also very much involved in the decision-making process. The *anterior cingulate cortex,* the ACC, guides your brain into decisions based on your experiences and the outcomes of prior decision-making. When something goes wrong, the dopamine neurons in the ACC become active trying to figure out why.

Dopamine neurons remember and learn from past experiences. Have you ever been on a cruise and gotten seasick? Seasickness is the result of your dopamine neurons having certain expectations of how your body responds in space, and then being surprised by the motion of the ocean. A sensory conflict begins and, until the dopamine neurons "learn" to change for the motion, you feel sick.

You can make technical decisions using veridical decision making, but you need to use adaptive thinking to make leadership decisions. Adaptive thinking requires feelings. Dopamine is essential for making the connections between higher-level thinking and emotional thinking.

Dopamine works in two ways:

- ✔ In the prefrontal cortex, dopamine inhibits unnecessary and unwanted thoughts from the focus of the problem.
- ✔ In the reward system, dopamine remembers what works and what made you feel good, as well as what didn't work and brought you no reward.

The Frontal Lobe: CEO of Your Brain

Most people envision the CEO of a large company residing in the penthouse suite and working on the top floor of the building in an enormous office surrounded by windows that take in a beautiful view. The CEO of your brain, the frontal lobe, has a similar setting. It resides at the highest level of your brain, takes up quite a bit of brain geography, and has a view of the world like no other.

The frontal lobe is where decisions are made. Your rise to leadership depended on your frontal lobe abilities. But your frontal lobe didn't work alone. The interaction among many brain areas and the emotional center enabled you to work with others, handle relationships with clients and other employees, organize, plan, and make decisions.

Train your brain, change your life. You did this through your experiences, your relationships, your reflective thinking, and your ability to work with your emotions and feelings rather than against them or letting them run the show. When you decide, you can base your decision on intuition, a more automatic process, or use a more analytical and reflective method. Both are overseen by the frontal lobe, in particular that prefrontal cortex.

Time is a factor in decision-making. Whether you have to make a spur-of-the-moment decision or you have time for researching, analyzing, and consulting others affects your decision. Many people had to make split-second decisions during the terrorist attacks of September 11, 2001. Some became helpless; they couldn't decide what to do because time was limited. Others became leaders and took care of the helpless; they used their feelings to create actions. After those events, many people changed their decision-making processes because they looked at the world differently. They took a "life is too short" attitude, and as a result some of their short-term decisions were made from a different perspective, and some of their goals were changed.

Giving yourself time to decide

Whenever you face a decision, the problem or decision comes to the attention of the *reticular activating system* (RAS) in the brain stem. If you need to attend to the problem or are interested in solving it, the dilemma is transmitted up to your amygdala, the brain's emotional center, where you begin to feel uncertain, afraid, frustrated, or angry. If you don't act on those negative feelings right away, you have a chance to examine the issue at a higher brain level. The frontal lobe and the prefrontal cortex take over.

Give yourself ten seconds for the predicament to get up to the brain's executive areas and apply some logic to the issue. By doing so, you suppress those overwhelming negative emotions, and so you don't act without some reflection but take those feelings into account as you analyze, devise a plan, organize your resources, determine possible consequences, and then share your decision.

Becoming more aware of your body's responses to stress helps you control your emotions and take them into consideration along with your rational thoughts as you consider an issue.

For instance, Keith operates a chain of stores that cater to runners. Running is big business. He sells the top brands that many runners stay with year after year. He also sells walking shoes, aerobic shoes, and cross-training shoes. To keep overhead low, his stores are not in the most fashionable parts of town. Sometimes he opens a store near a university to get the college runners, but even then he saves money in rent by staying off the beaten path. Because his stores are out of the way and in older neighborhoods that are run down, the sale of soft goods like walking and aerobic shoes is slowing down. He hates to lose this part of the business, but he has to make a decision.

Because he doesn't have to make the decision in a hurry, Keith can look at different aspects of the problem and even do some research. His gut tells him it's time to focus only on running, because that part of his business is doing so well, but his head keeps counting the profit on those other kinds of athletic shoes.

Keith can follow a typical decision-making format similar to the one that follows:

1. **Define the situation and the decision to be made.**

   Bottom line is bottoming out on shoes other than running shoes, possibly because of the stores' locations. Drop the lines or change the locations?

2. **Identify the important criteria for the process and the result.**

   Sales in running shoes continue to rise. Aerobic and walking shoes used to sell well enough to stock, and they provide a good profit margin, but people — especially women — are reluctant to shop in the neighborhoods where Keith's stores are located.

3. **Consider all possible solutions.**

   Keith's solutions include the following:

   • Carry only running shoes and accessories, which may save money because Keith will need fewer employees.

- Remain in current locations with low overhead.

- Change locations, pay higher overhead, and hope for larger market share in other products.

- Add an Internet storefront.

- Try moving one store and measuring the results after one year. If the profit is great enough, consider moving other stores.

4. **Calculate the consequences of these solutions versus the likelihood of satisfying the criteria.**

   Keith faces the following possible outcomes:

   - Moving can be difficult and time consuming, and it doesn't guarantee that business in soft departments will increase.

   - Dropping the soft lines means risking losing some impulse buying on the part of runners' family members or runners who want a second pair of more casual shoes for another purpose. Some employees could be cut, and those salaries would help balance the loss of sales.

   - Selling on the Internet would provide a whole new market. A technology person would have to be added to the payroll. Sales could increase.

   - Moving one store is a financial risk, but it's not as big a risk as moving all of them. Employees would remain the same.

5. **Choose the best option.**

   Get assistance from others if you need more input. You want to come to a decision that matches your values and your finances, so take whatever steps you can to calculate the risks.

Keith chose to move a single store to a new location. The rent is about 30 percent higher than he currently pays, but he hopes to make up the difference in sales. Because he has never operated in an upscale area, he is curious whether overall sales will increase. He has overridden his gut feeling, but he's taking a small risk instead of a big one. He decided taking a chance might even change the look of his business and an expansion in product lines if he gets more traffic.

Often, decision-making breeds further decision-making. To act on his decision, Keith must choose a location. But he has the time to check the demographics and figure out where to make his first move.

Deciding in the blink of an eye

Split-second decision-making, which doesn't happen often in the business world, follows a different pattern in the brain. Your RAS is alerted because your brain anticipates a survival situation. Information goes up to the limbic brain, where emotional reactions occur. Chemicals released as the fight-or-flight response begins increase blood flow to your extremities. With less blood flow to your brain, your thinking might also be interrupted. Mild though the fight-or-flight response may be in such instances, it takes place when you face a novel challenge that has time constraints. Your heart beats a bit more rapidly and your head begins to swim. You decide to go with your gut and make a decision based on the emotions the current environment and conditions inspire.

When you rely on your gut, do you make a good decision or a bad one? In his book *Blink*, Malcolm Gladwell explains that you may have made a very good decision. Your gut has some very good information. Some studies suggest that making a decision over time using analytical strategies is not better than relying on your gut feelings and making quick choices based on those feelings.

No gut, no glory

Tony is the vice president in charge of new product creation at a software company. His job is very demanding as he has to keep producing cutting-edge software. The latest project Tony's section is working on is security software for large corporation networks. The normal procedure is to take a beta version of the software and install it onto a few nonessential computers and run a proof of concept trial run, during which users compare the new software to the old software to see whether the new product is easier to use, requires less technical support, and provides better security.

A large customer of Tony's company reported a major breach in its current security system. Because the breaches were getting out of control with the old software they demanded new security software immediately or they would switch to a new vender. Tony had to decide whether to release the beta version of the new security software or lose this customer to another vender. If the software works, he would be a hero and would have saved the account. If it doesn't work, he will lose the account. But he will lose them anyway if he doesn't have something to offer them right now. Tony took the risk for the company. Although it was a quick decision, Tony had that gut feeling, based on his previous experiences, that this would work. And if it didn't, he had a bit more time to come up with something else.

Your gut feelings come from years of experience at making decisions and using critical thinking skills. When your brain stores all of the choices you've made and their consequences, you have a huge file of information from which to choose. What seems like a snap judgment is really based on your experiences and the wisdom from them.

Working Memory: Bigger Is Better

Your brain lets you to store your previous experiences, learn from your mistakes and successes, and to learn from the mistakes of others. What enables you to juggle all of those situations including the results? Your wonderful working memory.

In this section you find out how to increase your working memory power. The bigger your working memory becomes, the better able you are to consider more options for your decisions.

Making up your brain

Working memory — the process that enables you to hold information in your brain for a brief period of time — enables you to manage the activity of the outside world and the activity inside your brain.

Think of working memory as a sheet of paper. You are asked to make a decision regarding your business. You write the situation on the paper. Then you go through a decision-making process such as the one that Keith used in the section "Giving yourself time to decide." All of the information from your decision-making process goes onto that sheet of paper. Perhaps new information comes into the picture. Onto the paper it goes. You begin to think about prior decisions you've made that apply to this issue. Onto the paper they go. Then you think about what someone else might do in this situation: a famous executive like Bill Gates, your father, or a friend of yours. Those names and the thoughts you have about them go onto the paper as well.

Your working memory (sometimes called *scratch pad memory*) is like this sheet of paper, and it has a lot to hold. When you have the luxury of writing things down from your working memory (as you do when you have time to consider a decision), you empty your working memory to allow more information to enter.

But what about those rush decisions? The ones that don't allow you time to write anything down? Even when you're deciding on the fly, you still go through the decision-making process; you just have to do it all in your head. Working solely in your head requires more space in your working memory, or enough stored experiences in your brain to hook to the vital information that can help you make your decision. That scratch pad in your head has to be big enough to consider the information, your prior experiences, and what others might do. You start to juggle the information as though you are juggling balls:

- ✔ Ball 1 is the problem or situation.

- ✔ Ball 2 might be how the decision can affect you, your employees, the bottom line, and so on.

- ✔ Consider Ball 3 the way this situation compares to others you have been in.

- ✔ Oops, where were we? Ball 4 — what would daddy do?

If your working memory is large enough, you can examine all of these thoughts without losing any of the balls. You increase your working memory by working your working memory!

You're a busy person, of course, but if you always write things down, if you never memorize numbers but have them programmed into your phone, or if your assistant reminds you of every appointment, then you are not working your working memory. You cannot increase your memory without using it. Remember as a student you had to memorize poetry, preambles, and amendments? That exercise was good for your memory.

Practice the following memory-building strategies:

- ✔ Play memory games. For example, place a deck of cards face down, and then turn over two at a time, looking for pairs. Try to remember each card you look at so that when you turn a card that has the same number on it, you easily find its match.

- ✔ Do mental math. Forget the calculator for a while.

- ✔ Try to remember the names, occupations, and personal information of new people you meet.

Living in the past

Your past situations and decisions stay with you. You rely on the results of some decisions to help you in the future. Much of the time those experiences enable you to make good or better decisions right now.

Wishy-washy leadership won't work

Your decisions affect more than just yourself. Max is the owner and chief pilot of a small *fixed-base operation* (FBO — a service center for planes and pilots) at a large airport. Max has trouble keeping good employees, from his mechanics and electronics people, to his flight line and office personnel. Max prides himself in keeping up with what's going on in the industry. He reads all the aviation management periodicals and belongs to an aviation managers' association.

Every time Max is inspired by an article or swayed by a fellow owner's idea, he creates new rules or systems that sound like they would help the business run smoother, but he usually replaces his latest and greatest within a few months with an even newer idea — if it didn't fail in the first few weeks from lack of guidance. Employees bet on when Max's next change of

heart will come. Max once took down the aviation memorabilia and painted the customer waiting area pink trying to make the room look more modern. He surveyed some of the charter customers afterwards, and they said they enjoyed the old memorabilia because the room was like a museum, and that made it less boring to wait. Max changed it back. Max also constantly changed the weather minimums under which a flight could fly. Employees couldn't tell whether these changes were based on profit or safety.

Max's lack of focus and indecisive leadership creates an environment that's too unstable. His indecisiveness makes the predictability element that the brain loves impossible, and hence, his employees are uneasy, and few of them stick around.

But you can't live in the past. The world has changed too much. Do you want your heart surgeon to use the methods and decisions he made 20 years ago on you today? Probably not.

People use the past to assist with the present and predict the future. But getting stuck in the past is disastrous for leaders. Living in the past can leave you stuck. Leadership is about change. For change, you have to look to the future.

Deciding for the future

Leaders who always focus on the present may stagnate. The leader who focuses on the future, stays on the cutting edge, takes some risk, and makes decisions based on possibilities. She has ideas that no one else has, and they may not necessarily be the most popular ideas. Leaders know that if they do something, if they make a decision, then something will happen. They count on that something to be positive, exciting. lucrative, and challenging.

Leaders make decisions based on wisdom from the past, knowledge from the present, and hope for the future. They use their gut feelings to guide their rational thoughts.

Part III
Working with the Brains You Have

The 5th Wave   By Rich Tennant

Remember Robin — lead, follow, or get out of the forest.

In this part . . .

A leader enables her current staff members to excel. In this part, I show you how to bring out the best in your workers, including how to create an environment that primes them for success, and how to overcome differences — in brains, communication style, generation, and opinion, to name a few.

You also find out how best to add new members to your team, and how to support and encourage the teams you lead.

Chapter 10

Enabling Your Current Employees to Excel

As I point out in Chapter 4, a leader's job is to bring out the best in her employees. You may have exactly the people you need to meet your goals and fulfill your mission. Helping your current employees excel makes your organization stronger and more productive. All of the different brains in your organization bring their own experiences and abilities to help solve problems, make decisions, and move your organization toward its goals.

Meeting face-to-face with each member of your organization helps you discover who's really following your lead. Leaders need followers, but sometimes not everyone is in step with you. You face the hard decision of whether to keep or fire employees who aren't helping fulfill your vision. You can avoid some of the stress of letting people go by discovering more about them, teaching them more about the organization, and helping them become the employees you need.

At every organization, you find toxic people who may cause a ripple effect that spreads negativity. Just like other emotions, negativity can be contagious. You need to seek out the toxic people and determine whether they understand your vision, agree with your values, and want to work on the mission in a positive, encouraging way. Making clear to everyone that you expect positive, encouraging behavior is particularly important if you have team leaders who have become part of that negative crowd.

In this chapter, you find out how different brains work together, how stress affects your mission, how to deal with toxic people, and how to help good employees develop into great ones.

No Two Brains Are Alike: Working with Differences

There has never been a brain like yours and there never will be. This statement tells you how special you really are — and that everyone with whom you work is just as special. Your experiences, diet, sleep, genetics, environments, hobbies, career, and all that you do go into making your brain unique.

Understanding the uniqueness of each of your employees helps you understand how they function best and how you can bring out the best in them.

If employees grow, so does your business

What keeps employees from excelling? Opportunity? Fear? Complacency? Or you? Mike owns a profitable business, and he does well because he does it all. His employees are perfectly capable, but Mike has two concerns: He doesn't want to train his people for fear they will then leave and find another place to work, and he needs to micromanage. Mike doesn't believe anything can be done without him.

As a result of his attitude, he loses employees. They leave because he doesn't make them feel valued. But Mike is happy that he hasn't trained them for anyone else. Mike is so concerned that his business can't succeed without him that he doesn't take time off, which — according to his ex-wife — led to their divorce.

If Mike made his employees feel important and valued, they would stay. If Mike trusted his people to do the right thing and trained them according to his vision and values, they would stay and grow. They would feel that they're a part of something and can make a difference.

If you want your employees to excel and your business to prosper as a result, do the following:

- ✔ **Keep them growing.** Use on-the-job training, provide onsite professional development, and send them to offsite trainings.

- ✔ **Let them know you value them.** Acknowledge each individual's work and point out the connection between their work and the company's goals.

- ✔ **Create a learning environment.** Keep stress low, and ask team members to shadow other workers to get a complete understanding of how the organization runs.

✔ **Build trust.** Emphasize the skills of each team and team member so employees feel confident that their own work is in good hands.

✔ **Build relationships.** Get to know your employees on a deeper level. Use the emotional intelligence training from Chapter 8 to reach them. Help them build and maintain relationships among themselves.

✔ **Have fun.** Encourage employees to socialize; make the work day more fun by adding humor and telling stories.

✔ **Appreciate their differences.** Types of intelligence, sex, and generational differences are part of what makes everyone unique. Accepting and valuing these differences in order to celebrate employees' contributions creates a better place to work.

The outcome of any endeavor depends largely on the perception that each employee has of your vision. Often, leaders share their vision using emotions, facts, and symbolic language and then assume that everyone has received the same message and has the same big picture of what the organization is about.

Find a happy medium with each employee. Some want your input on a regular basis; others don't want to hear from you and can come to you when their project is complete. Make sure you can live with what you decide works best for you and each employee. Even though you may not be a delegative leader, some people need free rein to become creative and feel in control.

If you're like Mike — afraid of losing well-trained employees to other companies — look into the possibility of a non-compete clause in their contracts that can keep them from working for a competitor for six months if they leave your business.

If you're new to a leadership position, review what you need to know about each employee. The human resource person, team leaders, and personal conversations can provide you with a wealth of information. It may take both intrinsic and extrinsic rewards to keep employees happy. The extrinsic, or external, rewards can be monetary or other perks to show your appreciation of a job well-done. Intrinsic motivation, that internal feeling of knowing you have done a good job, may be even more important. Show your appreciation for jobs well-done by offering verbal or written feedback.

Using differences to your advantage

When you work with employees who have different intelligences, their points of view on problem-solving or their approaches to projects may differ. Respecting and acknowledging those differences can increase creativity and productivity. Presenting basic information may begin a series of suggestions, or because of the differing views, employees may hold back waiting for a request for their input.

Seek approaches to your projects and solutions to problems from employees. Multiple answers provide choices for you and for your employees. You will be meeting the need that the brain has for choices as well as honoring diversity.

Get employees talking — to you, to each other, and to their teams. If like-minded people are always interacting with each other, no one is going to change his mind. Get over the idea that everyone loves to collaborate. The brain is social and likes to interact with other brains, but collaboration is a skill that can be learned. Here are some ideas for how you get people talking:

- ✔ Share the topic and why it's important.

- ✔ Explain what you hope to take away from the conversation.

- ✔ Lead the conversation. Someone has to begin; it's easiest if you find the starting point.

- ✔ Be honest about how the conversation is going; share your feelings throughout the conversation.

- ✔ Ask others to share how they feel about the conversation, but don't hesitate to step in and redirect the conversation if it gets off track.

- ✔ Keep saying "thank you." Every comment deserves a response, and "thank you" is safe. If you say "good point" to one person, you have to say that to everyone or you'll slowly stop the conversation. Show that you are grateful to them for sharing.

Create diverse conversations by making sure that friends are separated. Encourage confrontation. Get employees to share their feelings. One method to get the ball rolling is to simply have these diverse groups brainstorm words that they would use to describe the company, what other people might say about it, and what the customers are saying. It doesn't matter whether they're positive or negative, let the thoughts flow and get them posted on a white board or flip chart. After they jot down thoughts in one big list, ask them to separate them into positive and negative thoughts. Discuss that negative list first. Then see if everyone agrees on the positive. Ask each group to come up with more positives that they would like to be able to say about the company. You may be redesigning your vision, but if it makes everyone more productive, perhaps it is time to do just that.

Encouraging confrontation and the sharing of feelings works only if people feel safe, so try these ideas:

✔ Focus only on facts. Leave personalities out of the conversation.

✔ Ask questions, and keep accusations out of the conversation.

✔ Begin on a positive note.

✔ Get everyone involved in finding solutions.

Discovering How Stress Makes a Mess

Within every organization — or for that matter, every group of people or animals — a hierarchy forms. Wanting to know who's in charge is part of human nature. Some therapists believe that the youngest child in a family wields the power. And I believe that you're only as happy as your unhappiest child. Could that be true in business as well? Your most unhappy employee may well cause enough stress and negativity to bring the rest of your team down. Business has a formal hierarchy, but social hierarchies develop within the formal structure.

Utilizing stress at the top

As a hierarchy develops, someone takes the top spot. This person has the power to influence others and may well be your best employee. A true leader may have emerged to lead others to your vision.

The person at the top of the hierarchy experiences positive stress — the kind that drives you to accomplish things. Positive stress enhances memory and people skills, and it enables you to feel the emotions necessary to win and to achieve.

Positive stress is a tool for getting things done. A little rush of adrenaline that gets the heart beating faster and puts employees in action can go a long way to getting things done. Try some of the following strategies to increase and harness positive stress:

✔ **Set short-term goals.** Time limits increase stress levels but only enough to create positive responses in those who are equipped to meet the goals.

✔ **Offer incentives.** The promise of a reward gets those stress juices flowing.

✔ **Promise new learning.** Some employees experience positive stress when they get excited about a doable challenge.

Most research shows that money is not the reason people work for an organization. The reason is they share the organization's vision.

Combating negative stress at the bottom

Where there's a top, there's also a bottom. Being at the bottom of the heap affects the brain in many not-so-pleasant ways. Take a look at the following common progression of problems for the employee feeling stress from being the low man on the totem pole:

- ✔ Feeling uninvolved, unwanted, kept in the dark, constantly reprimanded, useless, or helpless may induce chronic stress.

- ✔ Chronic stress may lead to an inability to think clearly and to health problems.

- ✔ Health problems may lead to absenteeism.

- ✔ Absenteeism means the job isn't getting done.

- ✔ Returning to work after an illness may cause additional stress because work has progressed and the employee doesn't feel informed.

- ✔ This new stress may cause further health problems.

And so on and on and on. . . .

Because stress is a response to a survival mechanism, another scenario is common for the employee on the bottom of the hierarchy. The reflexive or reactive part of the brain that includes the brain stem and the emotional area of the brain, the limbic system, acts to protect you because it doesn't know the difference between physical stress and emotional stress. Such action may cause the following kinds of unconscious thought and harmful actions:

- ✔ Being at the bottom of the heap makes the person feel inadequate.

- ✔ Whenever the person "on top" asserts her authority, this person feels even more insecure and inadequate.

- ✔ This person may feel that everyone on the team knows his rank and be embarrassed by it.

- ✔ In order to avoid scrutiny of any kind, this person works to make the one on top look inadequate.

- ✔ The person creates a situation in which the top dog can't continue her work, thus shifting negative attention from the bottom to the top.

Is there room at the top?

Include your employees in the glory and the profits to keep them feeling important and experiencing less stress.

John and Lois work hard to keep their e-business going. It began with a few creative ideas dealing with baby gifts. As young parents, the couple realized how excited they were to receive clothing and other items with their baby's name on them. Through a larger online company that would produce the items, John and Lois opened their e-store. They designed and created until the wee hours of the morning while they kept their day jobs and parented their children. It was a labor of love, and it was exhausting. But their efforts paid off. Soon the business was making enough profit that Lois could quit her day job and split her time between the children and the business. John continued to work evenings on the business after the kids went to bed.

Life was good. Until things changed. The e-business that made and mailed their orders changed its way of doing business. The percentage this company now wanted left John and Lois with a mere 10 percent profit. The company also wanted to standardize the price of items in each of its e-stores. As John and Lois saw their dream of an ongoing business that offered a service to parents, grandparents, aunts, and uncles going down the drain, they were distraught. And then they found Jeremy. Jeremy had a small shop that made many of the kinds of items that John and Lois sold. Jeremy could produce and mail the orders just as the e-company had done. It would cost more, but in the long run and with plenty of volume, John and Lois could still offer their service and make a living.

It worked. John and Lois began to see their income rise. Orders came in quickly, and Jeremy filled them as fast as they came in. Because the business was unique, it attracted press attention and was featured in a story about Internet "mom and pop" stores. John and Lois were interviewed, photographed along with their products, and even made an appearance on television. After all of the hoopla, they noticed that a few customers complained that their orders hadn't come as quickly as in the past. Jeremy began to fall behind. It was true that business was growing, so John asked Jeremy if he needed more money to hire someone else to take care of the load. Jeremy refused. He complained that people were just whiners. He was angry and sometimes hostile. John and Lois offered to buy the business from Jeremy, so they could hire others to do the work. Jeremy refused.

Just as John and Lois were considering finding another business to replace Jeremy, it dawned on Lois what had happened. Jeremy wasn't included in any of the publicity. John and Lois had taken all of the credit for their wonderful business. In reality, Jeremy had done a great deal. The vision and mission and goals of the store remained the same, but Jeremy had to be moved to the top. John and Lois made a new arrangement with Jeremy, who would henceforth be included in any promotions that were done. His name and bio were placed on the Web site along with John's and Lois's. Jeremy began to promote the products himself, and the three found that Jeremy's knowledge of what went into production was impressive to customers. Jeremy moved up and shared the top. His stress levels dropped; his enthusiasm soared.

This scenario isn't pretty, but it happens universally. You probably remember someone in your elementary school being the class clown. That child may have been bright, but he just didn't catch on to many things. The class clown's job was to get the teacher off her task of teaching because teaching made him feel stupid. He thinks that if the teacher isn't teaching, even if he gets into trouble as a result, he's not looking stupid. He looks instead like he doesn't care, and he entertains the class because he believes they will like him for it.

At work, this scenario may play out a bit differently. Your team is preparing for a launch of a new product. One employee feels that he has been overlooked for a special position on the team. Because he feels he won't receive proper credit for the work he has done, he wants to sabotage the project in some way. He disrupts each team meeting with questions and concerns about the launch. He argues with a few of the team members over details.

What happens if you fire or transfer the person on the bottom? If you think life will be good then, you may be greatly mistaken. You see, someone has to be on the bottom. The question is, how do you fix this? Can you make everyone equal? Yes. If the team can clearly see your vision and share it with you. If every single member can get on board with your mission and has the same values that your company has, and is willing to take this journey together, then the hierarchy may not be a problem. You have to realize that you cannot do it alone and you need to make every member of your organization a member of your team.

Not everyone is unhappy at the bottom of the hierarchy. Many people don't want the stress of trying to climb their way to the top. They do their jobs so that they make a living and can participate in whatever hobbies or interests they enjoy. They retire happily with their pension, and may be better off for doing so.

Neutralizing Toxic People

Toxic people are those people in your life who are so negative that they drain you of your energy and make you miserable, but for some reason you either feel forced to be around them or think you can change them. It's bad enough when they infect your personal life, but when they infect your business, your employees, and your future, it's time to detox.

Recognizing toxicity in the workplace

Because negativity and toxicity spread like germs in the workplace, you need to recognize the characteristics of the toxic worker. Watch for the following signs that a toxic person is on your staff:

- ✔ **Gossip:** From the water cooler to the washroom, the toxic person talks about others at work to whomever will listen.

- ✔ **Unconstructive criticism:** He can do it better, would have done it another way, or doesn't believe it should ever have been done.

- ✔ **Drama queens:** Her life is a mess! She couldn't get the work done because her dog ate it!

- ✔ **Drama kings:** No one understands him; he's highly creative but can't let it out in this environment.

- ✔ **Bitterness:** Because she wasn't asked to be on the project; she tells everyone that the project is beneath her.

- ✔ **Constant complaining:** The environment stinks; the lighting's not good; the equipment is archaic.

- ✔ **Blaming others:** The project would have been successful if a certain someone hadn't been involved; it's not her fault.

Describing the ripple effect

If your employees listen to a toxic person's negativity enough, they leave your company or succumb to the toxicity. (If you can't beat 'em, join 'em.) Joining the toxic person adds fuel to her fire.

What does this toxicity do to your workplace? The more negative the work environment becomes, the more likely you are to see

- ✔ Lower productivity

- ✔ Lower emotional intelligence

- ✔ More time spent soothing feelings

- ✔ Lack of enthusiasm

- ✔ Loss of interest in your vision

- ✔ More interest in personal agendas

- ✔ Loss of key employees

Fortunately, the ripple effect works both ways. Just as negativity spreads throughout the company, so too can a positive attitude. If your employees know that you are going to look into this problem and do something about it, they will be willing to work with you. Let them know you will find the source of the contamination and do whatever it takes to get back the positive environment that you desire.

Detoxing brains

Discovering what makes people toxic is the key to creating a better work environment. Anytime a person feels so uncomfortable that he needs to be toxic in order to function, he is in a survival mode. The fight or flight response is in effect.

A toxic person's behavior interferes with her own work and the work of others. The following are some possible causes of toxicity:

- ✔ Not understanding the company's vision
- ✔ Having become disconnected from the purpose of the organization
- ✔ An unfulfilled need to connect with others
- ✔ Nonexistent emotional intelligence skills
- ✔ Not knowing what you expect
- ✔ Problems at home
- ✔ Feeling underappreciated

To begin detoxing your business, work to uncover the root problems of the negativity. You do so by opening the lines of communication. Speak individually with each person who is bringing negativity to the workplace, and speak to those who are caught in that negativity and may be spreading it as a result. Take the time to find out what they feel is expected of them and reiterate your expectations. Clarify and emphasize your vision. Show them where they fit into your vision and your mission. Find out how things are for them at home. Offer counseling or other resources if the problem does stem from somewhere outside the office.

After you have face-to-face conversations with the toxic people in your company, meet with each team or department. Review your vision and your mission at the beginning of every meeting. If you find that additional employees are not in sync with your purpose and do not know where they fit in, begin individual meetings with everyone, both toxic and nontoxic. Make your presence known throughout your organization. Be present. Observe. Listen.

As you look for solutions, note that you may be part of the problem. Are you modeling the behavior you want to see? Are your words or actions negative? Meet with the executive team and discuss the problem. Make sure that they have an opportunity to speak up if they're having difficulty with expectations, purpose, or next steps.

A coaching or mentoring program (see Chapter 4) may help you fight toxicity. Although such a program can make a difference, approach coaching toxic people warily. Problem employees may or may not be good candidates for coaching. Choose wisely.

Just as toxic people spread their negativity in the workplace, they may also spread it to their mentors. Choose strong mentors who understand the problem. Be certain that the mentors have strong positive attitudes and can explain to the toxic mentee that he's valued and how he fits into the vision and mission of the organization.

Offer each employee a chance to join you in your mission. Leading people where they already want to go is easy. Those who aren't willing to work up to your expectations and who get in the way of those who do must really be looking for a different vision. Give them the opportunity to find it elsewhere.

Moving Them from Good to Great

Good employees are not hard to find. You already have good employees. Great employees are like great leaders: they aren't born but made. Sometimes you inherit employees as you take over a leadership position. Rather than replacing workers with others who don't know the company, you may be better off evaluating their strengths and weaknesses and helping them develop the skills that you need. If you're dealing with a company that isn't performing and you have been given the awesome opportunity to recreate the company or, at least, . get them up to speed, some major changes may be in order. You have the opportunity to bring out the best in everyone you lead.

Developing people

The only person you can really change is yourself. If you've been trying to change a spouse or a loved one, you probably know this to be true. But when it comes to employees, certainly you can offer the opportunity for change.

In any of my positions, I always feel my job is to reach people where they are and then help them stretch.

Setting the bar is better than bellying up to the bar

Creating a warm and friendly atmosphere helps the brain feel secure. Many people view socializing with employees off site as beneficial. But when it comes down to it, your employees need to know what your expectations are and whether they can meet them. Setting the bar and making sure they understand what exactly you expect of them is an important step in helping employees grow in their jobs.

Because leaders have stored in their memories what they want others to do, they may expect their employees and team leaders to also know. Many people make this mistake. Think about proofreading a speech or an article. When you proofread yourself, you often miss errors or omissions. This is because your brain fills in the blanks from your memory banks. Others who proofread can spot these mistakes right away.

Expecting employees to read your mind isn't an option. Make your expectations clear. Write them down and review them during meetings and personal conferences for reinforcement and for change.

Setting the bar requires contact with employees. Some suggestions for this include:

- ✔ Yearly retreats at which time everyone gets the big picture and employees gain a greater understanding of goals and expectations
- ✔ Semi-annual or quarterly planning meetings with team leaders to reinforce expectations
- ✔ One-on-one meetings with your direct reports to model the meetings they can be having with their team leaders and teams

Make expectations visual and don't forget the top line: the vision of your organization. (See Chapter 12 for information about creating visuals.)

Encouraging employees' accomplishments

Meeting expectations is a great accomplishment for every employee. Feeling in control is a great accomplishment for every employee's brain. Leaders create opportunities for employees to make things happen and to make a difference in some of the following ways:

- ✔ Even if you think you can do a job better or faster, don't. Delegate responsibility to your employees.
- ✔ Set the bar. Outline, define, draw, or tattoo the expectations and skills employees need to get the job done. Make them clear and specific, and be certain your employees can see how they contribute to the achievement of a goal.
- ✔ Help employees visualize success using emotion, fact, and symbols.
- ✔ Keep lines of communication open. Assure employees that they can ask any questions they may have along the way. Their input is important to you and to the success of the company. They may find a better way to reach your goals.

✔ Allow for differences in intelligences and learning style. You may be better at visualizing and expect others to be able to see your picture, but some may get messages or get things done by listening, talking, or acting. Getting to the same place through different channels is perfectly acceptable.

✔ Let employees know that you're available to help them problem-solve. Show them that you are passionate about your company and want to help if they need it.

✔ Celebrate the small successes. Growth can be slow and sometimes a little painful. Be the head cheerleader.

✔ Celebrate when expectations are met. If you see room for more growth with just a little stretching, offer employees the opportunity to keep growing. Don't diminish what has been accomplished, but show them that you always stretch yourself and that they may do so as well.

✔ Be prepared to make changes. Good employees sometimes find themselves in the wrong place. If you can, offer options whenever an assigned project isn't working for a particular person. People don't excel in every situation or in every environment. Give yourself and your employee a chance to grow under different conditions.

Retrain and retain or fire and rehire?

Good employees can become great employees. When your business grows, it also changes. Some changes require new skills, and so you add new employees, replace current employees, or retrain current employees. Which do you do? Rather than firing current employees and hiring others, you may be able to retrain some of your employees. Some may be resistant to change. But if they're good employees and can see your vision, they may be more willing to be retrained.

Good reasons to retrain rather than rehire include the following:

✔ **Hitting the ground running.** Current employees know their way around the organization.

✔ **Security for other employees.** Rather than wondering who's next on the chopping block, employees may trust the company to at least offer them a chance to retrain.

✔ **Increasing productivity through self-confidence and motivation from learning new skills.**

Although some leaders believe that change is too difficult for most employees, you can determine who is changeable. Those who are on board with your vision and see the big picture are doing their jobs with the goal of benefiting the company or doing something for others. Those who may not get that don't see beyond their jobs.

There is a story, or perhaps a legend, about the difference between doing a job and being part of a vision. In 1969, when the United States was about to send a man to the moon, NASA was crawling with reporters. One reporter approached a custodian who was sweeping the floors and asked, "What do you do?" The custodian stopped sweeping, leaned on his broom, and very seriously replied, "Why, I'm here to help put a man on the moon."

Find the employees who see beyond their cubicle, their team, or their procedures. Meet with those who you believe want to be part of your vision and ask them what they do. If the answer is something like, "I am in charge of advertising," he may not be the one to make changes with you. But if he says, "I'm helping this company sell more cars than any other company," you've got a winner.

Chapter 11

Hiring the Best Brain for the Job

. . . .

In This Chapter

▶ Choosing the brains that will work for you

▶ Ensuring that values and goals align

▶ Making effective hiring decisions

. . . .

Humans are a social species, and so every brain has two components: a personal brain and a social brain. When hiring the perfect brain for the job, you must check to see whether your candidate works exclusively from his personal identity or if at work he operates from his social identity. The personal brain involves itself entirely in what's in it for the individual. Of course, no one takes a job without some personal benefit. But the social brain uses socialization for survival and for getting along with others for the betterment of the group. You want your employees to be thinking "we" instead of just "I."

The best brain for the job may not be the "smartest" brain — the one with all of the appropriate degrees and the highest grades. This brain may have the highest IQ, but as I describe in Chapter 8, emotional and social intelligence lead to success in an organization.

This employee must be enthusiastic — as excited about your organization as you are. You also want him to share your company values and fall in step with the way you do things. That's not to say you don't want a brain that thinks outside the box, you just want that thinking to match your thinking and your goals for the organization. Finally, you want people with good communication skills, whether they're communicating with you, other employees, or your customers.

People don't necessarily buy your product or your service. They buy you and the people who work for you; they buy the way you make them feel. Top salesmen can't sell only their product to their customers, they can sell almost any product to their customers. They know how to include others in their social identity.

What skills or talents does it take to create these strong relationships? This chapter helps you consider what characteristics you want in an employee. You get the opportunity to take a look at yourself as a leader, and you find out how to pick others who follow your lead and walk your walk.

Picking Brains: Approaches to Hiring

When you look for new employees, you pick brains, as in choosing the ones you want to hire, and you pick brains, as in checking those brains to determine whether they have what you need.

If you're just starting up a business, you may be picking a lot of brains to fulfill the mission of your organization. If you have a small business, one wrong person can make a big difference in the group dynamics and productivity.

The upcoming sections introduce you to approaches for hiring employees, whatever your situation.

Look for those who love the work

Love sounds like a "soft" word to use in business, but love of work has the strength to make things happen. The more people love the work and the vision you create, the more likely they are to share that vision and make the entire company more productive.

How do you really know that the person you are considering for a job loves her job? Look for these indicators:

- ✔ Her job is also her hobby. For example, people who work in animal shelters usually have animals at home that they love and care for.

- ✔ She has personal skills related to the position. Home improvement centers hire employees who are not only skilled at building, decorating, or fixing things around the house, they also want employees with the ability to teach others how to complete those tasks.

- ✔ She has done the kind of work you want previously.

Work that you love energizes you. During an interview, ask the candidate what he does after work. If he says, "I work so hard that I'm too tired to do anything," either he is trying to impress you with his hard work or his work doesn't energize him. I'd rather have an employee who went out running or worked in the garden than one who is totally exhausted at the end of the day. Energy is particularly important if your organization works in teams. If employees are truly collaborating, the interaction motivates and energizes them. If your people are really dragging at the end of the day, the work they are doing may be too stressful.

Look for workers that you love

A second approach to hiring is to choose people you would like to work with — even if this employee is not going to work directly with you. If you already like the people who work for you and you feel good about the person you're interviewing, you can reasonably expect that they can all get along.

Finding employees with whom you'll enjoy working relies upon your emotional intelligence — that ability to listen to what your gut tells you. Being a good judge of character is a valuable leadership trait. You have to trust yourself. But that doesn't mean that you jump into hiring anyone who sits down at an interview and you happen to like. You need to give yourself time and several meetings to determine whether that instinct continues.

A tale of two pities

Ronnie gets up at 6:30 a.m. to get ready for work. He hits the snooze button at least four times because he really doesn't want to get up. He hates his job, but he needs the money. While he's at work, he rarely speaks to anyone, unless he's complaining. What does he complain about? Ronnie says he was meant for greater things. He doesn't get paid enough, and his department supervisor is a horse's rear end. Ronnie has his own pity party everyday. When he is asked why he feels that way, Ronnie just shrugs his shoulders and rolls his eyes.

Ronnie works with a team, but he doesn't participate at team meetings, no matter how hard his team leader tries. Ronnie spends a lot of time looking at the clock. By the end of the day when Ronnie turns in his work, he's tired and can't wait to get home, lie on the couch, and veg out.

Steven pities Ronnie. He just doesn't get why anyone would work where he was so unhappy. Steven loves his job, and if Ronnie weren't so negative and participated at meetings, Steven would like it even more. Steven knows Ronnie thinks he's stuck at a dead-end job, but the truth is, there is room for advancement. Yes, Steven pities Ronnie, and he's beginning to pity the whole department that Ronnie is in. Ronnie takes a lot of fun out of work when he's around. Steven hopes the team leader will move Ronnie to another department.

Employees like Ronnie emphasize the importance of finding people who like their work and are energized by it.

Whether you're leading ten people or a thousand, you want them to wake up every morning looking forward to coming to work, and putting together a team of personalities that mesh goes a long way toward that goal. One successful salesman for a wholesale clothing company told me, "I look forward to my work week because every day I get to have lunch with my friends. I get paid to hang out with great people. I've got the best job in the world." There were months when this salesman made a lot in commissions, but even when times were bad, he wouldn't leave his job because he would miss his friends!

Of course you want someone who can do the job. But given two candidates who can do the work, hire the one you like best. Some hiring managers even choose the lesser qualified person if they think she can fit in better with the team of workers. A quarterback whose arm isn't as strong but who can unite the team is more valuable than one who doesn't get team rapport and can throw a little farther.

Use the multiple intelligence assessment in Chapter 7 on all of your employees and then use it on your interviewees. See how they fit together. Your gut may be more important than any written assessment, but learning-style assessments and Meyers Briggs Inventories often help predict how individuals will work together.

Looking for leaders

If you believe that every employee you have can't be a star, you're probably hiring the wrong people. Every single person in your employ should be a potential leader. As the leader, you already have followers, many with great leadership potential. Hiring someone who simply wants to follow the followers shortchanges you and your organization.

Seth Godin, author of *Tribes,* calls people who fight to keep everything status quo *sheepwalkers.* Sheepwalkers do what they're told to do and nothing more. Do you want a bunch of sheepwalkers working for you? You want people who are thinkers and risk-takers, employees who shake things up a bit and make your business better.

Building a Brain Trust

In Chapter 9, I talk about the combination of your cognitive skills and your emotions to make good decisions. Hiring someone who is going to help you take your organization to the next level is one of the biggest decisions you will ever make. Can you trust your brain? And what about that instinct? Potential employees come to you with data, with personality, with a work ethic, and with values. You need to examine all of these factors to determine whether they are the right brains for the job.

Waving the white flag

Dale Tate is a great guy. He's one of those people that everyone likes. He values his family and his friends. When he thinks back to the interview he had with the president of the company he now works for, he realizes that the guy wasn't walking his talk, but because of hard economic times, Dale had to take the job. Dale is a regional manager for an accessories firm that has kiosks in malls throughout the mid-Atlantic states. Rent for kiosk space has gone up, and the president of the company has called a meeting of all the regional directors.

What Dale thought would be a motivational and informational meeting turned into a declaration of war. Threats were issued. ("If things don't improve, there will be no more regional managers.") Cutthroat techniques were suggested. ("Do whatever it takes to get the business from the other mall stores.") Statements that gnawed at Dale's stomach were issued. ("In this business, you have to work every single day. Watch those kiosk salespeople. They'll steal from you. It's kill or be killed in today's economy.")

Dale's stomach churned during that meeting. When he was sent off to complete the new mission, "Kill the competition," Dale could barely stand to get up in the mornings to go to work.

At the next month's meeting, the president spoke again. This time he humiliated a few of the other regional directors because their sales were so bad. Dale sat frozen in his chair as he waited to be belittled by the president. When it didn't happen, Dale was relieved. But later as he thought about it, he realized that he shouldn't have to live this way. He felt like a zebra waking each morning in the Serengeti hoping that there would be no lions around.

When he could take it no longer, Dale quit. He had actually been doing the best job of all of the regional managers. The president had just given Dale a raise. But all of the tension and negativity were still there. Dale found something for a lower salary, but he worked for a company that values the contribution of others. Dale felt like he had given up and that just wasn't like him, but he was much happier after he left that company.

If Dale had been clearly told what the values of the company were, he probably would not have accepted the job in the first place. You don't want to spend precious dollars training people who really don't feel comfortable with your values and therefore may leave.

Valuing the values

When you hire people to become a part of your organization, you want to be sure that their values are your values. Make sure you are personally clear about those values and ask any possible employee what theirs are. You are after shared values, for if you share the same values, then this person should conduct herself in a similar manner to you and your other workers.

Your values determine the relationships you have. When you're open about your personal and business values, your current and future employees admire your openness and honesty.

Your *values statements* describe how you treat other people in your organization, how you treat your customers, and how you treat any other stakeholders involved in business with you. By sharing your values statements with your interviewees, you are telling them "the way things are done around here":

✔ How you expect them to behave

✔ What they are allowed to do

✔ What behaviors are inappropriate when dealing with others

Perhaps before you spill the beans about your values, you may want to ask a few questions about their values. You might begin with some questions like these:

✔ If you could work for any leader in the world, alive or dead, who would you pick?

✔ What about that particular leader that led you to choose him?

✔ What guiding principles did this leader follow?

✔ In what way are those guiding principles the same principles that you value?

✔ In what type of culture or environment do you like to work?

The more personal clarity you get from job candidates, the more they may be worth considering. The brain that knows itself and is committed to its own values is much more valuable than a brain that doesn't know what its guiding principles are. Truly knowing yourself and what you value requires good communication between the executive areas of the brain and the emotional areas. Without knowledge of her own values, even someone who can recite your values statements to the letter may have little dedication to your values.

Scanning brains

As you look at the files or portfolios of each candidate, you may become overwhelmed. Resumes can be wonderful tools, and they can be misleading.

Interviews give you further insight, but one just isn't enough. What do you do to separate the best from the rest? Try these steps:

1. **Search the Internet.**

   Yes, search the Web for all of your candidates, using a search engine like Google or Bing. Check out Facebook, MySpace, LinkedIn, and any other social or business networking site. You may be surprised by what you find.

One large corporation brought in a CEO based on her resume, which listed some pretty impressive accomplishments. All of the accomplishments checked out.

An extensive Internet search would have revealed newspaper articles that would have dissuaded them from offering her a contract. (She had pulled the wool over the eyes of several top companies. After these former organizations had hired her, she refused to work on community relations and had a closed-door policy.) Less than two years after hiring her, the board couldn't wait to get rid of her; members discovered that they weren't the first company to be taken in. Deficit spending and poor community communication hurt the company badly. They ended up buying out the last year of her contract.

2. Look closely at candidates' credentials.

A potential hire's educational background may look terribly impressive on paper, but is it the real deal? People lie. Others tweak the truth. Just changing a few words can make someone look fabulous on paper.

Confirm any candidate's educational background. If you have been given false information, scratch that candidate off the list.

3. Confirm the applicant's work experience.

Even recent graduates have previous employers from college jobs, internships, or fellowships. Although most employers no longer provide much information for legal reasons, at least make sure the candidate did work where they say they did. If your instinct tells you something doesn't sound quite right, scratch a candidate or at least put her in the "hold" stack until you've checked out everyone else.

4. Ask around.

Find out whether your business contacts have heard of or even interviewed the candidates you're interested in. Ask around about the companies your candidates use to work for. You may find some valuable information.

For instance, a chain of upscale hair salons in Chicago was looking for a manager for one of their suburban shops. A woman from Indiana applied for the position and listed on her resume four years' experience with a large salon in South Bend. A member of the senior team in Chicago recognized the name of the salon because her sister lived in South Bend. Upon checking up on the South Bend business, they discovered that it had let several stylists go in the wake of embezzlement. No further information was available, but nevertheless, the Chicago firm took a pass on hiring the woman.

Keep an eye out for red flags

Jim hired Jana because she came highly recommended by the owner of a business that had to downsize. Jim needed a new director of sales and was told that Jana Schmidt was the best. Her resume was very impressive. She graduated from a prestigious university and had worked for companies larger than Jim's. She was available not only because of the downsizing, but because she had moved to this small southeastern city because her husband was transferred.

Jim didn't take much time with the interview; he needed someone now, and on paper Jana was perfect. But that was the only place she was perfect. After he hired her, Jim soon found out that Jana's values didn't match up with his or his company's values. Jana valued herself. She wanted a title, power, and a good income. (Jim paid her more than he had thought he could afford but imagined she would be worth it if she did the job.)

Jana treated no one with respect. She was snooty because of her educational background and the fact that her parents had money. The sales department suffered terribly under this change in the culture. Jim began receiving complaints and decided not to say anything to Jana. After all, she had just begun the job. She

was probably a bit nervous. Actually, Jim was nervous about the situation; hiring a new sales director was one of his last-ditch efforts to get the company headed in the right direction. He told the sales people to be patient.

As Jana ranted about low sales, motivation went down. She started threatening her sales force, and one of the best sales people found a job with another company. Jim tried talking to Jana. She was as sweet as could be whenever they conversed. She told him she didn't understand what the problem was. She said these people just didn't have proper motivation and her style was simply to raise expectations. The problem was she offered no help to her team. She told them what to do but not how to do it.

When Jim explained how the company was run, that they were all in this together like one big happy family, Jana just shook her head. Her values were so mismatched with the company's that she would never fit in. After several months, Jim let Jana go.

Jim's hastiness in hiring someone who looked good on paper led to problems that he would not have had to deal with if he had taken more time to get to know his seemingly golden candidate.

Going deeper in a second interview

You're down to the short list. It's time for the second interview and some tough tests for the several candidates you're considering. Sometimes a corporation creates a situation to see how the candidate does in as natural a situation as possible to check on stress levels and responses.

For instance, a corporation of nursing homes wants to hire some employees for a new location. They need registered nurses, licensed practical nurses, certified nurse's assistants, a social worker, a manager, a dietician, an activities director, and a receptionist — just for starters.

Dealing with the geriatric set is different from dealing with other age groups, and so this corporation sets up second interviews and has candidates wait in the reception area for at least 30 minutes. During that time, older people enter the room and require some help. One may be confused about where she is, for example. Another may knock something over. A keen eye watches to see what candidates do in each situation. Who jumps up to open the door for the elderly? Who gives up his seat when the waiting area is full? Those who are kind and caring, do not show any irritation, and go out of their way to help are more seriously considered for the job.

Second interviews outside the office in a more casual setting often offer good information about how candidates might handle themselves with customers. You can learn a lot over a casual meal. The ways that candidates treat the wait staff, taxi drivers, and people on the street can be revealing.

Honest, purposeful questions reveal a lot about the candidate. For example

- ✔ If you become part of this company and work with us toward our goals, how would you like to be remembered?
- ✔ How are you going to approach the work you do here to make that happen?
- ✔ How do you think our company can make a difference? And how can you help?

Bringing employees into the mix

After candidates make it through the resume search, the networking search, the Internet search, and the first and second interviews with you, you're ready to bring in the big brains. Rather than relying exclusively on yourself to choose your employees, let those who will work with the new hire conduct an interview. Try the following:

- ✔ Pick out two of the employees in the department for which you are hiring — two who truly display the "we" attitude.

  Be sure they get along well with you and with others on their team.
- ✔ Let them get to know the candidate first in a formal meeting and later in a more social situation, like lunch.
- ✔ Find out whether they were able to build rapport and find common values. Compare your experience with theirs.
- ✔ If a candidate passes the first interview with his potential co-workers, let the interviewers take the candidate to their department and get to know the others who they may be working with.

If the entire team wants this candidate and you like this person as well, you have your new employee.

Mirroring the behaviors you want

Nothing works better than modeling the behavior you want to see. Abraham Lincoln and Martin Luther King were respected and followed because they believed in what they lived and they shared what they believed. Whether you are interviewing, showing others around your business or interacting with your employees, what you do is what you get. Some of this stems from the fact that your shared values inspire your employees or employee candidates, and some comes from the action of mirror neurons, which are linked particularly to empathy and inspire mimicry. Chapter 8 tells you more about mirror neurons.

Providing some interaction between you and your candidates in the work setting gives them a better feel for how you live your values. Let them see how you treat others, talk to customers, and consider everyone's feelings. Doing so also gives you the opportunity to see how well the candidate follows your lead. Can she mimic your welcoming smile, your sincere handshake, and your desire to please the customer?

The sales manager at an upscale dress shop always takes her job applicants out on the floor to meet customers. This shop thrives on regular clients and the place is busy all of the time. Introductions are made and after the manager chats with the customer, he leaves an opening for the candidate to jump into the conversation. If the candidate fails to engage the customer, he falls out of consideration for the position.

Ready, Aim, Hire!

Slow down. You wouldn't get married after just one date. But if you have had at least two interviews, researched the candidate, and watched him interact with the other members of the team or with good customers, you may be ready.

You don't usually buy a new car without taking at least one test drive. Give the employee a trial period if you can. A new employee is similar to a student on the first few days of school, she's on good behavior. When the honeymoon period is over, the true behavior comes out. Let the candidate now spend some real time on the job working with his possible team members. Doing so benefits both of you. If he hates the work after the trial, off he goes. If he doesn't fit in with others, you have the option of saying goodbye or trying him out in another capacity.

If you haven't found the perfect brain for the job, don't hire because you're desperate or frustrated. Keep looking and you can find the right person. You're better off taking your time to find that person who loves your work, loves your workers, and shares your values.

Chapter 12

Optimizing Working Conditions

*P*roductivity flourishes under the right conditions. If you want a successful business, make your employees happy. If you want a successful and profitable business, make their brains happy. Chemicals in the brain create pleasure, motivation, kinship, and inspiration when working conditions are optimal.

Think about the places you have worked. Pick out the one in which you were the happiest, the most secure, and the most productive. Under what conditions were you working? Unless you love being alone, I doubt that you chose the cubby hole that separated you from other employees. And unless your job found you playing in a band, I would be surprised if you were happiest amongst loud music and a bit of chaos.

In this chapter you find out how to create an environment in which the brain thrives. Using visuals, providing music to help stimulate the mind and the body, creating the right temperature for thinking and making connections, and providing time for an occasional nap may be just what your employees are looking for.

Stimulating the Brain's Visual System

You actually do get the picture more than you "get" words. Most studies show that adding a visual to information increases retention from a mere 10 percent to 65 percent. The brain is set up for visual representations, and the eyes can be trained to see what is important.

If you put your hand on the back of your head, you're touching the part of the skull that protects your *occipital lobe* — the area that processes vision. Columns of neurons cover the outer layer of the occipital lobe; each column is responsible for a different aspect of what you see. One column may see only 45-degree angles or the color blue. Your visual experience relies on these columns coming together and forming a complete picture.

But that picture is not completely reliable. What you see is biased by what you know. For one thing, you have blind spots — areas in your vision that don't hold visual information. Nonetheless, you never see a dark spot. Your brain calculates what should be in those spots and fills in the blanks.

Your employees take in the visual information that surrounds them. I was doing some trainings for a chain of hardware stores several years ago. At one of the locations, I walked into the office to wait for the manager. I sat down in a not very comfortable chair and found myself directly across from a calendar displaying June 1972 (It was 1995.) and a young, scantily clad girl bending over to pick a tool out of her toolbox. The remainder of the walls were bare. I was surprised and a bit disappointed that the manager I was working with thought this image was appropriate; the calendar made me uncomfortable as I carried on a conversation with him.

What you place on walls might be a personal choice, but my question would be, "What do you want your employees thinking about?" I think most leaders want their employees thinking about work. Whatever is on display at work affects all those who see it.

You can keep employees' eyes on the prize, so to speak, by placing their goals within visual range in offices, workrooms, meeting rooms, and labs.

Help them get the picture by giving them the picture! Your targets are words. The brain remembers pictures more. Create a poster or sign with the target or goal and add something visual to it. For instance, "We'll Nail Your Problems at Stein Hardware!" Pictures of employees helping customers in different departments of the store appeared with the slogan on posters. Nails held the posters to walls throughout the store. Employees had a visual reminder of the bottom line — helping the customer.

Think of your workplace as an opportunity to sell your employees on working for you. Where you place visuals makes a difference in what people see, how they perceive it, and what they feel about the visual. Table 12-1 gives you suggestions for hanging visuals effectively.

Table 12-1	Placing Visuals for Optimum Impact
Location	*Reason*
Place material you want employees to talk about at eye level. You company's current goal is one example. Others would be reminders, messages, and so on.	Eye-level visuals are easy to see and so catch employees' eyes often.
Place information you want employees to remember higher than eye level. "How to" instructions are one example.	Employees tend to look up when they're relaxing and taking a break.
Put feel-good information, like charts that show growth and improvement, below eye level.	You look down when you access your feelings.

Posters can be fun and inspiring, or they can provide messages that you might not want to have around the office. For example, "Hang in there till Friday!" doesn't send the message that work is a good place to be. Choose your messages carefully.

Utilizing color

Many studies suggest that color affects the brain and behavior. Color affects mood and emotions. It makes you wonder if UPS, United Parcel Service, has brown uniforms to show less dirt or to instill confidence.

Understand how color works before you determine the colors of your visuals, the color of your walls and carpet, and even the colors your employees wear. The following are some common effects that various colors produce:

- **Black** represents strength, power, and luxury.
- **Blue** creates a feeling of reliability and trust; blue also increases creativity.
- **Brown** denotes confidence and security.
- **Burgundy** represents warmth, strength, and status.
- **Green** brings to mind prosperity and success.

- ✔ **Red** is associated with alertness and helps you focus.
- ✔ **Yellow** energizes.

Studies show how color affects emotional states. Painting a locker room bubble-gum pink actually calmed football players down — calmed them too much for the coach's taste. (The color also is used in jail holding cells to create more passive prisoners.)

What color is your conference room, waiting room, or sales room? Some suggest that painting these rooms blue to provide the feeling of reliability is a great idea. And some businesses are carefully choosing uniforms according to what customers might perceive from colors.

Shedding some bright light on the subject

If you want to avoid accidents, eyestrain, and stress in your workplace, check out the lighting. Work productivity increases with appropriate lighting.

Many businesses use fluorescent lighting because it's cheaper. But fluorescents increase stress hormone levels like cortisol. These lights flicker and hum and can negatively affect the nervous system, causing symptoms like attention problems. Even though many employees stop noticing the flickering and hum, a few hours into the workday they find themselves deeply fatigued.

Natural sunlight is best for mood, energy, and generally feeling good. Lack of sunlight may prevent the brain from producing serotonin, which affects moods in a positive way. You know how everyone wants an office with a window? The view may be great, and the sunlight not only provides Vitamin D but helps the brain release those feel-good chemicals.

Full-spectrum bulbs mimic sunlight. If you have offices without windows, the full-spectrum lighting may be even more important. Make sure workers in these windowless environments get frequent breaks that take them to rooms with windows. Sunlight provides vitamin D, increases the release of serotonin, and decreases depression.

Getting Comfortable on the Job

Your brain is always tracking your environment: what it looks like, how it makes you feel, and how your senses are affected by it. Taking care of the physical environment for your employees and making them comfortable shows them that you care about their needs. Comfort leads to better performance and more productivity.

If the chair fits . . .

Sit up straight and you pay better attention. That's what all my teachers told me. But some people work better slouching, standing, or lying on the ground. Meeting the needs of your employees means making them feel comfortable in their environment. Making them comfortable means happier, more productive workers.

Back pain can lead to absenteeism, physical and emotional stress, lower cognition, and less efficiency. A good chair can go a long way to preventing the pain that causes the trouble, making employees feel better in general and even encouraging healthy brain activity. An ergonomically designed chair includes a footrest, armrests, and support for the small of the back.

Successful seating takes some consideration so that you can address the different body types in your workplace. Give special concern for the seating of those who spend most of their days in a chair. Try the following suggestions:

✔ Take into consideration the size of the work space.

✔ Chairs should support the worker in a comfortable position.

✔ Height should be adjustable.

✔ Provide good lumbar support to encourage good posture.

✔ Padded seats promote circulation.

When you're hot, you're hot, and when you're not, you're probably cold

Climate control. Two of my favorite words. Many heated conversations have gone on in organizations about who should control the thermostat. Temperature is a somewhat personal choice, but studies show that there are optimal temperatures for the brain.

Some people have a different body thermostat than most — for those few I suggest fans and sweaters! When temperatures rise, the brain tends not to work as well. Comprehension tends to become a problem when the temperature rises above 74° Fahrenheit. Computation can become a problem when the room warms up to 77° Fahrenheit. Some studies show that accidents increase and productivity decreases when the heat goes up. A too-cold environment decreases productivity, as well. As one administrative assistant said, "I don't type well with gloves on!"

You need to provide a comfortable and healthy indoor environment for yourself and your employees. Bringing in outdoor air dilutes building contaminants and replenishes oxygen. You have probably attended or presented in an enclosed room and felt sleepy or witnessed others becoming sleepy. The low level of oxygen in the room may be the culprit. (Or it could be boring slides or speakers!)

Ultraviolet lights installed in the duct system or air purifiers (which take the place of the furnace filter) in the heating and cooling system help stop the spread of colds and viruses. These options also make those who suffer from asthma or allergies more comfortable. These products can be added to any forced-air system by a heating and cooling contractor.

Humidity is an interesting factor in climate control. People can be comfortable at 80 degrees if the humidity is only 20 percent or at 75 degrees with 55 percent humidity. Air conditioning normally dehumidifies in the summer, but during the cold winter months you must humidify to keep employees comfortable at 68 degrees. Heating and cooling contractors have a variety of products, from a steam system to evaporator pads, that enable you to add humidity.

Putting a Song in Their Hearts — Or At Least in Their Cubes

Auditory stimuli bombard the brain every second. Buildings have all types of acoustic problems that can be stressful, distracting, and even provoke anger. Addressing all of the problems may be difficult, but covering them with some brain-stimulating or relaxing music is a relatively simple task.

Choosing music: If it ain't baroque, fix it

The brain responds well to music. Dr. Georgi Lozanov, a Bulgarian psychiatrist and professor of education, was the first scientist to systematically research the factors involved in rapid learning. His major premise was that learning is a natural, joyful process. He found that music synchronized breathing, heart rate, and brain waves to relax the body and mind. Relaxed alertness is a very receptive state for learning. The types of music that produced this effect were classical and baroque.

Chapter 2 explains that brain cells communicate through chemical and electrical activity in the brain. The electrical activity is measured in terms of waves, which cycle at different rates per second. Table 12-2 shows you the four levels of brain activity.

Table 12-2	States of the Brain	
Brain wave	**Description**	**Cycles per second**
Beta	Most common conscious state	15 to 40
Alpha	Quiet and relaxed state	9 to 14
Theta	Between conscious and unconscious; daydreaming	5 to 8
Delta	Deep sleep	1 to 4

You spend most of your waking time in the rapid Beta state, which enables you to do all the things that your busy schedule requires. However, Beta waves do not provide an opportunity for creativity and deep thought; Alpha or Theta states do. Specific kinds of music help relax your body, slow down your breathing rate, lower your heart rate, and offer the opportunity for creativity and learning:

- Much **Baroque** music, which was composed between 1600 to 1750 has 40 to 60 beats per minute, making it ideal for relaxation.

- **Classical** music was composed between 1750 and 1820 and is more energetic and forceful than baroque music. Classical is excellent for teamwork and problem-solving. It usually contains 60 to 80 beats per minute.

- **Romantic** music was written between 1820 and 1900. It is very energetic with a lot of variations. Because it has more than 80 beats per minute, romantic music is perfect for working toward deadlines.

Music tends to stimulate both the left and right sides of the brain. The left and right hemispheres have different functions and, although you use both sides when you listen to music, each hemisphere responds to it differently. The left hemisphere is involved with analyzing the music, while the right appreciates the sounds. Studies also suggest that when music stimulates the right side of the brain, it eliminates day dreaming and aids concentration.

Music also helps you remember information, in large part because it affects your emotions. The same part of the brain controls emotions and long-term memory. Attach music to learning, and you add an emotional element that stimulates retention.

Mozart doesn't make you smarter

In 1991, Alfred A. Tomatis described "the Mozart effect" in his book, *Pourquoi Mozart?* Tomatis asserted that listening to Mozart healed and developed the brain. Research conducted by Gordon Shaw and Frances Rauscher at the University of California, Irvine, in 1993 suggested that listening to Mozart "primes" the neuronal connections that are used for abstract reasoning. The subjects of the study listened to ten minutes of Mozart's Sonata for Two Pianos in D before taking a test. Another group listened to minimalist music by Phillip Glass, and the control group didn't listen to music at all. Those listening to Mozart did better on the test than the other two groups, but the replication of this study was unsuccessful for the most part. The media loved this research, and headline after headline proclaimed "Mozart Makes You Smarter." Books were also written on the topic and many Mozart CDs were sold. You can increase your brain power, sure, but listening to Mozart is not going to do it.

Music also appears to stimulate the release of serotonin and dopamine. These same chemicals are released when you eat chocolate, have orgasms, and partake in other personal pleasures. Most people admit that music does make them feel good.

Music in the workplace can change employees' emotional states. Calming music may lower stress. Music can also get people moving faster. A faster beat when teams are working together may help them get the job done faster.

Examine the following positive effects of music to decide whether it should be part of your working environment. Music can

- Increase focus and creativity
- Calm and lower stress
- Energize
- Increase concentration
- Make people happy
- Cover distracting noises
- Stimulate conversation
- Pump up celebrations
- Signal meeting times, closing times, and break times

Some of your employees may have negative anchors to certain music; they associate certain songs or tunes to specific, unpleasant times in their lives.

These pieces of music may elicit a mental state that you do not want and that is not conducive to working. You can't avoid this pitfall entirely, however, you can minimize it by using lesser known classics.

Setting the tone with music

The office manager for a physicians' office tells a very interesting story about music. Music played for patients who were on hold because one of the physicians had read that callers stay on the line longer when compared to those listening to nothing at all. The phone was set up to have callers listen to a radio station. The office manager knew little about radio stations and asked her son which station to put on. He chose one of his favorite stations.

The wife of a recent open-heart-surgery patient called because she was concerned about her husband's breathing. Put on hold without time to explain her call, she immediately began listening to hard rock music, which she found unsettling and which stressed her further. By the time the receptionist came back on the line, the woman was hysterical. Her own heart rate and respiration had increased from listening to the fast-paced selection.

Table 12-3 offers suggestions for matching music to departments and situations. I based these suggestions on work done by Eric Jensen (*Music with the Brain in Mind*), Jeff Green (*The Green Book of Music*), and Steve Halpern who has researched healing music. Steve's Web site is `www.innerpeacemusic.com`. Use these resources to learn to match your music to your environment.

Table 12-3	**Suggestions for Choosing Music**	
Department or situation	*Type of music*	*Possible selection*
Complaint department	Baroque Music	Pachelbel's Canon in D
Break room	Baroque Music	Vivaldi's Four Seasons
Team meetings	Upbeat	We Are Family (Sister Sledge)
Brainstorming	Instrumental	Rhapsody in Blue (Gershwin)
Problem-solving	Waltz	Blue Danube (Johann Strauss)
Celebrating success	Disco	Stayin Alive (The BeeGees)
Challenge	Theme song	Mission Impossible
Beginning a project	Disney	Whistle While You Work
General meetings	Popular	Walk Right In (The Rooftop Singers)
Focused concentration	Classical	Water Music (Handel)
Meeting deadlines	Romantic	William Tell Overture (Rossini)

The Rest of the Story: Naps

Most people do not get the sleep they need at night. And even if they do, 16-hour days require some rest periods. Providing a nap time for your workers may sound silly, but it could be very beneficial to you.

Sometime in the late afternoon, usually around the three o'clock mark, everyone hits a wall for a short period of time. Suddenly, the computer screen looks fuzzy, you can't focus on your paperwork, or running that machine takes more effort than it did just minutes earlier.

The black hole hits us all. Maybe you've noticed employees nodding off in afternoon meetings. Those heavy eyelids aren't a pretty sight, and they certainly don't enhance productivity. Maybe you get angry when you see employees drowsing as you speak; maybe you wonder whether you're a boring person. You might be, but even if you're the world's most engaging speaker, the black hole wins in the mid-afternoon — hands down and heads down.

Some large organizations incorporate a nap time into their day. In other countries taking a siesta is expected. NASA conducted a study with airline pilots and found that a 26-minute nap boosted performance by 33 percent. Research shows that nappers outperform non-nappers. Sixty to ninety minutes' sleep gives brains a chance to dump some of the information that accumulated throughout the day. The nappers scored as though they had slept six hours.

Many employees nap during their lunch hours by catching a few winks in their cars. You might take a survey and see whether your employees are already napping or feel they need a nap during the day. Happy brains work better, and rested brains are more likely to be happy.

Some corporations, such as Ben and Jerry's Homemade Ice Cream, have created nap rooms for their employees to use when they get tired. Because sleep needs vary, offering the opportunity for a short nap makes more sense than setting up schedules. Comfortable chairs and soft music may be helpful for some employees.

Working Well, Even in Cubby Holes

When evidence became available that the brain can produce new neurons, researchers examined rats in labs for neuron production and found none. Perhaps the brain couldn't create new cells, after all.

Later research showed that in order to grow new neurons — the brain cells that learn and connect — brains need an enriched environment, one that is social and meets the needs I describe in Chapter 3. Research conducted in the 1960s by such famous neuroscientists as Dr. Marian Diamond and Dr. William Greenough compared rats kept in normal psychology rat labs which encompassed a life in a small cage with two fellow rats to rats placed in a large cage with plenty of things to do and play and a host of other rats to interact with. Theories about enriched environments were born. (And so were many rats!) The rats in the normal lab environment had few connecting fibers on their brain cells. Those in the enriched environment, however, had cells with a lot of fibers. The interaction with rat friends and rat toys caused new growth in the brain.

To save viable brain cells and encourage the growth of new cells, I suggest the following:

- Encourage workers to decorate their cubicles or offices. A personalized space is more fun to be in.

- Provide visual goals for them to display. Being separated from others may make keeping eyes on the prize more difficult. Make goals visible.

- Use productive color combinations in those cubicles. Energize them with yellow, help them focus with red.

- Provide music for motivation. Background sounds help most people feel less alone and less stressed.

- Provide bright lighting and appropriate lighting for close work. Dim lighting increases the production of melatonin, the chemical that makes you sleepy.

- Encourage employees to take frequent breaks, to leave the cubby and see daylight and fellow workers. These social and movement breaks give the brain a rest; seeing others reminds workers that they aren't in this alone.

- Offer time and opportunity for play, exercise, and interaction. Movement and interaction release chemicals that help with focus, concentration, and feeling bonded with others.

- Give employees work to do in small groups, so they're not isolated most of the day. Isolation can lead to depression. Groups provide conversation, interaction, and an opportunity to ask questions and solve problems.

Putting Humor to Work

You have good reason to get serious about humor in the workplace. Research on humor suggests that laughter

- ✔ Increases productivity
- ✔ Burns calories
- ✔ Lowers blood pressure
- ✔ Strengthens your immune system
- ✔ Bolsters coping mechanisms
- ✔ Enhances memory
- ✔ Increases alertness by adding oxygen to your blood
- ✔ Energizes
- ✔ Increases bonding and communication

People who are happy at work keep their jobs longer. Try mixing business with pleasure:

- ✔ Use humor to get employees to attend meetings: begin with a funny story or joke.
- ✔ Give an award to the employee who makes people laugh the most each week.
- ✔ Create a laughter bulletin board that employees can contribute to with cartoons, jokes, and so on.
- ✔ Send a joke of the day through e-mail or your intranet.
- ✔ Set a humorous tone. Encourage banter among your employees. You must begin. Try making fun of yourself or situations that you find yourself in.
- ✔ Funny posters placed strategically can add laughter and humor.
- ✔ Look for humor at work. Some work situations (but not people) are funny, but your employees won't laugh about them unless you or their team leader does.

Humor is not always a funny thing. Make sure that everyone knows there are rules for using humor. Jokes that poke fun are not allowed. Sarcasm is not good humor. Anything that you must follow up with "I was just kidding," is not good humor.

Chapter 13

Understanding Male and Female Brains at Work

*Y*ou may have heard the outdated notion that women are right-brained (meaning creative, intuitive, freer with feelings) and men are left-brained (analytical, detail oriented, less emotional). Fortunately, that insulting idea went out with shoulder pads back in the '80s. What stuck, though, is that men and women do indeed have different brains, and researchers have backed up that idea in studies that examine brains with high-tech imaging devices.

The ways that men's and women's brains are different shows up in pretty much everything humans do, and the workplace is no exception. This chapter examines the characteristics of male and female brains, giving you knowledge that can affect how well you understand yourself and your leadership style. You can use the information you find here to become a better supervisor, manager, and negotiator as you develop a deeper understanding of the people with whom you're working.

Ultimately, your organization benefits by becoming a *gender-intelligent organization* — a balanced workforce that utilizes the skills and talents of each gender to reach goals and create a workplace that retains the best workers, trains the best leaders, and has the best woman or man for each job.

Biology Basics: Size Doesn't Matter, but a Lot of Other Stuff Does

The male brain is larger than the female brain. Both weigh in at about three pounds, but the male brain is about 11 percent heavier. Decades ago, researchers assumed that a larger brain meant higher intelligence, but intelligence tests found that males and females are equally intelligent. So, in this case, size doesn't matter.

Testosterone most likely is responsible for the larger size of the male brain. Men have a lot more of this hormone than women do.

Size might not matter, but in the sections that follow, you see that the physical development of male and female brains can affect the workplace and your ability to manage and lead.

Why gray matter matters

The male brain has six and a half times more gray matter than the female brain. As I discuss in Chapter 2, *gray matter* refers to the brain cell bodies that process information. The female brain has approximately ten times more white matter. The *white matter* transfers information to different processing centers throughout the brain. The fact of the matter is that both males and females have the same cognitive abilities, yet they utilize different pathways in their brains.

The prevalence of white and gray matter affects how people work together and alone. Take a look at the difference in these two ways of working:

- ✔ **White-matter approach:** The female brain uses all that white matter to integrate information from many areas, which adds to her language abilities (something I talk more about in the upcoming section, "Hearing, Listening, and Talking: Communication Differences") and encourages her to utilize relationships to reach her goals. The white-matter approach goes beyond local processing, connecting to some of the brain's geography where male brains rarely tread: emotional areas, speech centers, and memory centers on both sides of the brain. In the workplace, the female brain is processing the work, the people, and the context surrounding the objective.

- ✔ **Gray-matter approach:** The male brain tends to process locally — within all that gray matter — which assists in accomplishing singular tasks and keeping focused on a given target. The gray matter approach is to get the job done; relationships are secondary. The male brain processes the objective and finds the most direct path to that objective.

The multitasking female brain

You've probably heard the pervasive notion that women are better able than men to do several things at once. Although current research suggests that multitasking is a myth — the brain is incapable of attending to more than one thing at a time — there may be two reasons for the multitasking assumption for women.

One is the ability of the female brain's white matter allowing it to collect and distribute information easily. Secondly, access to each hemisphere is accelerated by the size of the *corpus callosum,* a bridge of fibers connecting the two hemispheres. Many studies suggest this that the female corpus callosum is larger than the male's, and it certainly appears to account for the multiple brain areas used by the female in various endeavors.

A mixed gender team often works well together. Leslie is a very successful car dealer. Paul is one of her biggest assets. Paul sells cars, too, but together the Leslie and Paul team sell lots of cars. Leslie uses the white matter approach; she integrates information from her emotional areas in her brain along with her uncanny ability to speak to people from different walks of life on a level that gets instant rapport. Leslie has honed her empathy skills and knows just what to say. Paul closes the sale. His gray matter approach allows him to specialize in the financial end of making deals. He uses local brain areas and creates financial deals that meet the budgets of the people buying cars. Customers feel that they have been taken care of and are confident they are getting a great deal.

Both the white and gray matter approaches to accomplishing tasks and achieving objectives can work equally well, but in a gender-intelligent organization, balancing these two approaches offers leadership the opportunity to see the big picture and be sure that nothing is missed.

Considering emotional differences

From birth, males notice things while females notice people. The larger right hemisphere in males may be the reason for this phenomenon. The right hemisphere houses several areas that focus on spatial ability. This creates men who are skillful at spatial reasoning, manipulation of objects, and gross motor skills.

Because males notice things rather than people, they have difficulty becoming aware of and responding to signs of emotion. In a study at Stanford University, males and females were placed in scanners and shown emotional scenes. In the female brain, nine different areas showed activity, while in the male brains only two were active.

The emotional structure in the brain, the *amygdala*, is always filtering information for emotional content. The amygdala is larger in the male brain, but rather than making the male more sensitive to his own and other's feelings, it seems to affect aggression. If a stressful situation arises, the amygdala alerts the *hypothalamus*, the structure in charge of internal responses, to get ready for the fight or flight response. Males are more likely to run or to defend themselves in a threatening situation.

Males have emotions, but they are just not always great at sharing those emotions or recognizing emotions in others. In an analysis of hundreds of studies where men and women were shown pictures of people expressing various emotions, women outperformed the men 80 percent of the time.

Not being able to recognize emotions makes it difficult to share emotions, use them in conversation, or make decisions. Some males are at a disadvantage in this area. Men's brains work very hard at reading emotion, but they sometimes use more primitive brain areas that lead them to reflexive behaviors rather than reflective ones.

Females tend to be emotional experts. Their busy brains allow them access to both emotional areas and language areas at the same time. Simultaneously, their communication skills include reading body language and facial expressions. Because relationships are important to them, reading other's minds through their expressions and movements has become a large part of their communication skills.

Reacting to stress

The male and female brains respond to stress differently. Stress in either brain causes the release of the fight-or-flight chemicals, *adrenaline* and *cortisol*. These cause blood pressure to rise and prepare the body to flee or fight. The male brain stops there, which means that males become agitated and try to release stress through competition and debating or through escape. They bottle up their emotions and don't want to talk about them. Males also try to "play through" their stress through physical activity like golf.

Female brains let loose adrenaline and cortisol, too, but they also release two other chemicals: oxytocin and serotonin. *Oxytocin* is a bonding chemical. For instance, it is released in mothers and fathers upon the birth of a child to help them bond with and therefore care for the infant. Oxytocin has been called the "tend and befriend" chemical as it makes people feel close to each other. Females have a tendency to want to talk about and talk out their stress with others. *Serotonin* is a calming chemical that naturally occurs in high levels in the female brain. The combination of the release of these two chemicals makes stress a very different experience for the female brain.

In high-pressure situations in the workplace, the female brain has a tendency to remember details and talk about them, and the male brain frames the big picture but does not necessarily want to talk. Having both types of brains onboard for such situations provides a fuller scope of the situation.

Differences in memory

The male brain has a smaller *hippocampus* — the brain structure that helps form factual memories — than the female brain. Neuroscientists believe that higher levels of *estrogen* (the "female" hormone) are responsible for this biological development. Females tend to have better memories for details.

Because the hippocampus sits next to the emotional center in the brain, the *amygdala,* memories that contain emotions are easier to remember for male and female brains.

Even though females use more emotional centers and more pathways in their brains for emotions, males also respond to emotional situations and emotional content. For this reason, adding emotion to your trainings, meetings, and professional relationships helps your workforce and clientele remember more of their experiences with you.

Going with the flow

The brain is the only organ that can't store energy and so needs constant feeding. Females seem to be better brain feeders. About 15 to 20 percent more blood flows to the female brain, bringing the oxygen and nutrients that feed this organ.

Female brains are active even when at rest; male brains show much less activity during restful states. In fact, some research suggests that male brains go into a state of rest under various circumstances such as stress, exhaustion, and even during conversations.

Blood flow is initiated by the brain's activity. At any given time, a female's brain is more active than a male's. In fact, the male brain requires resting states throughout the day, while a female brain does not. This can translate into a male zoning out during a meeting. A female, on the other hand, utilizes so many different pathways in her brain that she may easily appear off task as she calls on different brain areas to make connections. Keeping your male employees alert and your female employees on target are two important tasks for you as you conduct your meetings.

Understanding risky behavior

Most risk takers don't believe that what they do is risky. The chemicals in their brains fill them with confidence and a feeling of control. Risk-taking and thrill-seeking are more common in males, who sometimes go to extremes that affect their health. Three young men die for every young woman. Men often choose riskier careers or seek thrills in their personal lives.

Risk-taking has its upsides and downsides. Frank Farley, PhD, studies risk-taking at Temple University. He calls a risk-taking personality *Type T*. The T stands for thrill. Type Ts need a high level of stimulation.

Risk-takers can be good for business. They're often inventors, explorers, and entrepreneurs. These workers may be more creative and respond positively to challenge, but managers need to make sure they don't take unnecessary risk.

Along with testosterone, the male brain releases adrenaline and cortisol during stress. In small quantities, these chemicals are motivating; in larger quantities, they're a recipe for disaster. The feeling of confidence and control is amplified until the risk becomes greater than the reward.

Males mature later than females. This immaturity is linked to the part of the brain called the prefrontal cortex, located behind the forehead, where higher-level thinking, future planning, and decision-making are processed in the brain. (See Chapter 2.) A less mature prefrontal cortex may indicate less impulse control.

You may want to assess how your future employees respond in stressful and competitive situations. Impulse control is necessary when working with clients. Some corporations put their interviewees in stressful and competitive situations. One corporation places each potential hire in a hotel room that serves as his office. Over the course of the day, he's given large stacks of documents to prioritize, sent memos for spur-of-the-moment meetings and given only minutes to prepare for them, and asked to negotiate problems. At the end of the day each interviewee must explain why he performed as he did. The candidates know that others competing for the same job are in the same hotel working on the same problem. Note the amount of risk each candidate is willing to take to get the job or complete a task. Many walk out of the hotel without notice before the end of the day.

Hearing, Listening, and Talking: Communication Differences

Leaders know that they need to communicate clearly to get the best out of people. Recognizing how males and females engage differently in two-way communication helps you overcome barriers and meet the needs of your organization.

Men really are hard of hearing

In general, women have a better sense of hearing than men. The cochlea is in large part the culprit. The part of the ear called the *cochlea* converts sound to nerve impulses. The male ear contains a longer cochlea, which slows down the brain's recognition of sound and its response to it.

Males also have difficulty with higher pitched sounds and soft sounds. Female voices are often higher pitched, and so men accused of not listening may actually not be hearing. Women's voices are more complex than men's because of differences in the size of the larynx and vocal cords.

In schools, boys tend to sit in the back of the room and girls sit in the front. Teachers often find that they need to raise their voices in order to be heard by the boys. The girls, who are sensitive to this increased volume, are often upset because they think they're being punished. In the workplace, a similar dynamic can unfold.

To prevent misunderstandings based upon the different ways in which male and female brains hear, you can take a number of steps:

- ✔ **Educate your team as appropriate.** You don't have to hold a training session on the way in which males and females hear, but you can always get the information across in the course of normal conversations if you feel the issue has led to misunderstandings.

- ✔ **Bring males to the front of the class.** In meetings and training situations, bring the male brains to the front of the room or place them closer to the primary speaker.

- ✔ **Get a male's attention before speaking to him.** Saying his name loudly or tapping his arm alerts him to pay attention to your softer tones.

Verbal communication is more than just words. Only 7 percent of a message is based on the words a person says. Tone of voice comprises 38 percent of the communication, and the remaining 55 percent is body language. Females do well with their ability to read people. However, with today's technology, at least some of our communication relies on e-mails, text messages, and instant messaging, which offer no tone or body language for others to read and therefore create confusion. Choose your words very carefully when you communicate by using these means. Chapter 15 goes into greater detail about maximizing electronic communication.

Listening cues: Understanding his and hers

Dr. Deborah Tannen, a Georgetown University Professor of linguistics, has studied communication differences in men and women at work. She found that

- ✔ Males give little or no eye contact as they listen. They sit with others side by side and avoid looking at faces.
- ✔ Females sit face to face and contort their bodies in order to give and receive eye contact. This adds to their unique ability to read facial expressions and body language.

Imagine then the frustration that can occur in the female brain when speaking with a male at work as he avoids looking her in the eye.

Understanding different listening styles helps you and your employees work together more harmoniously. Here's how:

- ✔ When females realize that they aren't being rejected by not receiving eye contact, they're less stressed and work more productively.
- ✔ Accepting the female listening strategy of searching for eye contact keeps males from feeling that they are being targeted in some way.

He says; she says more

According to research, the average male speaks about one third as many words as the average female. This is an average — certainly some males talk a lot and some females do not. Current estimates state that males speak about 7,000 words a day while females clock in at 20,000 words per day. (For some interesting theories on what accounts for this difference check out the "A conversation on hunters and gatherers" sidebar in this chapter.)

A conversation on hunters and gatherers

Scientists, marriage counselors, and psychologists agree that the male brain is one of few words. Perhaps it goes back to the hunter/gatherer days when men had to be silent as they went out hunting. Bursting into conversation would scare the prey away or turn them into prey. Better to hunt for lunch rather than *be* lunch.

The "survival of the fittest" interpretation is that a male's offspring would never have entered the gene pool if Dad had not survived by successful hunting. Perhaps that need for silence has carried over to our modern day.

As gatherers, women cared for children, prepared food, and shared the history of their people with their offspring. Their need to communicate may have changed their brain development to fulfill the duties that were then part of their survival.

Conversations between men and women may be disappointing for women, who like to add details and feelings to the conversation and to receive them from the person to whom they're speaking. Men may believe that time is wasted on too much conversation. An understanding of each other's needs leads to better relationships and dialogue at work.

Making Meetings Work for Males and Females

The differences in male and female brains that this chapter highlights mean that male and female leaders run their meetings differently. (And what is work without meetings? Blissful, maybe, but probably not productive or realistic.) To make sure your meetings are as effective as possible, you might want to evaluate how you organize your meetings and address the needs of all of your employees.

Meetings run by male brains may

- Keep explanations short and hold descriptions to a minimum.
- Discourage responses by employees.
- Include a lot of interruptions in an effort to keep conversations short.
- Not address prior meeting conflicts or conversations. (Men tend not to remember them.)

✔ Support risk-taking.

✔ Downplay emotions.

✔ Encourage immediate action.

Meetings run by female brains may operate quite differently. These meetings

✔ Include lengthy explanations.

✔ Encourage and expect opinions from employees.

✔ Rely on group consensus to drive the direction or the results of the meeting.

✔ Attend to details or emotional interactions from prior meetings.

✔ Resolve any emotional conflicts that occur during the meeting.

✔ Minimize risk-taking and competition.

When running a meeting, keep in mind the needs and expectations of each gender. For the females in the workforce, allow time to offer opinions and get consensus. For the males, cover the main points briefly and remind them of prior conflicts or conversations that may be pertinent to the topic at hand. Balance the emotional needs with the need for action.

As you look at the employees attending your meeting, you may see very dissimilar behaviors from males and females. Table 13-1 contains various meeting scenarios and gender-based responses to be on the lookout for.

Table 13-1	Comparing Men's and Women's Behaviors	
Scenario	*Male brain reaction*	*Female brain reaction*
Stressful meeting	May become competitive and aggressive because of rise in testosterone	May withdraw; oxytocin produces a need to talk to someone about the problem
Lengthy meeting	May go into a resting state because they're overwhelmed by long discussions	May be so busy making connections that they appear to be off task but usually are not
General meeting	May take over a meeting because of their more aggressive nature	May feel undervalued if their opinions aren't requested

The organization can suffer as attendees lose their ability to share what might be brilliant ideas. Short breaks that provide movement may wake up the resting brain and provide time for dialogue for those brains that require more talk.

Competing in the Workplace

Testosterone levels rise in both males and females during competition, but testosterone increases more in the male brain. Just attending a competitive event as an audience member usually increases testosterone in both male and female brains. The degree to which each is a stakeholder in the event can affect the levels as well. (Think "hockey moms," gamblers, and workers competing for promotion.)

Males like to compete. They compete over who is brighter, stronger, faster, or better. Competition is motivating, activates emotional areas of the brain, and when used correctly enhances productivity, lowers absenteeism, and makes males happy. Some females prefer not to compete in the workplace. The female brain wants to build and maintain relationships. Interpersonal skills override the need to find out who is better. Females tend toward team work in which everyone wins.

The female's lack of competitiveness led to the conclusion that females always cooperate and males always compete. That's not quite true: Males actually compete very cooperatively.

The less the undercurrent of threat, the better the competition. In one Tony-Award-winning play, employees were offered a contest. The first prize was a Cadillac. The second prize was a set of steak knives. The third prize was being fired. This kind of competition increases fear instead of motivation.

Competition comes in two flavors. *Direct competition* is a one-to-one experience that produces only one winner. *Cooperative competition* occurs when a team works together to achieve a goal for the good of the group. The upcoming sections give you details about each form of competition.

Direct competition

Competition between two individuals can be destructive — if there can be only one winner, then there is always a loser. Too much competition within the workplace can lead to lower productivity, hard feelings, and a loss of focus. Anger and even hostility can arise to a point where people or teams won't accept others' ideas. As a leader, you need to carefully oversee competitive situations.

Competition increases levels of chemicals like testosterone and is motivational in many situations. An extrinsic reward for the competition — monetary compensation, extra perks, or a more prestigious position — can cause stress for some employees.

Stress can be motivating, but recognizing the ways men and women handle stress may affect your approach to competition. Female stress and female competition look very much alike. Females compete in a more subtle manner than males, using relationships to get ahead. The extrinsic reward may be motivating, but most females still believe in the idea that "we're all in this together." Stress in males leads to a more aggressive approach to competition, and the extrinsic reward challenges the male brain even more.

Intrinsic rewards for competition offer another approach worth considering. The feeling of accomplishing a goal can be reward enough. Acknowledgment from management and fellow workers might be sufficient motivation to get all employees to work harder and contribute more to the company. Because the male brain likes to compete, the intrinsic reward is in winning or being the best. Intrinsically, female brains consider acknowledgment by others motivating and yet still want others to feel good and be a part of the praise.

The question among many leaders is, "Do I praise them or raise them?" Offering bonuses for work well done has always been part of the business climate. Some research suggests that praising an employee in front of his peers motivates him or her more than money. Of course, either approach may be better for a particular individual. Direct competition without an extrinsic reward may increase productivity, but generally males respond better to direct competition.

Cooperative competition

In cooperative competition, a group or team sets a goal and pursues it together. Working together and helping each other provides not only a release of testosterone for motivation but also the release of the brain chemical dopamine. *Dopamine* is the pleasure chemical and is also involved in the feeling of bonding. Oxytocin, which enhances bonding, is also released.

The brain strongly desires these feel-good chemicals, and so the team is intrinsically motivated. They want to continue to have these good feelings and be a part of something greater than themselves. Research suggests that team composition works best if teams are divided by gender or have an equal gender split. A feeling of being a minority in any team is a problem. For instance, a team of four men and two women often results in the women contributing less. Mixed teams generate better ideas than single-sex teams.

Working toward a personal best is also a healthy cooperative type of competition. For example, each employee tries to raise her level of productivity not in competition with others but rather in competition with her own established best. The collaborative groups support each person's quest to excel. Post a team chart that shows each individual's current production rate. Together the team brainstorms ideas that work for each individual. Individual workers implement strategies; results are tracked on the chart. The whole team celebrates a person's increases.

Using competition in the workplace can be healthy and productive. Teams made up of males and females may bring different ways of thinking about the goals to the table. All-male teams are more likely to become overly competitive.

Considering competition and reward in action

A distribution company I worked with on sales motivation offered a trip based on sales to winning dealers. The trip was extravagant and offered leisure activities as well as competitive sports. (Keep in mind that the competitive games may have increased testosterone levels in the males.) During the trip, the dealership owners competed with their local competitors as well as those outside their own territories. Dealers received awards at a gala evening event. One of the top producers for the distributor had been receiving awards at these functions for years. This high-producing dealership was owned by a man and a woman who were stunned when their names weren't called to receive a sales award. The dealership had failed to meet the specific qualifications for the award.

Angry and embarrassed, the dealers left the room, checked out of the hotel, and hopped on an early flight home. Their account manager thought surely he would lose the dealership's business forever. He immediately went to meet with these clients upon returning home. Although the male owner was still upset, he looked at the facts when the account manager gave him the data and copies of memos that had been sent to the dealership detailing what they were in need of accomplishing for the award. The female owner and partner, however, refused to give the account manager a meeting and remained angry with him until he used brain research suggestions for dealing with the female brain. He asked her how she felt while looking her directly in the eyes. He showed empathy for her distress at losing the award, and then showed her the data and discussed how they, as a team, could move forward. The dealership continued doing business with the distribution company.

Checking Out Working Relationships in Action

While training a regional group of team leaders on male and female brain differences, many of the brain differences in this chapter presented themselves. Here's what went down and how the actions illustrated the concepts in this chapter:

1. **Matt, one of the younger participants, interrupted my opening remarks to reject this material immediately.**

   "I want to see the research on this," he began. "I know this won't make a difference with my team. I know how to lead men and women." His male brain showed competitive stress.

2. **Before I could respond, Paul, another team leader, spoke up.**

   "This research has been around for awhile. Don't you read trade journals?" he looked directly at Matt. Paul was having a competitive reaction.

3. **One of the female leaders, Tammy, very quietly explained Matt's behavior.**

   "Don't take this personally. Matt just has to get his two cents in. He doesn't mean anything by it. Most of the women on his team tend to ignore him. They've tried talking to him, but they mostly feel sorry for him because he's so young." Her female brain reacted empathetically.

   Tammy smiled at me. She then slumped over her place at the table as if to remove herself from the loud remarks. Her female brain was shutting down from the bossiness.

4. **Tall, confident Oscar stood up and commanded the others.**

   "Let's just get on with this! We aren't going to know if any of this is true unless we get to the details." His male brain wanted just the facts.

5. **Everyone's attention turned to me.**

   I wanted to ask everyone how they were feeling. My female brain focuses on relationships. But I knew better and so asked the team leaders to participate in a short activity to get the men moving and give the women a chance to talk. I continued the training a few minutes later.

At the end of the training, Matt still wasn't sure that I had proven anything. I asked the leaders to get in small groups and discuss what had happened during the day that would tend to corroborate the research findings about the differences between the male and female brain. As they shared their anecdotal evidence collected from that single day's training, even Matt couldn't deny that there was something to this research.

Chapter 14

Making Teams Work

You can't be a leader if you have no followers. Your teams are the vehicles through which you get the job done. With the multiple generations you probably have in your organization, creating teams can be challenging but interesting.

Everyone in your organizations must live up to your expectations. They must be productive and creative change agents. Building teams and making them work can increase motivation, productivity, relationships, self-confidence, and timing throughout your organization.

Just as a sports team works together to accomplish goals, work-related teams progress toward the organization's goals as well as their own specialized goals. You choose the expert team that runs your organization. Individual agendas, egos, or career status cannot enter the picture.

In this chapter, you find out about building the right team, setting goals, monitoring progress, and encouraging everyone along the way — you're not just the leader, you're the head cheerleader, too!

Building an Executive Team

Your executive team is going to be the most important group of people you need (besides investors). This is the "first" team and must consist of those people who make your business run, make it profitable, solve problems that you don't need to be involved in, and help you solve other business problems.

So, who is on first? You or the person you designate to run the show for you. You are the ultimate decision-maker. The buck definitely stops with you when it comes to taking responsibility for mistakes, failures, and miscommunications.

Other members of your first, or senior, team depend on the kind of business you are running. Large and small organizations have some executive team members with similar responsibilities, but a retailer and a wholesaler have some differences, and so do a physician's office and a nonprofit organization.

Fill the jobs with the right people. Sometimes these people are available within your organization, other times you need to go elsewhere to find them. Look for the following in your leadership team:

- ✔ Leaders who are interested in and have knowledge of every aspect of your business; even though they lead their own departments, they have a good understanding of the business as a whole

- ✔ Leaders who can help make decisions, even though some of the decisions may not directly impact their department

- ✔ Leaders who can see the *vertical dynamics* (communication that goes in a top-down fashion) and the *horizontal dynamics* (communication across levels) and can switch from one to the other

- ✔ Leaders who don't criticize after a decision is made

- ✔ Leaders who are excellent role models

Your executive team is going to help you make decisions, move the organization forward, and keep you informed about what's going on in every department. This team should be able to get you through the rough times, help you celebrate successes, and determine how you're going to reach your goals.

Keeping this team functioning at its highest level is a challenge for every leader. Everything may be going well, and then complacency sets in. To keep this team running smoothly try the following:

- ✔ **Cultivate collaboration:** Have a meeting before the meeting to build community and get to know each other better.

- ✔ **Promote trust:** Show your vulnerabilities, admit mistakes, and ask for feedback.

- ✔ **Make the time for off-site meetings:** Hold two- or three-day retreats with a facilitator. Getting away from the office provides a fresh perspective, and because employees can't tend directly to office business, they stay focused on the meeting.

Discovering How Teams Develop

All teams go through developmental stages, just as the brain does. The upcoming sections detail the way a group of people matures into a team.

Infancy

During the *infancy* or *forming* stage, everyone is excited about entering this new world, doesn't really know the team members, and has little idea about what the vision, mission, expectations, or norms of the team will be. Members are tentative as they determine whether they can trust their fellow players. Just as the brain during infancy is making new connections, adapting to its environment, and learning from experiences, so is the newly formed team.

At this stage of team development, the team members have the following needs:

✔ Getting to know each other

✔ Discovering their roles and the roles of other team members

✔ Defining the team's purpose, values, and norms

✔ Reaching harmony on authority and on personal and professional boundaries

✔ Outlining decision-making processes

At this stage, the team reviews the vision statement and mission statement. All teams within your organization require a team purpose. Every team's purpose is to model both the vision and the mission statements.

During the infancy stage, the team develops its own team norms. *Norms* are the ground rules for the individual and team behaviors. For instance, one norm shared with me by a leader is "early is on-time; on-time is late." In other words, meetings must start at the designated time. In order to accomplish this, every team member must be present, seated, and ready to begin at the designated meeting start time. Getting there just in the nick of time causes the meeting to begin late.

Each team sets its own goals based on the goals of the entire organization. Infancy is a "getting to know each other" period and a time to set up the framework for the work. Teams really depend on their leaders during this stage, which can last a few months.

Playing nice within teams

You can compare the infancy stage of a team to early social development. Children begin "playing" by standing next to each other and playing with individual toys. As they gain confidence and trust, they begin to play with another child, and eventually move on to small groups and then larger groups.

Individuals who have been assigned to a team may be smiling and excited to be on the team, but most know little of what is expected of them. They may not know who's in charge, and they may wonder who to trust. They may introduce themselves to those sitting on either side of them. For the most part, interaction is minimal.

As with the small children, the team members play side by side.

At the next meeting, team members are a bit more relaxed and may have small group discussions as the leader reviews and revisits information from the previous meeting. They may have run into their team mates while at work and may feel some camaraderie with them. The leader may provide a "get to know each other" activity to help define roles and create a climate of trust. All of the "kids" are playing together instead of side by side.

The leader's tasks include the following:

✔ Help the team outline its values and goals

✔ Help team members get to know each other

✔ Guide the team in setting up their norms

✔ Provide structure by scheduling regular meetings

Adolescence

Adolescence refers to the stage in which the team seek more independence. This stage of development is one of the necessary evils associated with teams, but its outcome is really what makes a group a cohesive team. Some call this stage of development *storming,* and if you remember your own adolescence or have raised an adolescent, you can understand how well this stage fits with the behaviors that result from the growth of the adolescent brain.

Adolescents often are

✔ Moody

✔ Difficult to work with

✔ Emotional

- ✔ Confrontational

- ✔ Frustrated

- ✔ Confused

- ✔ Challenged by communication

- ✔ Convinced that they are incompetent or have low self-esteem

- ✔ Prone to unrealistic expectations

The adolescent brain is underdeveloped in areas of decision-making, controlling emotions, and understanding consequences. As this brain develops, all of these areas improve and the brain begins to work in a more cohesive fashion.

Characteristics of the storming stage of team development include

- ✔ Conflict

- ✔ Frustration with authority

- ✔ Confusion with goals, mission, and norms

- ✔ Desire for independence from leader

- ✔ Lack of self-confidence

- ✔ Unrealistic expectations

The team, like the adolescent brain, can mature and learn to work productively. The emotional and social intelligence of the team is an important aspect of becoming a productive and healthy group of people who understand each other's differences and can work together using those differences to make change. And as one leader said, "Change is good. But I prefer dollars!"

The adolescent stage can last a few months. The leader assists in this stage by doing the following:

- ✔ **Helping the team resolve conflicts:** You might need to remind the team of their previously established rules.

- ✔ **Building trust:** Share stories about some of the problems your own team has faced.

- ✔ **Encouraging independence:** Allow them to speak freely.

- ✔ **Being prepared for challenges:** Assist them in planning to achieve their goals.

The challenge for this stage of development is to firm up the goals and norms. If the leader steps back and lets team members make their own decisions, the team will become less dependent on her.

Maturity

When the brain reaches maturity, it begins to function at a higher level. High-level thinking skills, problem-solving, and attention to goals and roles lead to better decision-making. The mature brain controls emotions and reads others' emotions; its improved ability to handle relationships means that the brain can be more productive, be more task- and goal-oriented, and feel more 'like part of the team.

At this stage of team development, sometimes referred to as the *norming* stage, you may see these characteristics:

- Focus on specific topics
- Dividing into smaller groups to accomplish more
- Reviewing previous accomplishments and seeking areas of improvement
- More commitment to vision, mission, and goals
- Spending more time on decision-making
- More energy to produce
- Respect and trust among team members
- Cohesiveness

A mature brain has a developed prefrontal cortex; as Chapter 2 details, this area of the brain integrates information from all other areas and gets a rational picture of what is happening. The prefrontal cortex also is aware of emotions and works with them, so the mature brain is much like a team beginning to truly work together. At this stage, team members start talking in terms of the team instead of just themselves. The team has taken shape and can now make great strides.

The leader is more of a coach for a team at this stage and should do the following:

- Provide feedback to guide them toward the goal
- Continue building positive relationships
- Help focus on specific areas of productivity
- Assess team function
- Continue to address conflict

At the maturity stage, the team is closer to becoming a powerful entity for your organization. Its members have learned from the first three stages of development. The team needs a few more months to move to the next stage.

Wisdom

As the brain continues to develop beyond the maturity level, one of the most respected aspects of humanity, wisdom, develops. Team wisdom is a combination of knowledge and skills that enable the team to solve problems and make decisions easily. People become wiser by working with others, and they become better able to make decisions that produce positive results.

Dendrites, the fibers in brain cells that receive information, continue to form and grow longer when you learn. As they grow, more and more tiers of fibers develop in order to receive messages. The highest tiers that indicate the achievement of wisdom. Turn to Chapter 2 to find out more about how brain cells grow.

Wisdom comes from experience. Your team is now achieving wisdom. This stage is often called the *performing* stage. And you have given them the stage on which to perform!

Characteristics of the wise team include the following:

- ✔ Problem-solving proficiency

- ✔ Clear purpose

- ✔ Shared leadership

- ✔ Optimal productivity

- ✔ High levels of motivation and drive

- ✔ Initiative

- ✔ High level of team loyalty

- ✔ Relationships built on trust and experiences

- ✔ Respect for individual differences and the need to disagree

- ✔ Quick conflict resolution

As the wise team works toward its goals, you see continuous improvement and soaring productivity. They regulate themselves and make changes to their goals as necessary. This team still has needs. Those needs include the following:

- ✔ Autonomy to make decisions

- ✔ Continued professional development

- ✔ New challenges

- ✔ Recognition of accomplishments

- ✔ Celebrations of individual and team accomplishments

The high-performance team continues to gain wisdom as it helps you create the organization that meets your vision and your goals. Allowing every team the time and guidance to move from stage to stage is the responsibility of every leader.

Leading a Team from Without and Within

Leading your organization requires you to sometimes be on the outside watching teams achieve goals, or you may be completely involved in their work. As teams go through various stages, you may have to change your leadership style to fit their level of maturation. In this section, I share how to match your style, how to find others to help hold teams together, and how to train team leaders.

Matching your leadership style to your team's stage

As your teams develop, you may wonder which leadership style you need for each. (Check out Chapter 6 to get more information about leadership styles.) You can compare the process of leading to a classroom.

When class begins and the students don't know content, methods, or procedures, the instructor's job is to run the classroom — that is, to take an authoritarian approach to leadership. The authoritarian leader takes responsibility for running things. Telling others what to do and how to do it are part of this process. The infancy stage of team development requires a lot of guidance, and therefore an authoritarian leadership style works best.

The adolescent stage is a bit different. Although this stage includes a lot of dissatisfaction, much learning is taking place. This stage requires a slow leadership change. The leader begins with an authoritarian style to begin this stage, but as the "adolescents" learn, they need some leeway. Thus, the leadership style changes to a more democratic style.

The adolescent team is going through major developmental changes. As the changes occur, you must give the team opportunities to begin making some decisions and weighing risks that it might previously have automatically taken.

The maturity stage occurs when the team members are really learning to figure things out. They are working together but still need some guidance.

The democratic style works well with the maturity stage. Members seek input and make decisions under the guidance of their team leader. This is a productive stage, but it's still a learning stage. You need to do some coaching and support the work being done.

Socrates said that wisdom comes to each of us when we realize how little we know. The wisdom stage for teams requires little coaching, yet some support. When a team reaches this stage, switch to the delegative style of leadership. The team is ready to make its own decisions and may only occasionally need the support or advice of a leader.

Finding (or fostering) the glue people

Sometimes teams can find themselves in sticky situations. Even though they have managed to make their way through the four stages of team development, problems can occur. Even those in the wisdom stage of development can come across areas of dissension. This often occurs when a team member leaves a team or new members join.

One way of finding the balance and recreating the climate is to find what Daniel Goleman (author of *Emotional Intelligence*) calls the *glue people*— those who help hold things together with their high emotional intelligence. Friendly, interested, and positive team members set the stage for others as newcomers enter and others leave teams.

When the team runs into a problem with the work or interpersonal clashes, these glue people smooth the edges and assist in coming to terms with the problems. Team members such as these may be hard to come by, but you can develop them through emotional and social training.

As you assemble teams, be conscious of the value of the glue people and try to place one on each team. If you find yourself lacking qualified people with this skill, remember that it is a skill that can be learned. Select people you feel are destined to help your organization reach its goals and provide training in emotional intelligence.

Training team leaders

When it comes to the senior team, you may indeed be the leader. But what about your other teams? As you create them, or as your senior team constructs the teams they need for their department goals, discuss how the leaders of these teams will be chosen and trained.

You may choose team leaders based on need, availability, and — if you're lucky — positive team experience. The experienced team member has at least felt what going through the team-development process is like. She may not be able to name the stages of development, but she can relate to them as they are explained.

In most team leader trainings, the first step is for each team leader to describe a team experience in as much detail as he can remember. Make this a written assignment that is then shared in small groups to save time. Another useful activity is creating a list of ideal team leader characteristics. You do this in several stages:

1. **Each team leader writes down the first name of her favorite team leader and lists the characteristics that made this leader great.**

2. **Each team leader writes down the first name of a team leader that she did not enjoy working with and lists the characteristics of this team leader.**

3. **Each team leader writes down how each of these leaders made her feel.**

4. **In small groups, the team leaders discuss the characteristics of both leaders and create a chart with positive team leader characteristics on the left side and negative characteristics on the right side.**

5. **Display each small group's charts and discuss the characteristics as a whole group.**

6. **From these charts, create the definitive characteristics of a great team leader.**

The information you obtain from this exercise is a great anchor for training. From this point, I suggest the following steps for training:

1. **Review the styles of leadership that Chapter 6 describes.**

2. **Define the stages of team development that the section "Discovering How Teams Develop" outlines.**

3. **Allow participants to share experiences that they've had in each of these stages.**

4. **Let participants in small groups discover which leadership style would be most effective at each team development stage.**

5. **Provide scenarios in which the leader may need to change style during team development.**

6. **Discuss the importance of glue people.**

7. **Review the emotional intelligence competencies that Chapter 8 details.**

8. **Role play scenarios in which the team leader uses his emotional intelligence to defuse conflicts in a meeting.**

9. Discuss ways to build trust among team members and between the team leader and the team members.

10. Model and share activities in which team members can get to know each other.

11. Offer example problems and discuss who on the team should be making decisions to solve them.

And we're on the same team: A team-building activity

One of the most effective team activities for helping members get to know each other is one that I have used numerous times, and always with great results. It's fun, too! I call it "and we're on the same team" because it involves finding commonalities among people. The process is simple. Remember musical chairs? This activity is similar. Here are the steps:

1. Each participant brings her chair to a designated area of the room.

2. Participants form a circle with each chair touching the next. Leave no spaces.

3. Each participant sits down while I begin the activity by standing in the center of the circle.

4. I introduce myself by saying, "Hello, I'm Marilee."

5. Each participant responds with "Hello, Marilee!"

6. I then make a statement about myself that may or may not be true about someone else in the group. For instance, I may say, "I enjoy working with a team." I follow this statement with the phrase, "and we're on the same team!"

7. I ask participants to stand up if they also enjoy working with a team.

8. The standing participants and I try to sit down in someone else's seat.

9. The person who is left without a seat stands in the center and follows the same process.

10. This process continues until everyone has been in the center or whatever time is allotted is up.

You find out interesting information from this activity. From my first statement, if all are truthful, I know who likes teamwork and who doesn't. The other statements may reveal personal information about the people. For instance, someone may say, "I played collegiate sports," and those who also played rise. You also get to know people's names.

The activity provides movement, which gets blood and oxygen flowing to the brain and stimulates the brain to release dopamine — a pleasurable reward that helps participants focus as the meeting continues. And I have never had a group that didn't end up laughing during the activity. Laughing also releases feel-good chemicals in the brain.

The last statement, "and we're on the same team" emphasizes the goal of the group spending time together. You can vary this activity by making the statement more specific to your immediate needs — for example, "and we're going to increase productivity!"

Leading introductory team meetings

Any first team meeting can be awkward — people don't know what to expect or exactly how they fit in. When you train team leaders, show them how to make every meeting an experience. First meetings may simply be "getting to know you" meetings. If the team is a large one that will be broken down into smaller teams, the first meeting is the time to divvy up team members.

Here's a first-meeting plan that gets a project moving and gives team members a chance to get to know each other:

1. **Each person introduces himself.**

2. **Create your mini-teams, and separate the teams within the room.**

3. **Let each team get acquainted with simple questions or activities.**

   You may ask them to introduce themselves and then share three things with the team, one of which is false. The rest of the team tries to guess through questioning which statement was false.

4. **Determine mini-team leaders.**

   You can let team members vote for a leader, but this option works best if team members already are acquainted. I often ask each person in the team whether they want to be the team leader. If I get multiple yeses, the volunteers may share leadership. If there are no yeses, I go around again until I eventually get a leader.

5. **Give each team about three minutes to come up with a team name.**

   Yes, a name. Every sports team has a name. Why not a business team?

6. **Each team makes up a team cheer.**

   Cheers make people smile or laugh. They get people up and breathing deeply. These results enhance thinking. If you wish, have each team pick team colors or a logo.

7. **Each team leader introduces her team to the larger group.**

   The team then says its cheer. Applause is encouraged and modeled by the leadership.

8. **Schedule and set up the team meetings that follow.**

9. **End the meeting by asking each team to name one goal that they have for the next meeting.**

   For example, one team may say they want to know everyone's name on their team, or they may want to contact each other by e-mail or text by the next meeting.

The teams are assembled, the team leader has been trained, the mini-team leaders are selected, and that may be enough for one day.

Running routine team meetings

For brain-compatible meetings that keep their attention and make time fly as you meet the needs of your team members and keep the team on track, I suggest the following:

✔ Play music that sets the tone of the meeting. "Mission Impossible" for a challenge and problem-solving; "Whistle While You Work" for finishing up details. Or make your climate inviting in some other way. For example, welcome posters, standing at the door and shaking each person's hand, or offering a high-five.

✔ Use humor. Start with a story that relates to your team or its purpose.

✔ Review your goal for this meeting. Get consensus on that goal.

✔ Have a printed agenda for each person. If you've sent the agenda prior to the meeting, a quick request for changes or additions is appropriate and makes everyone feel included.

✔ Ask for feedback from the previous meeting.

✔ Ask each mini-team to do its cheer whenever it completes a task. Doing so lets others know that they're finished and may inspire others to commit to finishing their task more quickly.

Setting Goals

Goal setting is vital to the success of every team. Setting goals gives the brain a focus, it also increases performance — especially if the team helps to set its own goals. Of course, these goals are based on the goals of the organization itself.

The brain sees a goal as an extension of itself; it takes ownership of the goal and the accomplishment. Neurotransmitters such as dopamine and serotonin, which I describe in Chapter 2, are released in the brain as goals are set and worked toward. If the brain truly desires the goal, it is rewarded along the way to the achievement by the release of these chemicals. However, if the goal is not achieved, these chemicals are withheld and the individual feels bad. The brain therefore makes every effort to reach its goals.

SMART goals

A goal is a statement that usually focuses on attainment in one to three years. Goals are action statements. The goal-setting process is simplified by the often-used process of writing SMART goals. The following characteristics make up this acronym:

✔ **Specific:** Each goal specifies your target exactly. For instance, increasing sales may be your goal, but it's not specific enough. Increasing sales by 10 percent is much more specific.

✔ **Measurable:** One of the big problems with setting goals is knowing when you have met them. In other words, you must be able to evaluate your success. Increasing sales by 10 percent is measurable if you have the data on present sales.

✔ **Achievable:** A goal that is within your reach increases motivation and those brain chemicals that keep you or your team motivated. If you wanted to increase sales by 50 percent, your sales staff may see that goal as impossible to achieve and give up before they begin. The 10 percent mark, however, may be very possible for the sales team if they have a reasonable amount of time to achieve it.

✔ **Realistic:** A realistic goal is one that your team has the resources to realize. If the team has the skills it needs to increase sales, you have enough of the product to sell, you have plenty of customers in your sales area, and you have time to get the job done, the goal is realistic.

✔ **Time:** SMART goals are written with an end in mind. Increasing sales by 10 percent by the end of the next fiscal year provides a deadline. If you don't have a deadline, the goal is too vague and the target is unclear. Time is a motivational factor in achieving goals. (I want to lose ten pounds is a goal. But I want to lose ten pounds by Christmas provides a deadline.)

After you set your SMART goals, you want to examine who is going to be involved in reaching the goals. Ideally, everyone in the company plays a part in this process. For example, imagine your company's goal is to increase sales by 10 percent in the next fiscal year. This goal is lofty. The next step in working with this goal is to determine how it can be broken down into smaller goals. Who in your organization will be involved? Your senior team leads their teams in the following ways:

✔ **Chief Technology Officer:** This executive's team may be involved by creating an easier or more proficient way to keep track of sales, contact current customers, and expedite information to get products distributed more quickly.

✔ **Marketing Director:** A new or improved marketing program for the product may be designed by the marketing team.

✔ **Sales Leader:** Motivating and assisting sales teams can be one way that this leader contributes. The sales teams may create new sales approaches and new contact lists.

✔ **Customer Support Leader:** Communicating with customers the kind of support they will receive after purchasing this product may encourage an increase in sales. The customer support teams design print information that each customer will receive.

✔ **Chief Financial Officer:** The finance teams track production, sales, and distribution of products as well as allocate funds for promotional purposes. They also determine rewards for reaching goals to increase production.

✔ **Chief Operating Officer:** All senior team leaders report to the COO so that she can oversee all aspects of this targeted goal and keep departments up to date.

The SMART approach is linear, logical, and very left-brain oriented. Those teams that think in a left-brained format appreciate this type of goal setting. It is easy to track and measure goals that are created by this approach.

SAFE goals

If your teams consist of members who are creative, visual, and right-hemisphere dominant, SMART goals may not be motivating enough for them. Approaching goals in a nonlinear manner appeals more to the right hemisphere. You may want to consider a more global approach for reaching those goals. SAFE goals approach goals a bit differently. SAFE is an acronym for the following:

✔ **See it.** See yourself working toward that goal. For example, picture yourself increasing sales. Perhaps you visualize yourself approaching old customers and sharing valuable information about the product you sell. You then picture yourself calling on new prospects and pitching the product to them. Picture the goal already achieved.

✔ **Accept it.** Picture yourself working toward the goal and accept that you can achieve it. Accept the recognition you might get and the rewards your company will receive from the sales.

✔ **Feel it.** Adding emotion to your visualization is powerful. Feel good about your accomplishment. Enjoy the satisfaction of a job well done. Through visualization you can actually cause your brain to release dopamine and other brain chemicals that make you feel good.

✔ **Express it.** Visualize yourself telling others about the accomplishment and giving presentations at your team meetings about how you contributed to the accomplishment of this goal.

The SAFE method is especially good for those brains that need to have the big picture in order to accept the fact that they can accomplish their goals. You may not need to use SAFE for every goal of the organization or team, but it may help those who doubt their capability of attaining certain goals.

Keeping Score

Teams keep score. Doing so may cause healthy competition among teams or mini-teams. But keeping score really gives the team some reflection time to assess themselves. First, they get to rate themselves on how well they're achieving their goals. They then get to compare themselves to other teams who may be having more success. When the team leaders explain their team's successes and failures, make sure they have time for feedback or brainstorming to help them try a different approach.

You have many options for making team work more visible to the team and to others. Sparking healthy competition may be just what a struggling area of your organization needs. Scorecards in the form of charts, posters, or other graphics remind the team players who's getting the job done and offer opportunities for coaching and mentoring.

You may want each mini-team to create a team chart — a score card of sorts. It includes categories that relate to your purpose and the individual purpose of each mini-team. The team fills in the chart as a form of self-assessment, and may be used as a vehicle for reporting to the rest of the teams at weekly or monthly meetings.

Using the goal of increasing sales by 10 percent by the end of the fiscal year, a team's scorecard may consist of any or all of the following:

- ✔ **Dollars and cents:** Keep a running total of team sales on a weekly or monthly basis.

- ✔ **Number of units sold:** Display a weekly or monthly tally of products sold by the team.

- ✔ **Percentage increases:** Display a tally sheet of the sales increases thus far by percentage.

- ✔ **Countdown tally:** Figure the total number of units that the team needs to sell to reach the goal. ("X units to go till deadline.")

Keep teams informed in a timely manner of how they're progressing toward goals. Making the information graphic ensures that all team members see progress and that conversations begin over known results. You may need to change your approach from a countdown to a celebratory graphic of units sold if confidence is low or you're in an off season.

Chapter 15

Overcoming the Digital Divide

*T*he brain is plastic. Our experiences change the brain's structure and function. Research shows us that if you use your brain to specialize in specific tasks, you literally change it. Perhaps you decide you want to learn a musical instrument — a wonderful way to keep your brain young and to make new connections. From practicing and playing the violin, the areas in your brain that control your finger movements make new connections and probably grow new brain cells.

The business world today is comprised mainly of those whose brains have changed from constantly using technology, and those whose brains are only beginning to change as they slowly come on board. If you don't fit into either of these categories, it's time to join the global world.

If you're saying to yourself, "it's too hard to keep up," or "this too shall pass," get over it. You're wrong on both counts. With practice, you can catch up and keep up.

In this chapter, you meet your own generation and the generations you have to deal with in business. Your leadership skills must include understanding the way the brain adapts to our rapidly building technological advances. If a digital divide exists in your organization, you must lead the way to closing the gap. This chapter shows you how the brain adapts to rapid changes in communication, problem-solving, and creativity. You also find out how to work with brains that need face-to-face practice and emotional intelligence training because they have spent so much time in the global world communicating without face time, without gestures, and sometimes without meaning.

Generations Apart: Touching on Generational Identities

No one seems to understand the younger generation — no matter which generation that is. Several generations are at work in most organizations. Their ages and stages in the digital world make a difference in how they interact and work in the real world.

Some of you can't live without your digital doohickeys; others yearn for the days when you didn't feel you had to be connected at all times. Maybe you remember when you saw your first television program in color or when your family bought the first TV set. Or you maybe feel television is too passive to be entertaining. You send text messages constantly and think e-mail is too slow. In this section I introduce you to the generations currently in our workforce, describing some of their common characteristics and ways of working.

Traditionalists

Anyone born before 1946 is a member of the silent generation, the *Traditionalists*. These people come from the Depression era and know hardship from their own personal experiences or from their parents, who were farmers or who immigrated to this country.

Although Traditionalists are at retirement age, many of them still work. They may be valuable employees or leaders, but they likely work with three or four other generations, and that isn't easy for someone with a Traditionalist's values and work ethic.

Traditionalists expect to work from 9 to 5 but are willing to put in extra hours as well. Traditionalists tend to be loyal; many have kept the same job or have had few jobs in their lifetime. Many of the silent generation thought it appropriate that Mother stayed at home while Father worked. Raising the children was the wife's major responsibility.

Certain actions define each generation. For the Traditionalists, World War II, the Korean War, and the Great Depression were formative events. Each generation has an overlap. So some individuals born before or during World War II fit into the Boomer generation in which both spouses work for the extra income.

Traditionalists have a much more conventional work ethic than other generations. Characteristics that this generation is known for include:

- Hard-working
- Private
- Respectful toward authority
- Packrats
- Loyal
- Dedicated
- Formal in dress and manners
- Sacrifice for their families and their employers
- Believe work is a privilege

Baby Boomers

Those who fit into the well-known generation of *Baby Boomers* were born between 1946 and 1964. As couples put off having babies until the end of World War II, when the husbands returned, families grew. A lot of babies were born as the country flourished — 78 million, in fact. The events that define this generation are the Cold War, the civil rights movement, space travel, and the assassinations of high-level, influential people.

All Boomers grew up in a time during which most everyone had jobs. They enjoyed spending their money and were introduced to the credit card era. Many Boomers like to take care of themselves, stay young-looking, and buy gadgets.

As far as technology is concerned, Boomers grew up with television. In the earlier days, Boomers and their ancestors gathered around the radio and listened to shows like *Big John and Sparky;* they used their imaginations and visualized the stories. Television took those pictures out of their minds and put them on a screen in front of them. For the first time, people saw news stories firsthand and the horrors of war were revealed to all.

This generation believes in standing up for one's rights; they were part of the women's movement and the civil rights movement. The good news and the bad news for the Boomers is that with medical advances, they are going to live a long time. Many of them did not prepare for retirement and will remain in the workforce well past the age of 65.

Because this generation is so large, they're targeted by businesses. Health care, beauty programs, exercise programs, and brain programs aim at Boomers who want to live forever, avoid Alzheimer's disease, and look younger.

Boomers tend to

- ✔ Be hard-working
- ✔ Love prestige
- ✔ Believe in working long days and long weeks
- ✔ Encourage group decision-making
- ✔ Compete with others both inside and outside work
- ✔ Work past retirement age
- ✔ Achieve goals
- ✔ Do volunteer work
- ✔ Value personal growth
- ✔ Believe in the equality of the sexes
- ✔ Question authority
- ✔ Like teamwork

Generation X

Between 1965 and 1980, about 50 million people were born in the United States. This group has been dubbed *Generation X.* This era is defined by Watergate, the fall of the Berlin Wall, Desert Storm, and the energy crisis.

This age bracket faced high unemployment and saw parents getting laid off. It's one of the best-educated groups in history and use their education to set their own personal goals and create a life much different from their parents'.

This generation values parenting more than work. They prepare themselves to be flexible and portable. Loyalty to one company or employer is not important to this group. They want to create a job for themselves that caters to their personal needs and goals.

Many of the workers of this era are

- ✔ Hard-working
- ✔ Protective of family time

- ✔ Ambitious

- ✔ More comfortable with flexibility in their jobs

- ✔ Drawn to diversity

- ✔ Attracted to challenge

- ✔ Open to input

- ✔ Creative

- ✔ Protective of freedom and independence

- ✔ Unimpressed with authority

- ✔ Seeking experience so they can move on to the next job

Generation Y: The 'Net Generation

People born between 1977 and 1997 have accumulated several names. They are sometimes called *Generation Y,* because they follow Gen X-ers; occasionally they're referred to as the *Millenials;* and some call them the *Echo Boomers* because they're a rather large population. But they are most often referred to as the *'Net Generation.*

Columbine and other school shootings, the Bill Clinton and Monica Lewinsky scandal, the Oklahoma City bombing, and the technology boom are the significant events of this generation.

Because these people were exposed to different lifestyles and cultures while in school, they embrace diversity. Communication is their strength; technology is their world. Raised with digital tools, they're connected to more people all over the globe than any of the generations.

Many members of the 'Net generation

- ✔ Value professional development

- ✔ Want creative challenges

- ✔ Want to work faster and better

- ✔ Prefer flexibility in their work and work schedules

- ✔ Desire telecommuting

- ✔ Want to work part-time to have more personal or family time

- ✔ Tend to be optimistic

> ✔ Exude confidence
>
> ✔ Are civic-minded
>
> ✔ Are innovative

Don't underestimate the abilities of 'Net Generation workers. As Malcolm Gladwell points out in his book *Outliers,* experts become experts through opportunity and hours of practice. It takes about 10,000 hours of practice for someone like Michael Jordan to perfect his skills. These employees from Generation Y have put in at least 20,000 hours using digital technology since birth. This is the only generation to have practiced this long.

Understanding the Digital Brain

Research shows that technology changes the way the brain works. Some of those changes are beneficial. Other changes separate us more from the different generations and affecting the way people work. The upcoming sections look at the effects of technology on the brain.

Considering technology's effect on brains

Neuroscientists tell us that the brain is a "use it or lose it" organ. Using technology brings about new connections, new cells, and new learning. Other parts of the brain that are not used or are no longer used begin to wither away.

The good news is that current technology brings about the following advantages. People who use it

> ✔ Skim material more effectively
>
> ✔ Are more efficient
>
> ✔ May have better problem-solving skills
>
> ✔ Get information faster
>
> ✔ Communicate globally
>
> ✔ Respond to visual stimuli quickly

The bad news is that technologically savvy workers also may

✔ Have more attention problems

✔ Have shorter attention spans

✔ Experience more addictions

✔ Lose people skills

✔ Never develop good listening skills

✔ Have difficulty reading body language

Debunking the multitasking myth

The brain cannot give full attention to more than one thing at a time. Research suggests strongly that something, or all things, that you try to do simultaneously are cheated. Multitasking is not the wonderful skill it was once thought to be.

The female brain often gets accolades for its ability to do multiple tasks at one time. As I tell you in Chapter 12, that ability is a myth. You can't think about two things at one time and give them both direct attention. You probably have been in situations in which you were talking to a small group of people at a party and became interested in the conversation of a nearby group. You tried to follow the other conversation. In the meantime your group continued to chat, and someone asked you for a response. You didn't have a clue what you were supposed to say. It's a common problem, and it shows how the brain has difficulty switching from one cognitive area to another.

The brain has to go through several steps to switch attention. They happen in milliseconds, but for every exchange, the following five steps take place:

1. **The reticular activating system, which regulates what information enters your brain examines the new information.**

2. **The parietal lobe disengages from its current focus.**

3. **The cingulate gyrus shifts focus to new information.**

4. **The prefrontal cortex considers the choices and picks one.**

5. **The prefrontal cortex inhibits the other possible choices in order to focus and hold new information in working memory.**

The person at work who looks busiest may actually be the least productive. Attempting to move from task to task too quickly has been known to slow people down by 50 percent and add 50 percent more mistakes!

Do you see this person in your organization? As you walk by his office or cubicle, this multitasker is working at his computer with the phone on speaker so he can carry on a conversation with a client as he finishes a report that's due by the end of the day. His cell phone plays a special tune indicating he has just received a text message. Keeping one hand on the keyboard, he reaches for his Blackberry and begins reading the message. Seen enough? Wait a minute — another window on his computer opens up as he receives the familiar sound for incoming e-mail. He puts the Blackberry down after sending a brief reply to the text sender and double clicks on the mail he just received. It's his wife reminding him that he has a dental appointment immediately after work. He responds with a smiley face and switches back to his speakerphone conversation as the client has just asked him a question. He has no idea how he is to respond to "What do you think?" He asks the client to go over it again for him. You can hear the voice on the speaker becoming impatient. Is it any wonder that mistakes are being made?

Addressing Digital Differences

The brains of those who are digitally connected are different from those who are not. The upcoming sections offer suggestions for helping these different kinds of brains work together, communicate effectively, and be productive in their own individual ways.

The digital native

Today's world requires a new language and a new literacy — digital literacy. The late Generation X-ers and the generations that follow them are *digital natives* — they speak the language well. These people have grown up with video games, cell phones, computers, mp3 players, the Internet, and other techno toys. The ABCs of learning have been replaced with the XYZs of technology.

Learning and working for these generations has been a matter of action and interaction. Unlike the Boomers, and very unlike the Traditionalists, these digital natives grew up communicating in a very different and fast-paced way.

They're proud of their ability to come up with hard data quickly and easily. The working and learning gap between these generations and the prior groups is wide.

The digital natives who believe that their world isn't complete if they aren't constantly connected are always trying to multitask. They're working their hardest to switch from one task to another and then back again without skipping a beat. But doing so is difficult. Former Microsoft executive Linda Stone calls this problem *continuous partial attention*. Not truly giving anything complete attention has a number of negative effects, including inability to accomplish a darned thing. Efforts to stay connected may prohibit you from bringing deep thought and closure to any one project. A common result of this situation is stress. And stress is the enemy of getting the job done well.

The digital immigrant

Some Traditionalists, most Baby Boomers, and the early Gen X-ers fall into the category of *digital immigrants* — they didn't grow up learning this second language and speak it with varying degrees of fluency.

The following characteristics describe many of the digital immigrants:

- ✔ Insists on paper bills even though he receives copies via e-mail
- ✔ Prints out e-mails and attachments and relies on printed newspapers, books, and so on
- ✔ Is leery of paying bills online
- ✔ Believes that methods she was taught years ago should work for everyone
- ✔ Is outraged by the informal text used in e-mails and instant messages
- ✔ Believes "real math" is done without a calculator, let alone a computer
- ✔ Believes a social network consists of people he meets with for bridge or outings

Digital immigrants have much to offer to the workforce — wisdom derived from years of storing patterns in the brain gives them the ability to see the big picture, predict accurately, foresee future consequences, and draw on mental templates to help store impressive amounts of new information. Challenging tasks activate more areas in the frontal lobes of the brains of Boomers and Traditionalists than in the brains of younger subjects.

The immigrants have little choice because their brains change as they increase their skills with technology. The late Gen X-ers and the Gen Y-ers may need to practice more conventional skills that their brains haven't used very much, like building rapport face to face.

The digital dinosaur

Natives speak the language of their birth, immigrants are learning to translate the digital language of the natives, and then there are what I call the *digital dinosaurs* — those individuals or businesses that are hopelessly out of date. You may think that Traditionalists fall into this category, and some do. But anyone or any business can be a dinosaur.

Digital media is transforming organizations everywhere. If your business appears to be incapable of change, those who embrace digital technology won't find it appealing. If your customers are changing their minds and getting plugged into the latest in technology, you don't want to present yourself as stuck in an analog world.

Take a close look at what your competitors are doing digitally. If they're still dinosaurs, make some changes so your business can be the first to enter the global age. Rather than feeling safe because they aren't doing anything that you're not doing, get out of that reptile brain and use your thinking brain to take some risks to get updated.

Communicating Brain to Brain and Face to Face

As a leader working among several generations, your challenge is to find a way to keep the loyal Traditionalists, the hard-working Boomers, the wandering X-ers and the totally connected Y-ers working together in harmony so your business can flourish.

Table 15-1 provides you some basic comparisons of the generations and their responses to work.

Table 15-1 **Comparing the Generations**

	Traditionalists	Baby Boomers	Generation X	Generation Y ('Net Generation)
Work ethic	I work hard. Having a job is a privilege.	I will work hard and would like a prestigious job.	I will work hard with a flexible schedule.	I will get the job done at my convenience. I change jobs frequently.
Work relationships	I respect my overseers. I keep to myself and get my work done.	I want to work with a team to get more input and good results.	Working with others is okay, but I don't intend to stay in one place too long. I have plans.	I have relationships with people all over the world. I don't need to be close to colleagues; I may only see them on a screen.
Future	I will probably stay with this job until I retire.	I'll never retire. I want to keep my brain active, and I can't afford retirement.	I'll work with similar companies or try to get in on the ground floor of a new company. I want to make my money and retire young.	I want to come up with a way to get my job done faster because I don't want to work full time. Family time is important.
Major influence	The Depression.	Television.	Video games and computers.	Blogs, Twitter, My Space, Facebook, smart phones.
Technology	What?	Trying to get there.	Use it. Love it.	Live it.
Difficulty	Change.	Lack of change.	Loyalty and trust.	Communicating face-to-face.

Working together digitally: Plugging in

Harnessing the gifts of both digital natives and digital immigrants is your job as leader. Honoring each group's strengths and finding ways for them to work together successfully can be a challenge.

The two generations that are already plugged in have different needs. Generation Y may be high maintenance, but they're also high performing. They need attention, supervision, direction, and feedback. Generation X wants little supervision, but they do want feedback. The generations that are trying to plug in feel a little behind. They want their meetings in real life, don't need e-mail memos, want supervision and feedback. They stick with you through thick and thin, so playing the loyalty card works with them. (With the younger generations, not so much.) Negotiating time off with family may be more motivating for younger generations.

Here are some issues facing leaders who work with multiple generations:

- ✔ X-ers want a more relaxed atmosphere.
- ✔ Y-ers need structure.
- ✔ Boomers are still learning.
- ✔ Traditionalists aren't sure they want to learn.

And here are some commonalities among the generations:

- ✔ They all like a challenge.
- ✔ They all need feedback.
- ✔ They all value personal or professional growth.

Use the points the generations have in common to begin creating a work atmosphere in which your employees thrive together. Each generation has something to offer your organization; capitalize on it before you lose them. Try some of the following tactics for narrowing the digital divide:

- ✔ **Decide on the how, when, and where of feedback:** Before any project begins, discuss with the team or individuals how and how often they would like to receive feedback. Where to receive feedback includes face-to-face meetings, e-mails, text messages, memos, faxes, and the list goes on.

  For example, if the team working on the projects has a Gen X-er who wants feedback via text messages every day, but the Boomer on the team prefers e-mails once a week, and the Traditionalist wants a face-to-face at the end of the project, plan ways to meet the needs of each. Compromise by varying the feedback between text and e-mail for the X-er, duplicate the e-mail for the Boomer, and plan an end-of-project meeting time for all.

✔ **Offer intergenerational training:** Because professional growth is of interest to most generations, training them together provides an opportunity for them to get to know each other. Traditionalists can listen and learn from the younger generations about how to access information quickly. The X-ers and Y-ers can learn from the older generations about their years of work experience. Let trainees choose the way they want to learn, or have the training set up in a fashion so each generation gets a taste of what the other generations learning styles are.

✔ **Talk about generational differences:** Offer the opportunity to share points of view. If conflict arises, let the generations talk it out. Be a role model for accepting generational differences. Let your employees see that you value contributions from each generation.

✔ **Mentor and coach:** The social brain needs interaction and nurturing. Providing mentors or coaches who take an interest and provide feedback from another perspective. Create mentor/mentee combinations with different generations to help bridge the gap.

✔ **Offer challenging work:** All generations prefer work that challenges and interests them. Link challenges to their personal roles in reaching the company's vision.

Let each employee work from her strengths, whatever those may be. Those who are comfortable with teleconferencing or using Skype should be encouraged and enabled to do so. Your customer/client base provides the information you need to devise a plan. For instance, your Boomer client wants a face-to-face meeting; your X or Y customer prefers a phone or video conference.

If your business caters to the digital natives, your contact with them and your marketing techniques need to be technologically advanced. If you deal with Boomers or Traditionalists for the most part, then you need your workforce to cater to their needs. As you look to the future determine who will be taking on leadership responsibilities in your organization and who your clientele will be. Increase the technology as you look to the future of your business.

Working face to face

Because those workers in Generations X and Y grew up in a digital world, they never relied on face-to-face meetings with people. They did almost everything by using digital toys. And it worked well for them with their peers.

However, while they were wiring their brains for technology, some of them began to lose their social skills. You can't learn to read faces and body language if you don't see faces and bodies!

Some of your professional development dollars must go to training or retraining these employees in real-life interactive skills. Here are some tips for doing so:

- ✔ Once in a while, ask employees to disconnect. Plan some interactive events in which employees mingle without interruptions.

- ✔ Schedule face-to-face meetings.

- ✔ Place them on teams with projects that encourage group participation and interaction.

- ✔ Ask tech natives to teach immigrants in a friendly, positive manner; have the immigrants teach the natives about building rapport and relationships in real time with real people.

- ✔ Give them reflection time or have them trained in some mindfulness techniques. These are like meditation strategies that take them away from the digital world and let them examine what is going on inside their own heads.

Attracting the best of both worlds

You want to attract the best brains for your business, whether they're digital natives or digital immigrants. Appealing to both sides of the digital coin is easier when you

- ✔ **Make sure your Web site is informative, user-friendly, and has links to employment opportunities:** Most generations actively looking for work know to look online or have someone do it for them. Digital natives must be able to see a clear overview of your company online.

- ✔ **Offer flexible schedules:** Some Baby Boomers and Traditionalists are coming back to the workforce because they can't afford to retire. They may be as interested as Gen X and Gen Y in part-time work or flexible schedules.

- ✔ **Make retirement plans available:** All generations would like a retirement savings plan.

- ✔ **Update your perks:** The younger generations may like perks such as daycare facilities. All generations would benefit from wellness programs and workout facilities.

Part IV
Training and Developing Brains

The 5th Wave By Rich Tennant

"I think Dick Foster should head up that new project. He's got the vision, the drive, and let's face it, that big white hat doesn't hurt either."

In this part . . .

Here I share the importance of training and explain how to set up successful trainings. The novice brain and the veteran brain require different training methods, which you find in this part. Finally, your employees need to be kept up to date, and so I share information on creating memorable meetings and how to keep conversations going in your organization.

Chapter 16

No Train, No Gain: Understanding the Value of Training

Wouldn't it be nice if you could hire people who were already trained to perform the exact skills you need for your company? Rarely do you run into that kind of synergy. You have specific needs, and although you may hire people who have great credentials and experience in the field, you most likely need to train them to function at their best within your organization. Whether you're just planning a business or have been in a leadership position for some time, training should be at the top of your list of important expenses. In fact, scratch that word *expense* when you think about training. Training is an *investment* in the future of your company.

Some companies believe that training their staff and encouraging career growth is what makes them successful. Unfortunately, other leaders believe that on-the-job training and challenging projects create enough growth, or that training is a waste of money because employees will take that knowledge to other companies. In this chapter, you find out about the importance of training and the consequences of avoiding.

Avoiding the Knowledge Curse: You Don't Have All the Answers

A true leader recognizes the limits of his own knowledge and skills. Getting a company up and running and keeping it on track takes many kinds of talent. The knowledge curse is that phenomena wherein the leader either thinks he has all of the answers, or the employees believe he does. A true leader doesn't have to know how to program a computer to get the information he needs; he has to have the knowledge to hire a person with the proper skills and training.

Recognizing employees' capabilities

Authoritarian leaders don't believe that their employees are capable. They often tell them exactly what to do and how to do it. People tend to look at leaders of this type as know-it-alls. As you might guess, know-it-alls are not very popular with employees. They make them feel inadequate and can even cause real harm.

Know-it-alls create people who are helpless. *Learned helplessness* is a condition in which a person feels that her life is out of her control and that she's powerless to change it. No matter what this person does, in her mind, she cannot make a difference. She thinks, "Since I can't do anything right, why bother even trying?"

The term learned helplessness was coined by the psychologist Martin Seligman. He discovered the concept when working with dogs. Seligman found that a dog placed in a cage with a metal bottom would, when an electric charge was turned on, dance around looking for a place in the cage where there was no charge. When the charge was turned off, the dog would return to whatever he was doing. When the charge came again, the dog danced around again. Eventually, however, the dog gave up and would lay down and take the electrical shock. The dog figured it could not do anything to save himself. When the experimenters shocked only half the cage and tried to get the dog to the unshocked side, they had to drag the dog over repeatedly. They would drag him to the safe side, but because the dog had been trained to feel out of control, he returned to the shocked side.

When leaders don't give employees the opportunity to feel competent through training or by assigning projects and giving them agency over those projects, employees lose their motivation, inspiration, and drive.

Giving employees skills to perform

If you want your employees to take risks and to show initiative, you have to provide the opportunity for them to master their jobs through the appropriate training. A leader who makes all of the decisions instead of training employees to handle some of them loses out on the basic knowledge her employees have brought to the organization. Plus, if you allow yourself to be the last word on everything, you find yourself in a stressful situation.

The be-all-end-all leader who doesn't want to train employees isn't necessarily authoritarian. Instead, he truly believes that training isn't necessary. Perhaps he worked her way up in the business by watching others and on-the-job training. Or maybe he has so much information in his head that he doesn't understand why others don't just know what to do.

Many employers are just afraid of pulling people off the job for training. They're afraid of low productivity for those few days. They may be overwhelmed with the responsibility of being everyone's answer person. Yet fear keeps them from training, fear that they're setting a precedent and everyone is going to want to take time off and be trained, and this leader ends up with more fear as he discovers that the business cannot run well with only one person capable of making decisions and taking risks.

When I tell employers that they don't have time to be the "be-all-end-all" at their company, they don't believe that being interrupted and asked questions is really a problem. I think that being needed makes them feel good.

The CEO of a department store is the be-all-end-all for his business. Business was going well, and so he decided to expand and add some new locations. His untrained employees became managers of the new locations and proceeded to try to train new employees. The lack of training of his original employees produced a wide variety of outcomes. He was hit with questions constantly. His original, untrained employees still couldn't make decisions on their own; they either didn't know the answers or lacked the confidence to act on their own. The less than stellar job the original employees did when training new ones left the new people unprepared for their jobs. Instead of seeing what was happening and doing something about it, the owner began complaining about the new managers and new employees. The real problem was his need to feel important and his fear of training his staff.

Does this sound like the kind of person you would want to work for or have working for you? Because he's a charming man who makes people laugh, they put up with his shenanigans. I feel sorry for him and for his people. He needs to be the final answer in his business to make himself feel important.

Problems were easy to take care of when he had one location because he was always physically present to address any issues. Since he expanded, he works himself ragged trying to make it to each of his stores several times a week. He has customers make appointments only with him so that he can personally take care of big sales. He feeds his ego. And his company will fail if he doesn't change his tactics. His health and marriage will probably suffer, too.

Training Employees for Self-Sufficiency

Ask an employer what's in it for them to pull people off the job and send them to trainings and you probably hear "increased revenue" and "increased productivity for the long-term." In order to make training result in major benefits for a business, including self-sufficiency for your employees, you must consider the following:

✔ Look at the big picture to determine your priorities.

✔ Examine internal processes to identify those that could be done more efficiently.

✔ Determine where mistakes are being made.

✔ Prioritize your training needs.

✔ Find the right training company or trainer. (Chapter 18 gives suggestions.)

✔ Prepare to have employees off the job. (Chapter 18 tells you how to plan for the time off.) You need to

- Make training a commitment by the entire company.

- Let managers know they may be filling in for employees.

- Give employees motivation for doing more work while others are being trained.

A self-sufficient workforce feels better about itself. Your employees feel valued because you invest in them, and they are more self-confident. In the short term, profits or production may be affected in a minor way, but in the long-term, the organization is likely to be more profitable and productive with trained workers.

Gaining through office training

Many employees learn only what they need to know to get the job done. Creating a document, utilizing a spreadsheet, and sending e-mails might be the limit for some office workers. Technology can be intimidating, and these people need to be trained to a point of comfort.

Learning to speak a foreign language

Jose Menchaca applied for his job at the meat-packing plant knowing little English but a lot about meat. His interview consisted of showing Manager Lucas Andrews how he handled the beef. Meat packing is one of the most dangerous jobs there is, yet Jose handled himself with such ease that Lucas knew he was hiring a good employee.

After Jose had worked at the plant for several months, Lucas decided that his style of cutting should be taught to the other workers. Lucas asked Jose if he would be willing to train others. Jose didn't quite understand what Lucas was saying, and Lucas realized that perhaps some of the problems at the plant between employees and managers was a language barrier.

Never before had Lucas considered training his employees in anything but their specific jobs, but this time he decided that if everyone spoke the same language, life might be better at the plant.

Lucas planned trainings to teach the workers English. Those sessions made a huge difference in Jose's life and in the lives of many of the workers. Lucas lost some workers after spending money on them to learn English, but those who stayed were grateful and able to communicate their needs much better. Jose became the head trainer in cutting meat, got a pay raise, and eventually learned to teach more than just cutting. He taught many of the newly hired Hispanics how to speak English.

Knowledge is power, and those working in the knowledge industry need to concentrate on what they can do with that power rather than focusing their attention on how a program works. The brain's working memory, which enables you to hold incoming information is limited. If working memory is focusing on which button to push or how to use the mouse, the real power is then in the hands of the tool instead of in the mind of the user. Train office people to mastery. Then let them use their creative minds and their problem-solving ability to take your company to greater levels.

And don't stop with just trainings. Professional organizations in your field hold meetings and conferences. Attending these meetings can be motivating as well as educational. Give your employees the opportunity to feel like professionals by attending. They may learn cutting-edge approaches to your industry that save more time and increase production.

Offering tech training

One of the biggest mistakes companies make is in adding new processes or technology to their operations but not training the people who use them. And those older processes or technologies may not be the problem in the first place. Employees may not be utilizing them well because they were never trained to do so.

Instead of tossing out the old way of doing things because you think it isn't providing the functionality that you need, take a look at your employees. A program, for example, is only as good as the people running it. Make them masters in their area of expertise and then let them decide whether the program is what they need. Before you spend tens of thousands of dollars on upgrades, spend it on those people you entrust your business to.

When the training culminates in employees feeling very knowledgeable about their jobs, their approach to programs and processes includes the ability to make judgment calls. They will be able to tell you what the needs of their departments are. And they will feel more responsible for your goals and your vision. When they speak to others, they will speak with confidence and with respect for their employer.

Finding Alignment among Employees and You

The brain learns patterns and creates a *schema* — an organized unit of information stored in your brain that can be about anything. (I talk in detail about patterns and schema in Chapter 3.) You have a schema for your business, your job, and your employees. Everyone with whom you do business has a schema about your business, as well. Getting your schemas to match is part of what good training can do.

Your theories, expectations, behaviors, likes, and dislikes are based on the schema you have stored in your brain. These deeply engrained networks prevent you from seeing the world in the same way that others see the world. In one way, this individualization of perception is a very good thing. If you and your employees had exactly the same perception, then you may always agree, but not much would change. However, you sometimes want employees to see the world the way you do, and reaching consensus isn't always easy.

You expect your administrative assistant to receive all of your visitors, whether they have appointments or not. He's in charge of maintaining your schedule, when possible, and seeing that your guests are comfortable while they wait. But if your administrative assistant decides that those without appointments are merely wasting your time and asks them to make an appointment and leave, he definitely does not have the same mental map that you do.

You have two people representing your company at local malls during a weekend home show. One believes that the customer is always right. She speaks to every customer with respect and answers every question on the spot, unless she doesn't know the answer. In that case she either picks up her cell phone to get the answer or takes the customer's number to give her a call back. The other representative feels that people are asking too many questions. When he can't answer a question, he changes the subject and talks about what he knows. If they insist on an answer, he makes something up or tells them to come to the sales office. Both of these people feel they are helping your company, one by taking care of people's concerns and the other by saving you time and money dealing with stupid questions. Whose mental map matches yours?

If you want to change someone's schema, you must train him. For example, the rep above — who doesn't have the emotional skills to deal with people and questions nor the knowledge to answer those questions — needs training. I would first train him to give him the knowledge to answer the questions. Having the content stored in his brain may free up his mind and make him self-confident enough to handle customers in a better manner. If just the content knowledge training isn't enough, he may need emotional intelligence training as well.

In Chapter 18, I describe how trainings can change the brain. In Chapter 19, I tell you about emotional trainings and how powerful those can be to change old habits and instill new ones.

Saving your assets: Recognizing a call for training

Your employees are your assets — at least, they should be. How do you know when it's time to train them? Your direct reports and team leaders should have some answers for you, but you may find that each department needs training, and you can't afford to do it all at once. Here are a few examples of situations that demand training:

- ✔ Your business has changed. For example, you've installed a new computer program and the employees have yet to be trained. Or you're dealing with turbulent economic times. Outdated mental maps are becoming useless. Your employees need specific training to recreate mental maps.

- ✔ You talk to your customers, managers, and employees by providing feedback surveys and discover some inefficiencies. If your customers are complaining, you know it's time for some changes.

✔ You check out the complaint department. Are there more complaints about one area of business than another? There are those great months when you find no complaints, but when cusotmers start complaining about one area, like customer service, it's time to pay attention.

✔ You check the status of errors. Are there a lot of dented items? Irregulars? Whatever you're producing or whatever service you're providing, human errors based on a lack of knowledge tell you that you need to change their current schema and train them to create flawless processes and procedures. If the necessary changes aren't clear, get feedback from the employees through meetings.

✔ Check on employee turnover. Have you lost a lot of experienced people recently? First, you want to know why people are leaving. Some personal meetings may be necessary to discover the reasons. Do they feel they aren't up to the challenge? They may lack the training they need to feel productive and valued.

✔ Check the bottom line. Does your data indicate that the number of new customers is down? Are you making less money than you did last year? Try to isolate the areas, either within the company or geographically, to find the problem. Reevaluate the training you are currently providing. Does it address the problems you've found?

Using the information you have now gathered, meet with your senior leadership team. Together come up with a plan. Prioritize those training needs. Set up a schedule for trainings in every department that needs it. Determine whether the training will be held offsite, which is highly recommended, and who is going to do the training.

Creating change without pain

Most changes require training. If you want gains and are making changes, you have to keep your main assets — your employees — feeling like they're part of the change. And to maintain them as assets, their thoughts and behaviors need to change, too.

Change can be painful, and the less pain it causes, the happier you and your employees are. Allowing employees the opportunity to initiate change or define their own roles in the change makes change and training more acceptable.

The following steps provide opportunities for workers to take part in the changes:

1. **Share your new vision or goals, which now include the changes that require training.**

2. **Repeat that vision at all meetings for several weeks to make the new schema real.**

3. **Reiterate that vision at meetings with employees before you discuss their participation in fulfilling the vision.**

   Let employees ask questions about how the vision could be fulfilled or offer suggestions for their own participation.

4. **Ask employees for their suggestions on fulfilling the vision.**

5. **When they see how they fit into the vision, ask them what they would need to accomplish the work that keeps them in that vision.**

6. **Determine what content training is necessary based on their needs.**

   The training becomes their idea, and so they accept it more readily.

7. **Offer the appropriate training, and follow up with coaching.**

   Chapter 4 tells you more about mentoring and coaching.

Expecting the best

You get what you expect. That sounds easier than it is. But if you keep your expectations high for your training and your trainees, you are apt to get what you need.

Expectations shape perception and reality. In Chapter 4, I tell you about studies in which teachers treated less than average students as gifted; the students rose to teachers' high expectations and did very well.

The *placebo effect* is another example of expectations affecting reality. Some patients who take placebos (usually sugar pills) for pain or infection actually get better because they believe that they will. (In an episode of the television series *MASH,* doctors ran out of painkillers and so administered sugar pills. They explained to the patients that they were giving them very powerful pain killers and could give only small amounts. Many of the patients said their pain was gone.)

If all trainees enter a training expecting to learn something worthwhile that can help with their job, then they will. If you present the training as relevant to the success of the company and the value of the employee, trainees see it that way, too.

Keeping a Positive Focus When Bringing Change

Training someone to use a computer properly is different from training to change someone's behavior. The former is relatively easy: Trainees learn the process and practice a lot. Then they get opportunities to apply their learning and perhaps problem-solve if something isn't working correctly. The latter training, to change behavior, must come from within the person. In other words, they must gain insight into their own thought processes. That kind of change always begins with the positive.

If your organization is changing dramatically, and each employee must change her behavior, talking about the wrong behavior isn't helpful. Imagine two sales representatives who show a new product at a home show. One answers people's questions or takes their numbers to get back to them and so has 20 potential customers come in or call the company. The other representative doesn't take as much time with potential customers and draws no response. What should you say to the second representative to help provide insight into what might be more beneficial interactions? Try the following:

> **You:** "What do you think you could do to get more potential customers from working at the home show?"
>
> **Rep:** "Is there a quota I need to fill?"
>
> **You:** "Let's take another look at the goals for the customer representative department and see."
>
> **Rep:** "Our goals include increasing new customers by 10 percent and when we wrote that goal, we talked about the home shows bringing in new customers. I see that I can make some changes that would encourage more people to try our product. I could take the names and numbers of anyone who stops by the booth and asks questions. Then I could give them a follow-up call."
>
> **You:** "That's a good idea. You might share some of those contacts with the salespeople who are used to answering more of the technical questions."
>
> **Rep:** "There are some questions I have trouble with. I'll see if I can talk to the technicians, too, and see whether they can answer my questions."

During this conversation, you enable your employee to form connections in his brain that help him become a better public relations representative for your company. Your next step is to find the training that all of your employees need as you change your goals.

What would have happened if the conversation had begun on a negative note? Take a look:

> **You:** "Tanya had twenty potential customers call or come in about our product. You didn't have any."
>
> **Rep:** "Well, Tanya was at a better mall. There weren't many people at my mall."
>
> **You:** "So, no one stopped by at the home show?"
>
> **Rep:** "Well, I didn't feel very well, so I had to leave to go get some aspirin."
>
> **You:** "How long were you gone?"
>
> **Rep:** "Oh, just a few minutes, but that's when the big rush was."

You can see that this conversation led the representative to make up excuses. That is not going to get him to change his way of thinking.

Try to find ways to begin a brain-changing situation by asking the employee come up with solutions. Here are some suggestions:

- ✔ If the employee doesn't see the problem, begin by telling him what you see (the results, not the problem). Let the employee identify the problem. Then ask the employee for solutions.

- ✔ Ask questions on an emotional level. For example, "How do you feel about your productivity?" If the answer is "great" refer her to the goals of her department or team. Give her time to get the connection. Then you ask for solutions.

- ✔ If the employee recognizes the problem, but comes to your for a solution, ask him to come up with various solutions. Then let him choose which one is best. Support his choice if you can and have him try it.

Employees are much more likely to change their current schema with self-generated ideas. The more often you give them the opportunity to identify a need for change and implement their own solution, the more their problem-solving schema changes as well.

Savoring the *aha!* moment

You can see the look on someone's face when they have one of those *aha!* moments. There's nothing like that moment when a new idea clicks into place to make the brain release the chemicals that make you feel good. Those include dopamine, endorphins, and serotonin. If you have this moment of clarity with others, like your teammates, your brain releases oxytocin, which helps you bond with those people.

Chapter 17

Ensuring that Employees Are Fit to Be Trained

*O*ne of my favorite trainings involved a passionate presenter, a lot of movement, interaction with others, and music in the background. If you ask me what information I remember from this training, I would have to say "very little." The presenter kept me awake — most of the time. But I was so sleep-deprived from a project I had to get done for work that staying awake was very difficult. My stress levels were also very high because of the deadline. I didn't understand why my employer had insisted I go to this training when I had so much to do. I left the training every day at 5 or 6 o'clock. I then drove through a fast-food restaurant, grabbed a burger or a salad, and headed back to the office to work. At midnight or 1 a.m. I drove drive home and finally got to sleep about 2 a.m. The alarm went off at 7, giving me just enough time to shower and dress. Breakfast just didn't exist for me unless I ate a donut at the training.

What I remember about that training were the stressful events that surrounded it, not the content. Taking part was really a waste of my time, the company's time, and the extra time I spent on the job teaching myself what I had missed at the training.

Good nutrition, healthy sleep patterns, lowered stress, and proper hydration contribute to a healthy body and an open mind. The difference between a worthwhile training and a worthless training is not only the trainer, but the state of mind and body of the trainees.

If your workers are fit to be trained and not fit to be tied, then they should be looking forward to the training. The more positive you are about the training, the more positive your employees are. Remember, emotions are contagious. You can make a big impact on their attitude sand emotional states.

In this chapter, you find out about proper nutrition and how it affects the brain before, during, and after a training. I also tell you about hydration and dealing with sleep deprivation so that you get the most out of any training you offer. And I show you how the level of challenge correlates to the effectiveness of the training.

Providing Food for Thought

Trainings require work, and work requires sustenance. Provide your trainees with appropriate nutrition to keep their brains and bodies working at their optimal level. The upcoming sections explain how various kinds of "fuel" affect those brains and bodies.

Eating for the brain

If only you had listened to your grandmother's words of wisdom and eaten your veggies, you'd be a happier, healthier, and smarter person! She didn't know the science behind it, but she knew what she saw: People behave better, listen more carefully, and think more clearly when they eat well.

In Chapter 2, you find out about *neurotransmitters,* chemicals in the brain that influence behaviors, thoughts, and feelings. The foods you eat encourage the production of these chemicals. Table 17-1 gives you details about how food affects neurotransmitter production.

You are what you eat, and you think what you eat. The brain needs the right foods to most effectively produce neurotransmitters.

Your brain runs on glucose, which is a sugar formed from the good foods you eat. Your blood supply carries glucose to your brain, which uses this food for energy. Eating the right foods helps your brain remain healthy.

The old food pyramid has been replaced by several newer, healthier versions. You can find up-to-date pyramids from the U.S. Department of Agriculture (www. mypyramid.gov/pyramid/index.html), Mayo Clinic (www.mayoclinic. com/health/healthy-diet/), and Harvard University (www.hsph.har-vard.edu/nutritionsource/what-should-you-eat/pyramid/)

Table 17-1	Neurotransmitters and Nutrition	
Neurotransmitter	*Function in cognition*	*Foods that enhance production*
Serotonin	Assists in transmission of messages; enhances mood; calms	Carbohydrate-based foods like pasta, starchy vegetables, potatoes, cereals, breads
Norepinephrine	Necessary for retrieval of long-term memories	Almonds, apples, avocado, bananas, cheese, fish, most green vegetables, lean meat, nuts, grains, pineapple, poultry, tofu
Endorphins	Released from pleasurable experiences; if learning is pleasurable, endorphins are released and aid memory	Spicy foods, chocolate
Dopamine	Released to assist with focus and to inhibit other thoughts	Apples, fish, chicken, green leafy vegetables
Acetylcholine	Keeps brain cells healthy to transmit messages	Egg yolks, peanuts, wheat germ, liver, meat, fish, milk, cheese and vegetables (especially broccoli, cabbage, and cauliflower)

Here are some of the ways that what you eat affects your brain:

✔ **Proteins:** Proteins form the amino acids that your brain needs to help you feel calm, animated, and positive. Eating protein in the morning helps you remain more alert. Proteins are raw materials for producing neurotransmitters like norepinephrine and dopamine.

✔ **Fats:** There are good fats and bad fats. Bad fats are saturated fats and transfats. Good fats include monounsaturated fats and polyunsaturated fats. Essential to brain health, Omega-3 fatty acids are polyunsaturated. They help give the axons the myelin coating they need to aid in smooth and fast transmission of information. Fish oil capsules have become popular in the health industry to aid in memory, lowering cholesterol, and improving heart function. Depression, poor memory, learning disabilities, and inattention can result from low amounts of Omega-3s.

✔ **Sugar:** Along with red meats and refined grains, sugar should be used sparingly. Some studies show that brain activity increases after you eat sugary foods. But the effect is short-lived, and sugar causes a multitude of problems including a blood sugar drop that makes you sleepy.

- ✔ **Whole grains:** An important part of your diet, these complex carbohydrates go in to making the glucose for your brain.

- ✔ **Fruits and vegetables:** These foods provide the body with natural sugars, proteins, vitamins, and minerals. The Center for Disease Control has a Web site with a calculator to determine how many servings you need: `www.fruitsandveggiesmatter.gov/`.

Breakfast is the most important meal of the day. Your brain is the only organ in your body that does not store energy. When you awaken, your brain is running on fumes.

Many adults who skip breakfast exhibit a negative attitude toward their work and colleagues, lack of attention, and a decline in performance.

What are the possible consequences of all of your employees eating according to their brains' needs?

- ✔ Positive attitudes
- ✔ Happiness
- ✔ Sense of humor
- ✔ Productivity
- ✔ Friendliness
- ✔ Creativity
- ✔ Problem solving
- ✔ Peak performance

Good nutrition increases the production of new brain cells. New brain cells improve the brain's learning and memory capabilities. What prevents the process? Poor nutrition, lack of exercise, and stress.

Maintaining the training

Eat little. Eat often. Eat brain food. That's the best plan for feeding your employees and clients at a training. Sounds simple? It is. Your goal is to get your people trained and help them remember the training. Feeding them properly makes a difference. Here is a sample menu that gives employees' brains what they need:

- ✔ **Breakfast:** Whole-grain bagels and breads, whole-grain cereal; fruit, nuts, dried fruit, low-fat milk, 100-percent juices, eggs, turkey, lean meat, fruit smoothies, yogurt

- **Post-breakfast snack:** Fruits and vegetables

- **Lunch:** Green salads topped with eggs, cheese, turkey, carrots, broccoli, or cauliflower; whole-grain rolls with real butter; tea, low-fat milk, 100-percent fruit juice

- **Post-lunch snack:** Fruits, vegetables, cheese and whole-grain crackers

- **Dinner:** Salmon, asparagus, tossed salad, whole-grain rolls, butter

- **Post-dinner snack:** Fruits, vegetables, smoothies, yogurt

- **Hydration throughout the day:** Water, water, water

Although this is just a sample, these foods are very important to keep brains alert and to maintain the glucose levels for learning. In addition to the good nutrition and food breaks, provide plenty of *brain breaks* — time to move and stretch — especially if the training is a long one.

This example shows the training going into the evening, which is sometimes unavoidable but never a really good idea for brains. Trainees need down time and plenty of sleep so that they can encode information into long-term memory. By extending the day and fighting their need for sleep, stress levels increase and attention levels decrease.

Encourage your trainees to keep their brains hydrated. Do this by keeping ample bottles of water or icy pitchers and glasses within easy grasp.

Demonstrating the water-energy connection

One of the strategies I use to demonstrate the importance of hydration at my trainings is to use an energy ball, which is available at most science stores. An energy ball is a small white ball that looks similar to a ping pong ball. It has two metal strips on one side. When you touch both metal strips a light goes on and the ball makes a sound. This is a great device for teaching about connectivity and circuits. When another person joins me, I place one of my fingers on a strip and she places one of hers on the other. Then to complete the circuit we clasp our other hands together. Bingo! The light and sound begin. When I ask for a volunteer who has had little to drink that morning and we try to make the circuit together, it often won't work or the ball's light is dimmer and the sound lower. The volunteer then is asked to drink some water and try again a few minutes later. The result is a brighter light and louder sound. The importance of keeping your system hydrated to increase the electrical activity in your brain is proven.

Discovering the Importance of Catching Zs

Of course you don't want your trainees sleeping during the training, but sleep is going to be a factor in how well they retain what they're trained. You want them to come to the training refreshed and ready. Accomplishing that feat is a matter of education (yours and theirs), workload, and time.

As a trainer, one of the first questions I ask of my trainees is, "How many of you got eight hours of sleep last night?" Normally less than one-fourth of participants raise their hands. My next comment is, "So, the rest of you got more?" They think this is pretty funny, and they really don't stop to think about the consequences of this lack of sleep. But as their trainer, I know what I am up against. When I ask how much sleep participants usually get, I undoubtedly hear anywhere from four to six hours — they've come to me sleep deprived.

Some people may genetically be more resilient to sleep deprivation. In studies, such people performed well on cognitive tasks after a sleepless night. They are able to recruit more brain areas for these tasks than are those without the same predisposition.

The consequences of sleep deprivation include

- Memory loss
- Cognitive impairment
- Automobile accidents
- Work injury
- Illness

One possible solution to the sleep-deprivation problem is naptime. A regular nap or meditation time rejuvenates the brain. (Chapter 12 tells you more about naps.) Incorporating naps or other down times into your trainings may make the difference between your participants "getting it" or not.

Sleep studies show that memory storage takes place during sleep. Although this storage is ongoing most of the night, some studies suggest that most memory storage takes place during the last two hours of an eight-hour sleep.

If your employees are fit to be trained, they come to the training having slept well — preferably having had seven or eight hours' sleep. As they learn and store information in working memory to later be stored in long-term memory, they need the necessary sleep the night after the training and each successive night of the training. A brand-new concept may need three weeks of sleep to make it into long-term memory. That is why the training is never really over when it's over. Sleep and memory work together to make lasting connections in the brain.

To sleep, perchance to learn

By the third day of training, the trainer had fallen far behind. The reason was simple: He was an in-house trainer doing training in house, and so every possible interruption, from phone calls to client visits, hacked into the time planned for training.

The trainer consulted his supervisor, and they decided together that the training would have to go longer into the evening because only five days had been reserved for the training. Every salesperson had to know how to use the new software system before the first of the month when all of the associated companies would make the switch. The trainees were made aware of the time changes, and another thirty minutes was lost as employees made phone calls to change plans, notify families, and alert customers.

Although the training had been going well and everyone seemed to be understanding the new system, the extended time became a problem. By 8 p.m. that evening when the training ended for the day, 20 exhausted employees ran out the door. Some had been drinking coffee to stay awake after the quick dinner of fried chicken had been served. Because training would resume a mere 12 hours later, everyone needed to get home, go over some homework, and get some sleep for the next day.

That didn't happen. Every single participant stayed up until at least midnight doing office work, looking over the homework, finishing chores around the house, and finally hitting the sheets with a maximum of six hours to sleep before awakening, dressing, and driving to the training by 8 a.m. The employees arrived on time. They all walked in with a cup of coffee in hand, looking a bit more disheveled than usual. When the trainer began, the room got very quiet, a sure sign of stress. As the trainer started questioning the trainees, there were looks of surprise and shame on many of the faces. One hand raised.

"Are you sure you talked about this yesterday? I can't find any of this in my notes." Several others nodded in agreement. The trainer had to reteach the information from the previous day. More precious time was lost. She hadn't had to reteach on day 2 or on day 3, but extending the day made everyone more tired and anxious. Lack of sleep did nothing to lower stress hormone levels, so the participants entered on day 4 already stressed and sleep deprived. They hadn't had enough sleep to store yesterday's information. The coffee drinking from the night before may have kept them from falling asleep during the training, but it also kept many of them awake deep into the night.

Somewhere within this training a day had been lost. The circumstances were not brain-compatible: too much training and too little sleep. As a result, employees were far behind the rest of the organization in their software skills.

Many training rules were broken (Chapter 18 gives you the lowdown on running effective trainings), and participants' lack of sleep made matters worse.

To encourage a good night's sleep before a training, limit the projects that your employees might work late. Those projects are important, but for the training to be successful, sleep is imperative for most people.

Sleep-deprived trainees enter the training with melatonin (the chemical that induces sleep) still in their systems. One way to wake them up is to get some adrenaline flowing. At the beginning of the day, ask them to participate in some movement activities and assign a group activity in which everyone must perform. This may be as simple as creating a role play that demonstrates yesterday afternoon's topic.

Less Stress, Less Guess

Keeping stress levels low before and during a training produces the most favorable outcome. Creating situations in which your employees are in a safe, non-threatening environment sets the stage for success. Learning requires attention and focus; stress interrupts both. Employees who feel less stress retain the information.

The brain learns best when it's being challenged but doesn't feel threatened. The best trainings engage the emotional areas of the brain. The best leaders therefore create trainings that appeal to the emotions. A low-threat, high-challenge work environment and training environment motivates the brain to learn, to act, and to be productive.

Maintaining a low-threat atmosphere

Any threat causes a survival response in the brain, which releases adrenaline and stress hormones that cause a cascade of changes:

- ✔ The heart races.
- ✔ Respiration increases.
- ✔ Blood flow goes to your hands or your legs so that you're ready to fight or flee.
- ✔ The release of saliva stops.
- ✔ Digestion stops.
- ✔ The immune system gears up to help heal tissue damage.
- ✔ Ovulation and sperm production are delayed.

Low threat is the absence of the points above. Someone who isn't feeling threatened feels pretty good. She may be relaxed and curious about what's going to happen. Anticipation may be the emotional state she is in. These are positive emotional states for learning.

A low-threat atmosphere is an environment in which people feel physically and emotionally safe. Mistakes are considered part of the process and no questions are considered stupid.

Keeping employees challenged

Novel experiences and novel information alert the brain and keep it focused. Just as employees want to be challenged in their work, they want to be challenged in their trainings.

Assess trainees before training to determine each individual's understanding of the material. To obtain this pre-assessment, you can ask team leaders and department heads for observations, or the trainer may have a written pre-assessment that you can give prior to the training. Pre-assessment enables employees to be coached to higher levels of understanding.

Trainees know they're being challenged if they feel the work is stimulating yet doable. The key to getting employees to accept challenge is making certain they know they have or will have the skills they need to learn and accomplish whatever tasks are put before them.

To keep trainees challenged:

- ✔ Provide materials that explain the learning.
- ✔ Provide coaches for each team of trainees to help them stay on track and answer difficult questions.
- ✔ Hold trainees responsible for learning: use team challenges such as short competitions, role plays, written tests.

Working (and Talking) in Teams

When people work with others to learn new information, stress is usually much lower. No one feels as though they are put on the spot. Answers are team answers.

Introducing a low-stress training method

The trainer has a plan to lower stress in her trainings. After asking the trainees to form groups of three or four, she asks them a question about what she has discussed so far. The trainer then gives the groups a few minutes to discuss what they've heard.

While the groups share, the trainer walks around and eavesdrops. If she finds a group that isn't getting it, she stops the talking and asks each group to join another group to discuss the same question. In this way, the other participants repair the misconceptions.

When the groups finish the discussions and the trainer is confident that they know what they're talking about, she asks questions of the whole group. Any person who speaks, however, must say, "I heard someone say . . ." before providing an answer. Starting in groups and then crediting another person with the answer removes stress from the speaker and ensures that the trainer gets volunteers to answer her questions and discuss the content.

If you feel that your employees should be able to discuss new learning without any sort of "crutch," keep in mind that many of your employees are competitive, and their egos are sometimes at stake in a training, especially one with completely new information.

Teamwork provides many advantages for trainings, such as

- ✔ **Security:** Each trainee has someone to lean on and learn with.
- ✔ **Sociability:** Team members have the opportunity to get to know a fellow employee or fellow team member from work in a different way.
- ✔ **Knowledge:** Team members learn from each other.
- ✔ **Creativity:** Team members share ideas to reach common goals.
- ✔ **Accountability:** Team members feel accountable to each other for learning and completing tasks.

Before, during, and after a training your teams need time to share what they know. These meetings can prepare employees for training, and reinforce the training afterward.

A good trainer provides trainees with time to look at the training manual either days before the training or the morning of the first day. By previewing the material, the participants feel more comfortable with it. If the trainer introduces one of the concepts, vocabulary words, or part of a product that the brain has seen and read previously — even if only a few minutes earlier — it feels a bit more confident about the information.

Talking among teams during the training, at appropriate times, helps employees reinforce what they are learning. If all team members start off with approximately the same knowledge base, they can use discussion to help each other make connections to what they already know and do at work.

Meeting and discussing the training when the training is over is not only a rehearsal method, it is common ground for more communication. One question I suggest for these reviews is "How did you feel about the training?" This question begins a dialogue on an emotional level that can eventually lead to a team becoming more open and honest about how they feel about projects and working together. Sharing feelings with team members comes more easily as the team relates to each other through sharing.

Chapter 18

Holding Sticky Training Sessions

. . . .

. . . .

*T*raining is time-consuming, costs money, and is the best investment that your company can ever make. Training your novices as well as your veterans pays off in the end — but only if you manage training so that the new information sticks in their minds.

Research that shows how malleable the brain is proves that we *can* teach old dogs new tricks. If you have a trainer or training company that understands how the brain learns and changes, how to emotionally charge the learning, and how to get people to have fun, real, permanent change can occur. That change is most likely to happen if you expect and encourage employees to learn.

Most trainings and presentations are built to teach information, but that doesn't mean you learn it. In an old cartoon, a young boy points to his dog and says to a friend, "Hey, I taught my dog to talk!" The friend says, "I don't hear him talking." The boy remarks, "I said I taught him; I didn't say he learned!"

This chapter provides you with information to set up trainings based on how the brain learns and remembers. Your training can be more than a training; it can be a learning experience that is remembered on both an intellectual level and an emotional level.

Determining Where You Are and Where You Want to Go

A good training answers these three questions:

- ✔ **Where are you now?** Getting a sense of participants' background knowledge enables the training to find a starting point that includes everyone.

- ✔ **Where are you going?** Before embarking on training, determine exactly where you want it to take your employees. For example, a recent sales training at an insurance company focused on two goals, one for each day of the training. Day one's goal was finding new prospects. Day two's target goal was to sharpen communication skills to close the sale.

- ✔ **How can you get there?** Design strategies for reaching different types of learners, addressing multiple intelligences, and enabling participants to store information in various areas of the brain.

These questions give you a roadmap for your training. The trainer who leads your sessions needs to create this map with you and others in your organization who already know have reached these targets.

Following the leader

As the leader of your organization, you must model the appropriate behavior for a training. That means supporting your workforce by being present for the training. Showing your workers that you think the training is important and vital to the success of your business helps them focus on the new learning.

Emotions are contagious. If you act excited, that excitement transfers to the training participants. You also convey an important message to your trainers: you expect the training to be worthwhile and effective.

A colleague of mine once gave a training and was happy to see the CEO of the company in attendance to reinforce the importance of the information. During the training, although all of the trainees had been told to turn off their cell phones, the CEO's phone was on. He took calls and spoke as though he were alone in his office. To upset the training even more, he went to the back corner of the room and conducted an interview during the training. A few of the trainees were noticeably distracted, but most seemed to be fully attentive. The evaluation and assessment for the day, however, revealed that the portion of the training that took place during the interview was least understood by the employees.

Showing Employees What's in It for Them (And Other Motivational Ideas)

When it comes to training, one question hangs in the mind of every trainee: What's in it for me? Abbreviated WIIFM and pronounced *whiff 'em*, this question is the key to any training.

As the leader of the organization you can *make* employees go to a training. But making them go gets them there only physically. The real buy-in has to be an emotional one. Your job is to help participants find their individual WIIFMs. Making that connection from their jobs to their training makes a difference in how attentive they are and how much they remember. Meet with employees before the training to find and emphasize that connection.

Beyond what's in it for them, a great motivational tool is you! If your employees have a rapport with you and respect you, and if they know that this training is important to you, they may be motivated.

Speak to each employee individually about the training. Explain the importance of the training to you, to the future of the company, and to the employee. Reach each one on an emotional level. Share your excitement! Share your passion! If the training group is too big for you to talk with each person, talk with teams or whatever combination of people makes sense.

One COO went to his employees and told them they were getting a day away. He was truly excited about the training they were going to have on customer service. He also was impressed with the trainer, had personally observed one of her trainings, and knew that they were going to have a good time as well as receive some valuable information. The day away got their attention, but his excitement really convinced them that this was an important training.

What makes a highly motivated trainee? As I tell you in Chapter 8, the brain is motivated by two things: desire and need. The brain is alert to information that's going to meet its needs or its desires. Trainees must either feel the need to learn at the training, or they must want to learn.

Situations that might induce a *need* for your trainees include

- Earning a new position
- Keeping their current position
- Competing with others on their team
- Competing with other businesses

Situations that might induce a *desire* to learn for your trainees might include

- ✔ **Wanting to please you:** If you have built a good relationship with your employees, they are more likely to want to please you.

- ✔ **Wanting more recognition:** If you provide praise and recognition, they know that learning new information for the business may lead to more praise and recognition.

- ✔ **A desire to beat the competition:** This could be outside competition or healthy competition within the department or team.

- ✔ **Wanting to achieve a goal:** They may know that the training can help them achieve the goal of their team at work.

- ✔ **Wanting to meet others' expectations:** Their team leader, you, their team members

- ✔ **Wanting to be respected for their knowledge:** Who doesn't want to feel smart?

Dale Carnegie said that the sweetest sound anyone ever heard was his or her name. For this reason alone, be sure to have name tags for your attendees and the trainer. Carnegie also said that the one topic everyone liked to talk about was him- or herself. Fulfill this need by offering some "get to know each other" activities.

Managing Sticky Trainings

A training with the brain in mind is well-organized and has been well-practiced. Whether you hire an outside trainer or someone in-house can do the job, preparation makes all of the difference.

Choosing the content

The content determines the amount of time necessary for the training. "Spray and pray" trainings in which participants are given more information than their brains can handle and sent on their way to apply it are brain antagonistic and ineffective. The brain needs time to connect new information to already-stored information. It needs time to rehearse that information. (And as I tell you in Chapter 15, it needs sleep to convert short-term memories into long-term memories.)

Training content may be predetermined by a needs assessment. This assessment may be informal — for example, you may set training needs as an agenda item for your senior leadership team or for meetings with all of your team leaders. You may have your leadership team create a needs assessment or survey for every employee to fill out. There is no perfect needs assessment that's appropriate for every organization.

Here are some general questions you might include in a needs assessment:

- ✔ In which areas are you interested in further training? (List potential areas below question.)

- ✔ Select the most convenient day and time for you for training. (List specific days and times.)

- ✔ Which method of training do you prefer? (List options such as online training, on-the-job training, and so on.)

- ✔ What is the number-one topic you would like training for?

Selecting the trainer

If you hire an outside trainer, be certain that the trainer you hire knows your content and understands your business needs. This classic training story is always good for a laugh, but it is also food for thought. A company hired a trainer to work with employees on time management. The employees arrived at the training site eager to begin. It came time to start the session, but the trainer wasn't there. Ten minutes later . . . still no trainer. When the company manager called the trainer, he said, "Oh, was that this week? I thought it was next week." Know your trainer.

A trainer who understands the brain can vary her presentation to meet the needs of the trainees. Interview the trainer and be certain you're getting what you want. The trainer who says she can offer a training that meets the needs of each of the multiple intelligences as I describe in Chapter 7 should be able to offer you an outline of what she can do to meet those needs.

Following are some suggestions for choosing a trainer:

- ✔ Ask for credentials.
- ✔ Ask for references.
- ✔ Check out trainers on the Internet.
- ✔ Interview the trainer — preferably in person, but at least over the phone, and try to get a feel for the type of presenter he is.
- ✔ Ask for outlines of the material.
- ✔ Check to see whether the trainer provides follow-up for the training in the form of updates, coaching, or informal gatherings.

Choosing the setting, creating the atmosphere

The most effective trainings occur off-site. When trainings are given onsite, trainees are torn between concentrating on the new information and work they need to get done. Onsite trainings include more interruptions — trainees are often late returning from breaks and lunch because they try to complete work during that time, and less training takes place.

If you're simply stuck with the company training room in which every one of your employees has already been trained, change the setup of that room. For a training to impress the brain and make your participants interested and excited, you need to grab their attention immediately with a new atmosphere.

Check the room to make sure there are no distractions. Jack, an employee at one of the major automobile manufacturers told me about a training that he was really looking forward to. He had his entire work crew pumped up to learn a faster way to get their jobs done with fewer mistakes. When the training began, so did the noisy blower on the air conditioner. Every few minutes, it started up and made concentration nearly impossible. His coworkers thought it was a total waste of time, and it took a few days before morale sprang back.

An effective way to change the atmosphere of any training room is to play music. Research strongly suggests that the brain responds to music. I often have the Beatles or the Beach Boys playing as I begin my trainings. The music energizes me, and it provides a background for conversation as trainees arrive. Often people are reluctant to begin conversations in a quiet room. With music playing, the participants feel that their conversations are more private and no one can hear them. If the training is starting later in the day after participants have been working, play calming music.

If the set-up of the room has always been theater style or perhaps trainees always sit around a conference table, you can nonetheless design other formats. Check with your trainer to see what he or she is comfortable with or perhaps offers some of the following options:

✔ Round tables make trainees more likely to interact with each other. When the participants sit only halfway around the table, they have clear sightlines to the trainer and training materials, as well.

✔ U-shaped designs offer visibility if participants don't sit on both sides of the tables.

✔ Diagonal table set ups allow for visibility, interaction, and participation.

Many trainers prefer round table arrangements for participation and movement possibilities. If the room doesn't have windows, moods and attitudes may take a bad turn because they lack feel-good brain chemicals, like serotonin, whose release is affected by sunlight. If the training room is short on sunlight, be sure the training includes some short "road trips" to areas with natural light.

Organizing and Presenting Information

In order to present a training with the brain in mind, you might consider several basic brain rules. Brains handle information best if it has been chunked into workable, understandable, easily stored bits of information. If you want the trainees to truly attend to the learning, it must be interesting and engaging. Boring is not an option. Along with those needs, the brain requires occasional breaks, some downtime in order to process the new information. And finally, brains like to work together. Trainees gain from each other's experiences and group work lowers stress and raises memory.

Brains like chunks

Cognitive psychologists sometimes disagree on the amount of information that the brain can hold at one time. Researchers believe that the human brain can hang on to five, six, or seven bits of information for only about 30 seconds. The brain needs continual engagement with information to maintain it in working memory.

The best trainers understand how memory works and chunk information into memorable parts. The human brain remembers best what is presented first, and remembers second best what is presented last. (This is called the *primacy-recency* effect or the *serial position effect*.) The middle of any training session is the least-remembered section.

Dr. David Sousa, author of several books on the brain, calls the first part of a training, where retention is high, *prime time 1*. The second time for high retention — the information you hear last — is *prime time 2*. Researchers aren't sure how long prime time 1 may be. Most believe that ability to focus is age-dependent until the age of 22. After that point, focus time is about 20 minutes.

At the beginning of a training episode, most participants focus on the trainer with an interest in learning or finding out what this training is all about. During this time, the trainer needs to hook trainees with something novel or emotional and then begin teaching the new idea, skill, or concept. This prime time for retention may last no longer than 20 minutes, and so many trainers pause at the eight to ten minute mark for a minute or two to allow trainees to jot down information, share the information with another trainee, or compare notes with someone sitting close by. The training then resumes until the 20-minute mark in which another practice time, reflection time, or comparison of ideas might be shared.

Down time gives the brain an opportunity to organize information and connect it to similar information already stored for later processing. During prime time 2, the brain processes this information. This method is much different from the old training adage which allowed no processing time: "Tell them what you are going to tell them, tell them, and then tell them what you told them." The brain needs time to process if you want your employees to retain information. Prime time 2 may be a review or a different approach to the information that was presented during prime time 1.

In a 40-minute session, for example, you might want to schedule approximately 30 minutes of training and 10 minutes for processing. If the training is lengthy, fill it with segments of this kind. An all-day training, say from 8 until 4, would have roughly 10 to 12 of these training periods.

Brains don't attend to boring things

In this digital age where information doubles every two years, anyone can find answers to important questions by typing a few words into Google, and people spend about two seconds on a Web site before moving on to the next, the brain has become accustomed to fast-paced, novel enticements. Trainings can offer no less.

In 1933, Hedwig von Restorff conducted memory experiments that focused on novelty. She gave groups of participants lists of items that were similar — except for one isolated item. The lists looked something like this:

Bird
Dog
Horse
Cat
Tiger
Lassie
Cow
Sheep
Goat

"Lassie" stands out because it is different, a proper noun in a list of common nouns. Participants more often remembered "Lassie" than any of the other items in the list.

The point of these experiments and others that followed is that people remember novelty — in this case, something different from the things around it. Advertisers use this concept when they try to convince you to remember their product over others. The drawback is that the novel or surprising element, though very memorable, makes you less likely to remember the other information in the list. The trick is to make the novel idea a trigger for the other information.

Changes that make trainings more interesting include

✔ **Change of state:** After a period of time, the brain begins to wander to thoughts other than the training. Some ideas for revving up the brain include

- Having everyone stand for a few minutes as the training continues.
- Asking everyone to take a deep breath.
- The trainer and trainees changing positions in the room.
- The trainer changing her tone or volume.
- Asking trainees to stand, find a partner, and discuss the most-recently covered topic for two minutes.
- Asking trainees to stand and find three people in the room they don't know, introduce themselves, and tell why they're attending the training.

✔ **Change of presentation:** Lecture works for short periods of time, but the areas of the brain used to learn and understand lecture lose energy. By changing the format of the content, you let that brain area rest and rejuvenate so it can work proficiently again at a later time. Some ways to change the presentation include the following:

- Using small group activities to reinforce information.
- Showing video clips
- Asking for suggestions to connect the new learning to what is currently known or being done at work.
- Having participants create questions that others might ask about the information.

✔ **Change of activities:** Different people learn in different ways. Vary activities according to learning preferences by

- Using hands-on activities for those who need to learn with their bodies.
- Using visuals to show learners who need to see the information.
- Having participants teach each other the information that has been presented in whatever format they think is most effective.

The brain likes breaks

Some leaders shudder when they hear that the brain needs breaks. They think breaks are only for those who are unmotivated and care little for success. I remind them of the Dale Carnegie story about the two men chopping wood. One man rested only to quickly eat, while the other took frequent breaks. At the end of the day the man who worked continually was amazed to see that the other man had chopped more wood than he had. When he asked how this could be, the man who rested asked, "Didn't you see that while I was resting I was sharpening my ax?"

This is a wonderful metaphor for taking care of your brain and your memory. Breaks are necessary to rest and prime your brain for learning. The adult brain can focus for no more than 20 minutes. What happens when those 20 minutes are up can transform your effective training into one that is not only ineffective but into an outright nightmare.

If the trainer is lucky, before the 20-minute mark when he might lose all the participants to fuzzy thinking, someone in the session is blatant about the need for change. Some trainers use a 1-2-3 rule. If one person gets up to use the restroom, keep on training. When a second person is having trouble keeping their eyes open, it may have been a rough night and training can continue. But if a third person looks like he has mentally left the training or follows person number 1 into the restroom, it's time for a break.

Brain breaks do not have to be breaks from training. Brain breaks can be content-related. Consider the training format when fuzzy brain sets in:

- ✔ If it is a lecture and the participants are not climbing over each other in a desperate attempt to get away from the training, then the break can be content-related. For example, the trainer may ask the participants to take a few minutes to think about where in their job description this content would fit. She could then ask trainees to share their thoughts.

- ✔ If it is shortly after lunch and members of the audience have glazed eyes, a state change may take care of the problem — maybe a 30-second stretch during which the trainer continues sharing information.

- ✔ If a small-group discussion is in progress and some trainees are frustrated with the discussion or with someone in their group, redirect the conversation.

Changes such as these add to rather than detract from the training content. Training goals don't change, and if you're worried about loss of time, keep in mind that if you don't keep trainees' attention, they don't keep the information.

You might want to incorporate brain breaks directly into your training plan. Here are some ideas for brain breaks that work wonders:

- ✔ **Play Simon Says.** In addition to being fun, Simon Says wakes people up and emphasizes the importance of listening — all in just minutes.

- ✔ **Pair and share.** Trainees find a partner (preferably not one at their table) and share what they have learned thus far.

- ✔ **Review in groups.** Have trainees form groups of four. Ask each group to come up with a few key points that have been covered so far.

✔ **Get graphic.** Have employees form groups of four. Provide each group a piece of poster board and markers, and ask them to create a visual that depicts the main points of the training.

✔ **Conduct a mini-Q&A.** Instruct each participant to make up a quick question about the content and then ask the person next to them to answer it.

✔ **Connect the content.** Ask trainees to discuss in small groups one problem or concern with the information in the training as it relates to their job or their current approach to the topic.

The brain likes company

Some research suggests that putting trainees in pairs or small groups increases each trainee's retention of the material. Pairs might increase retention about 6 percent and groups of three or four people may bump that up to 9 percent.

Put participants in groups with different people from the ones they chose to sit with at the beginning of the training. Splitting up friends and friendly co-workers lowers the risk of trainees losing focus on the task and instead catching up on personal conversations.

Any group activity that includes working with content feeds the memory process in two important ways:

✔ It provides an opportunity to rehearse the information. If the training is for new recruits or revolves around new product lines or concepts, the amount of rehearsal time needs to be very high when compared to a training that brushes up employees on sales or product information.

✔ Whether participants form relationships or not, their reactions to other trainees cause some of this information to be tagged as emotional memory, the most powerful memory system in the brain.

Moving from Concrete to Abstract Information

Trainers often develop their trainings according to their own learning style, but they're better off varying their methods so that their trainings address each kind of learning. Although there are many ways of looking at learning styles, the brain stores information both concretely and abstractly:

✔ **Concrete learners** are inclined to focus on immediate reality and prefer real-life examples, explicit directions, and using their five senses. They learn best when they move from the concrete to the abstract in a step-by-step sequence. They value practical knowledge and tend to be precise and accurate in their work. They tend to excel at memorizing facts.

✔ **Abstract learners** are comfortable creating theories about what they hear and observe. They tend to look at the big picture to get an overall impression of what's happening and often leap to a conceptual understanding of material. They may be inattentive during sessions that predominantly give factual information.

Some learners can learn in either fashion; some require a concrete approach to then lead them to the abstract ideas. Many trainings share strategies and ideas, and so naturally abstract learners have an easier time. Concrete learners need a bridge from concrete to abstract.

To meet the needs of both concrete and abstract learners try the following:

✔ **Begin the training with the big picture.** For example, if you're teaching sales people how to sell a new product, the big picture might be that learning the three things this product can do to change the lives of customers. Abstract learners need the big picture.

✔ **Give real-life examples.** Show video clips, pictures, or charts that go along with stories of how this product changed lives. Concrete learners relate well to this step.

✔ **Use hands-on activities.** Enable the trainees to work with the product to see how it works and get a feel for how it might affect others. Concrete learners especially like the physical contact with the product; abstract learners may do more talking and throw out ideas about the product.

✔ **Step by step, show trainees how the product works and what the benefits are.** Have them work in groups or pairs to practice ways of sharing this information with customers. Together, abstract and concrete learners come up with big ideas and steps for selling the product.

Abstract and concrete learners make great teams. They cover ideas as well as facts, and they fill in any gaps for each other when they work together.

Creating Memories That Stick

Before it can begin the memory process, the brain filters incoming information for emotional content first. If you start a training by reaching trainees on an emotional level, you lay a foundation that makes remembering the important information to come easier and more effective.

Storytelling is one of the best ways to connect emotionally with trainees. A story often helps the listener relate to the trainer. I sometimes tell the story about how I became interested in learning more about the brain. I attended a training that included brain research applications for teaching my university classes. I was so fascinated that I continually tried to "pick the brain" of the trainer. At the end of the week, he asked whether I would like to be trained to present his training sessions. I immediately turned him down because I was apprehensive about traveling with strangers, leaving my family regularly, and change in general. I went home at the end of the week of training upset with myself and my fears. I pouted so much that my husband begged me to leave!

My story relates to many people on an emotional level. They think about their fears, the changes they want to make, and even their significant others at home. They laugh at the ending, and humor releases feel-good chemicals in the brain that facilitate learning.

For decades, researchers believed that information was stored in one area of the brain, and therefore how you learned or how you trained didn't seem to matter. Current research shows that memory is stored in multiple brain areas and that utilizing more of the brain's memory systems, or pathways, in training enables the brain to store more long-term memories.

If you want your trainings to truly stick, you want your trainer to access multiple memory systems. Two kinds of memory exist:

- ✔ **Declarative memories** are those that you can talk about. You are consciously aware of those memories. "My company has 50 employees" is an example. This is a fact and you can tell others that fact.

- ✔ **Non-declarative memory** consists of those memories that are not in our conscious awareness. This category includes things that you do almost automatically, like riding a bike and driving a car.

Declarative and non-declarative memory systems can be broken down into several more distinctive memory systems, each of which has unique characteristics and can be used effectively in trainings:

- ✔ **Semantic memory** is factual and conceptual. All of the text in the training manual, the lectures in the training, and any audio or video information is considered semantic. In other words — all the words! Semantic information is the most difficult type of information for the brain to learn. It requires high motivation and must pass through several temporary memory systems before it can be stored in long-term memory.

✔ **Episodic memory** relates to events, locations, and people. Research shows that if you learn something in an airplane, you remember it better when you're in an airplane. If you learn something underwater you remember it better underwater.

Episodic memory sometimes relies on location. The more unique a setting is, the more memorable it is. Transferring information from one location to another is easier if the locations are similar. If your employees are training in a technical skill that they will use in a specific location, have them practice these skills in the location where they will use them. Medical schools don't train surgical techniques in a classroom; they train future surgeons in an operating room.

✔ **Emotional memory** is a very strong memory system. If you learn something in an emotional way, your brain — which is always filtering incoming information for emotion — marks the memory and calls on many different brain areas to remember the information.

Emotional memory may be the most powerful way to make your training stick. If your trainees feel that the training will make a difference, they are more likely to remember it. If you have clearly established what's in it for them, they are more likely to remember. Your training must create excitement, passion, and drive. You establish these emotions through the environment, the passion of the trainer, and the modeling that you, the leader, provide.

✔ **Procedural memory** is sometimes called muscle memory. It involves movement and processes. This is skill learning, and it's vital to trainings in which participants need to learn how to use or repair a product or how to use a program.

Procedural memory may be a large part of any technical training. Just as location is important, learning the procedures in the correct location is also enormously important. This memory system can be associated with location as well. When trainees are learning how to run a computer program, physical practice places much of the memory of using the program in procedural memory.

✔ **Conditioned response memory** is sometimes best explained through antonyms. I say *hot* and you automatically reply *cold*.

Conditioned response memory is often used for information that is difficult to remember. Flashcards help trainees commit vocabulary via conditioned response memory, and so do memory devices like putting information to music or creating rhymes.

Sticky trainings utilize most of these memory systems. The more places in the brain a memory is stored, the easier it is to retrieve.

Not a lot of hot air

I was helping a trainer prepare a presentation to some heating and cooling distributors. As he went through the features and benefits of this new furnace, he said that the furnace had a two-speed blower that provided more comfort.

I told him that he needed to help his trainees convince customers that the statement was true, so I asked him to convince me. He thought a moment and then told me to hold my hand about four inches in front of my mouth. He then told me to blow on my hand like I was blowing out a candle. Next, he asked me to open my mouth wide and simply breathe on my hand. He asked, "Which feels warmer?" I told him that the slower-moving air felt warmer. When he pointed out that the air temperature was the same whether I was blowing hard or exhaling gently, I understood the benefit of the furnace's two-speed blower. He taught the trainees to use that example when explaining this feature and benefit. Because he had me participate and he caused an emotional reaction since I "felt" better with the warm air on my hand, this experience was more memorable.

Move It or Lose It: How Movement Enhances Learning

In recent years, staggering numbers of studies have shown convincingly that movement helps learning occur. In studies at schools, for example, physical activity led to improvement in grades and test scores, not to mention reading.

Promoting movement in your trainings takes little time and offers employees' brains more oxygen and better blood flow throughout the body. It promotes the release of brain chemicals that enhance motivation. And movement also helps wake up sleep-deprived employees! Here are a few ideas for working movement into training sessions:

- ✔ At the beginning of the training, have participants stand and find someone they don't know well. Give them a few minutes to introduce themselves and find three things they have in common.

- ✔ Ask trainees to walk around the room and make three appointments with three different people at times you set. (For example, have them make a 10 o'clock, 1 o'clock, and 3 o'clock appointment.) When those times arrive, trainees go to their appointments and discuss whatever aspects of the training you suggest.

- ✔ Instruct participants to stand up when they answer *yes* to a question.

✔ When you solicit opinions or agreement, send participants to one side of the room if they agree and the other side if they disagree.

✔ If weather allows, ask participants to take a walk with a partner and discuss points from the training.

✔ Give trainees time to physically demonstrate what they have learned. For example, role playing a sales pitch or repairing a machine.

✔ Tell participants that the last person at their table who stands up must answer the question that you have posted on a slide or flipchart.

Going through the motions: Procedural memory

Procedural memory is formed by making movements repeatedly. Procedures help free up working memory — the temporary storage process that everyone uses constantly. Working memory, however, is fragile and small — it can hold only about seven bits of information. As your employees are being trained, they hold information in working memory, and if their brains can connect this information to something they already know, they have a greater chance of working that information into long-term memory.

Remember that procedural memory is like a muscle memory. After the information is stored in the motor area of your brain, you don't have to consciously think about it anymore. Because you don't have to focus on it, it doesn't take up any space in working memory. For instance, in the retail clothing business, new merchandise is handled in a procedural manner:

1. **As soon as the delivery service drops off the boxes of clothing, the packing slips are removed and the merchandise on the slips are compared to the merchandise orders.**

2. **If the packing slip and the order match, the merchandise is taken out of the boxes and hung on the appropriate hangers.**

3. **Sales tags are printed out and placed on each garment.**

4. **Garments that need to be steamed are hung in the steaming room.**

5. **After the steaming is complete, the garments are checked in on the computer with the arrival date and the date they are displayed for customers.**

6. **The garments are then placed on the sales floor in an appropriate spot.**

This procedure becomes second nature to the merchandise team. If Helen is receiving packages and one of the salespeople comes back to ask her a question about sizes in an order that has yet to arrive, Helen can answer the question as she continues to work. She does not have to consciously attend to every step in the procedure because it has become second nature to her.

Procedures can save you time and money. Some managers ask trainees to watch for aspects of the training in which procedures can be set up. Employees more easily remember procedures that they create, and the procedures enable employees to be more receptive to the information they are learning.

Stressing the importance of exercise

You would be remiss as a leader if you did not understand the value of exercise for your trainees and all of your employees. Aerobic exercise can literally cut your risk of Alzheimer's by 50 percent, according to the research of Dr. John Medina, author of *Brain Rules.* Research shows that if you take a 20-minute walk each day, you cut your risk of stroke by 50 percent. Those are a few of the health benefits.

Some studies show that the continual integration of oxygen to the brain aids cognition. Here are a few exercise options to help training stick:

✔ Rather than sitting in chairs, have trainees who are interested and capable walking on a treadmill during the training.

✔ Provide morning and afternoon exercise breaks of at least 20 minutes.

✔ Conduct part of the training on a walking track or outside where trainer and trainees can walk one to two miles per hour.

✔ Keep the hours of the training within reason so participants have time to exercise as well as get a good night's sleep.

Exercise releases stress. Trainings can be stressful for some employees. If the stress is not relieved, stress hormones build up in the brain and body and compromise focus and attention.

Getting the Story through Pictures

If I ask you to picture the Eiffel Tower, what happens? It pops right up in your mind; whether you've seen it in Paris or in a picture, the vision is stored in your brain. Using visuals can make a difference in what trainees remember. The occipital lobe stores visual information and is attracted to certain types of information. What you see is sometimes what you get — as far as understanding information. The brain

✔ Pays attention to pictures

✔ Is drawn to color

✔ Notices different sizes

✔ Reacts to motion

Yes, a picture is worth a thousand words. You likely remember only 10 percent of information that you hear three days after the fact, but if you see a picture, the percentage of information that you remember goes up to 65!

Using visuals in trainings goes a long way toward making sure your employees "get the picture." Try some of the following tips for adding visuals to your training:

✔ Take a look at the PowerPoint presentations you currently use and redo them using more still pictures and animations.

✔ Look for opportunities to add visuals to your training manual. Think about adding color if your budget allows.

✔ Prime trainees' brains with pictures. Before the training, place pictures that relate to the training in the office or workspace. Prime their eyes and their brains for the new information or product. When they enter the training and see some of the same visuals, they may relax a bit because they feel somewhat familiar with it. This intentional priming may also wake up a few stored memories relating to the product, process, or idea.

Engage! Engage! Engage!

The trainer has presented information, and trainees seem to understand. It is time to engage them in rehearsals of the material. Some research suggests that a person needs 24 to 28 engagements with new material to move it into long-term memory.

If the trainer used different memory systems to help participants understand the new learning, then fewer rehearsals may be necessary. For trainees to benefit most they need to practice this material in an environment that is at least similar to where they will utilize the information. It is time to take the trainees' knowledge and do some elaborative rehearsal. *Elaborative rehearsal* goes beyond simply repeating information and engages participants in some kind of interaction with the material.

Review the newly learned concepts or skills throughout the day. At the end of the training day, review again. This review may take the form of a game. According to Bob Pike, professional training consultant, "Learning is directly proportional to the amount of fun you have." Make it fun to make it stick!

Practice makes permanent

When it comes to sticky trainings, practice is the glue. The old saying that practice makes perfect has been updated to reflect current knowledge about how the brain works. Practice can make perfect only if trainees really understand what they're supposed to store in their memories — that is, perfect practice makes perfect. One of the biggest pitfalls in teaching and training is not checking to make sure that the trainees really have the information straight in their minds. After you know that they have it, they need to practice it.

You may wonder how much practice is enough. In his book *Outliers,* Malcolm Gladwell hypothesizes that to be really great at something, an expert needs to practice about 10,000 hours. Clearly, one-shot training is not enough to create experts. Your employees need practice in order for any information to become second nature to them.

Try working the following rehearsal strategies into any training session:

✔ Pair up trainees and have them teach each other.

✔ Have volunteer trainees demonstrate the information. Doing so is particularly important for a sales training in which trainees are learning a new sales pitch. The pitch should sound natural and sincere, which happens through practice.

✔ Play games with the information. (Jeopardy is a favorite.)

✔ Have trainees write about the training.

✔ Have trainees draw pictures of the training.

✔ Ask trainees to share with others how this training information is going to change their jobs.

✔ Offer on-the-job training.

Feedback: Memory's Significant Other

The brain loves to know how it's doing. Continual feedback throughout a training is important for keeping trainees' focus on the road map. They need to think about where they're going and how they're getting there. Short conferences and conversations allow trainees to ask questions they might not ask in front of the group. Learning and feedback are ammunition for hitting the targets (goals). Rehearsal and review are the target practice.

Having a place for trainees to place sticky notes with questions and comments provides the trainer feedback from the trainees. Some trainers put a large piece of paper on the wall asking for concerns. Trainees write these notes anonymously, and the trainer reads them throughout the day and addresses their content.

Most trainings provide time at the end of the training for participants to demonstrate their learning in some way — demonstrations or role play, for example. After such an exercise, a written assessment by the trainer can offer suggestions for improvement and positive reinforcement for their efforts. The assessment of their work may be as simple as:

> *You did a great job at . . . .*
>
> *Your technique could be improved by . . . .*
>
> *I enjoyed having you in the training because . . . .*

Some trainings have written assessments that ask trainees specific questions about the training. Other trainings have participants write papers describing the training strategies or techniques in relation to their jobs. Written assessments are fine, but actively engaging trainees in formats that demonstrate what they have learned is usually more fun and allows yet another rehearsal for those observing the performance.

When trainees leave the training on a positive note, their brains are more likely to retain the information, and they will be happier about returning for more training.

Evaluations at the end of the day are valuable to you as the leader, and may help the trainer during a multiple-day training. However, if the training is one day only with follow-up at a later date, try asking employees for an evaluation of the training mid-day so that the trainer gets an idea of what trainees don't understand or don't like about the training. I often hand out index cards with a 3-2-1 format:

> *Describe three things you have learned.*
>
> *Write two questions that you have.*
>
> *Share one idea or strategy you can use immediately.*

On the back of the card, trainees write suggestions for the training. The trainer has time to review or make changes for the second half of the day.

Chapter 19

Changing Minds: Training by Redesigning Brains

. . . .

In This Chapter

▶ Addressing training for new employees

▶ Training tried-and-true employees

▶ Finding strategies for resistant brains

. . . .

*Y*ou have the opportunity to change minds and even to change brains. In Chapter 2, I talk about *neuroplasticity,* the brain's ability to change through experience. As a sculptor, you would mold your material or chip away at it to transform it into a beautiful or useful entity. As a leader, you can shape the brains of new employees through teaching and training so that they can make a difference in your organization.

When a sculptor discovers that his creation needs changes, does he throw it away and start over? No, he adds more clay and remolds it, or he chisels away at some of the stone to create a masterpiece. In much the same way, you can redesign brains of employees who've been on the job but haven't kept up with changes in the company.

Training minds to learn the skills that your organization needs is necessary to move your organization forward. Brain growth and change equals organization growth and change. Whether you're designing brains of new employees who need to understand the purpose of your company and learn skills to contribute to its growth or retraining those veterans who have helped make the business what it is today but need to refine their skills or learn new ones, you need to lead them to your way of thinking.

In this chapter, you discover how brains learn and change, how to help reshape and redefine veteran brains, and how to lead both to places they have not been before.

Designing Brains: Training New Employees

For years educators thought that the brain was a vessel that could be filled with information. Today, neuroscience knows that the brain is plastic — that it changes through its experiences. The brain can *bloom,* or grow new connections, and also *prune* by allowing no-longer-used connections to wither and die. When you have new hires with little prior knowledge of your business, you can design their brains and make them great employees.

Even brains that are new to your business and haven't been trained for specific tasks aren't blank slates. Everyone comes with her own background knowledge and experiences. You nonetheless have the opportunity to create networks in these brains that provide connections to your business and the skills these people need. You can design a brain for your business.

Imagine that you need a road from your house to your place of business. You have purchased a new home in an area that has never before been connected to the busy downtown area of your town. Using maps and satellites, you determine the best way to make a path. As you follow the path, you may find a few physical limitations, perhaps a river bed or a small mountainous area that did not show up on the satellite pictures. You refine your map and make the proper corrections to eliminate the need for extra work or extra time to get to your destination.

When you try out the new path, your car can't even get through, but as you walk the path and begin to remove bushes and rocks, you eventually have a trail. You can now get from home to work. But you have only a path, and you require a street. As you use this pathway and remove more obstacles, it becomes smoother and wider, and soon your car can make it down the road. You lay concrete to make your travel smoother and save some time getting to the office. As more and more other vehicles begin to use your street, you may find that it needs to be widened and perhaps made into a highway so people can travel even faster and many more people can use the path.

Certainly building this road was a process, but because there were few obstacles in the way, the project was easier. Newcomers to your business have fewer obstacle as they are trained and networks are laid down in their brains. The first time they are offered training information, their path from receiving it to storing it in their brains may be a little slow — after all, they're blazing a new trail in their brains. As they practice the skills and concepts, the path becomes a street. With application of the new learning, the network becomes even stronger and faster, just as the street became the highway.

These new employees who have a clear path don't confuse old learning with the new learning. They do not ask questions or make comments such as

"Wouldn't it be easier doing this the old way?"

"In my department, we found that a method like this took longer."

"I don't see how this is going to change anything."

These statements and questions stem from prior knowledge and fully ingrained habits of doing things in a certain way. Because these brains presumably don't have prior knowledge of old skills or strategies, they are less likely to challenge the learning.

Creating new brain places

Most trainings try to appeal to your semantic memory system. (See Chapter 18.) The trainer gives information and expects it to stick. However, the semantic memory system is the most difficult for the brain to use. Education has taken the semantic approach for years — read a text, discuss it, and then test to see whether students remember it. Because so many students learned to remember material for a test, the system seemed to work. But this process prepares participants for tests that occur immediately after the "lessons" have taken place. It doesn't involve long-term memory. Working memory holds the information just long enough for the test, and then the information is usually forgotten.

Business or corporate trainings must be designed differently. As Chapter 18 shows you, the more emotion involved in learning, the more easily you remember the information.

People remember information better when it's attached to an emotion. A model for training these new brains would include answering the following questions:

- ✔ **What?** Explain exactly what the new hires are going to learn. But add an emotional touch. "Today you're going to find out how to use the new widget" gets the job done, but this approach adds emotion: "Today you're going on a journey to distant lands to find the secret to making life easier for your customers and earning greater commissions." (Employees still find out about the widget but with an exotic spin that includes the widget's Japanese origins.)

- ✔ **Why?** Let them know the purpose of this training in relation to what they will do for the company and its vision. This is a great time to bring in the CEO to dramatically share her vision using visuals and speaking with the passion she feels about the company.

- ✔ **How?** Share with the participants that they will be immersed into the training in order to instill lasting beliefs and habits to make their jobs easier and to contribute more to the company. Begin with real-life examples, personal experiences, or a virtual tour via the computer. Demonstrate what employees will be expected to do, and provide a lot of opportunity for practice.

Use brain-compatible strategies for teaching content by utilizing some of the following:

- ✔ Games
- ✔ Role-playing
- ✔ Mnemonics
- ✔ Storytelling
- ✔ Brainstorming
- ✔ Projects
- ✔ Hands-on activities

Coaching the new brains

A strong new-employee training program can make all the difference between employees who know what they're doing and feel good about themselves, and those who still don't have a clue. Training works. But it requires practice to keep those new networks primed and ready.

Hold at least part of your training session in the location where employees will use the information or skill they're learning. Doing so gives these fresh faces and malleable brains the boost of *episodic memory* — the memory associated with location, people, and events. (Chapter 18 tells you more about episodic memory.)

Some experts believe that the first 60 to 90 days of coaching make the difference in retaining information from the training and in retaining the employee. And keep in mind that the person you want to coach a new employee is not the employee who is being replaced. Someone who is leaving your business to go somewhere else, whether the move was your idea or his, isn't the best coach.

The best leaders have a new employee program in place for at least the first several weeks to reinforce training, answer questions, and create relationships with the new staff members. Consider matching up each new employee with a mentor who stays with the employee throughout the day, introduces him to key people, reviews the employee handbook, and reinforces the first-day training. This mentor should spend some time with the new employee each day for several days and check in occasionally for the first three months through planned meetings, lunches, or drop-ins to check for questions.

The mentor provides expertise and enthusiasm. Choose mentors who really know what the new employee must do to make a contribution to the organization and cheer her along the way. (See Chapter 4 for more information on mentoring and coaching.)

Limbic learning

Terri was thrilled to get her new job. After graduating from college with a degree in history, she realized that few positions were available in her field if she didn't want to become an educator. By working for a temp agency, she was placed in an online human resource position for a software company. The company knew she had little training in this area, but she happened to be exactly what her employer wanted — someone without preconceived notions of how the job should be done.

Terri was given some training in using the software she would need for the job. She learned this easily enough by practicing with the software for hours. When it came time for her to really understand the purpose of the company she worked for and the leadership vision, learning online wasn't sufficient. She needed more inspiration than she was getting. She found herself mechanically speaking with employees when trying to help them find their spots in the company. Although she recognized their talents, her lack of emotional attachment to the company made her less than effective.

Terri's team leader began to question his decision to put so much effort into Terri's training. Upon having a personal meeting with her, however, he was convinced that she lacked only knowledge and not motivation. Acting quickly, the company sent Terri for a one-week training that involved limbic learning. That is, the training was set up to engage participants on an emotional level. The CEO of Terri's company came to the training and kicked off the meeting with a passionate presentation in which she shared her vision, the mission, and the company values.

Each day of the training was built upon that passion. With the CEO setting the emotional standard for the training and remaining visible throughout the week, the emotional temperature of the participants remained high. Their limbic systems activated the release of brain chemicals that made memories stronger. Terri left the training with a different outlook on the importance of the company, the talent it needed to fulfill its mission, and the ability to share the vision with the employees she guided.

Redesigning Brains: Helping Employees Train for Change

When organizations change, new job descriptions and new learning are part of the deal. The process of redesigning the adult brain brings with it the possibility of major changes. Change is not always easy. When current employees must change their way of thinking in order to meet new goals and challenges, resistance may be part of the process.

Breaking habits, changing networks

Some habits are harder to break than others. Changing the brain's networks requires breaking up existing connections and building new ones. This process takes a lot of brain energy, as the following steps show:

1. **New information enters the brain and is held in working memory.**

   Working memory holds only a limited amount of information.

2. **The brain compares the new information with stored memories throughout the neocortex.**

   Because working memory is limited to five to seven bits of information, it makes the comparisons only in small chunks.

3. **The work of holding on to new information and comparing it to old information exhausts working memory and causes it to lose some of the information.**

   Because of the working memory's fatigue, new memories may not be committed to long-term memory.

In the brains of your current workers, this attempt at learning new information may be frustrating. People feel discomfort when given information that is contrary to what they already know and believe.

You know that 2 plus 2 equals 4, for example, and so when you're suddenly told to change that thinking to 2 plus 2 equals 5, your brain detects an error and experiences a stress response that causes it to respond without thinking.

Changing networks that employees have practiced repeatedly is a challenge. To change the 2+2=4 network, for example, the brain has to override the impulse to activate the old network and instead activate a newly formed 2+2=5 network. The process takes some time and is similar to changing a habit like smoking a cigarette after dinner. If you used to be a smoker and enjoyed a cigarette after a meal, when you quit, the desire or the routine thought remains for some time. You eat, you think about lighting up, you toss that thought aside, and you find something else to do. Slowly, you overcome the habit. After several weeks, your thoughts only occasionally turn to having a cigarette after dinner. You have begun to replace that procedure with other things to do.

Imagine that you're an employee who has worked for a firm for years. You have just been told that your job is changing. You need to be retrained in order to follow the correct procedures. As you begin to try out the new process, you find yourself going back to the old routine. Your brain is used to following specific steps, and now you have to stop yourself from following the old habit and refocus on the new one. Your thoughts and reactions likely mirror some or all of the following:

✔ The old way was comfortable.

✔ The old process or program worked well — even better than the new one.

✔ You feel angry because you don't like the new system.

✔ You're afraid you won't be able to learn the system.

✔ Your stress levels rise as you try to learn the new information.

✔ Stress causes you to make more mistakes or forget some of the new information.

✔ You want to give up.

✔ You think you may lose your job.

✔ You think you may quit your job.

✔ You wonder why new employees caught on to the new system so easily.

As an employee's brain reshapes itself in response to new learning, he may experience all kinds of different emotions. The reshaping nonetheless can take place. But it may be slower for some of these previously trained workers whose old networks have to be disconnected as new ones are built.

Overriding old networks takes time and practice. The more emotional the new networks are, the stronger they are and the more easily they replace old ones. Motivation and commitment to the new networks also speeds up the process.

Reinforcing changes

In order to reinforce the changes that have taken place from redesigning brains, you need to do the following:

✔ **Apply new learning:** Although some employees may be a little reluctant to implement what they have learned, doing so is a necessary step to rid them of the old habits and instill the new ones. The changes work best if employees apply their new learning immediately. Expect them to need coaching, which can be supplied by your trainer or by other employees who have had more training in the area.

✔ **Integrate the changes:** Make sure that employees at all levels in the department integrate the new way of doing things. The emotional message is "we're all in this together." Employees are more likely to help each other if everyone is at similar levels of performance and working on the same strategies, programs, or techniques.

✔ **Hold employees accountable:** After a few weeks of repetition, the new networks in employees' brains can make smooth connections. At that time, you can start holding employees accountable for utilizing their training. The method you use to measure the level of responsibility that the employees have achieved can vary according to the kind of training they received. It may be a change in profit, productivity, or proficiency. If you find that you aren't getting the results you expected, you and your employees and perhaps the trainer need to examine where the responsibility lies.

✔ **Celebrate change:** Whether you celebrate onsite or off, recognition and praise are part of keeping employees' emotional connection to the changes strong.

As you reinforce the new learning, follow the progress of your employees. Doing so assists with the steps described above. You may want to do these three things:

✔ Collect feedback from your newly retrained employees.

- Provide surveys.

- Have team meetings.

- Speak to team leaders.

- Examine data on productivity.

✔ Use this information to identify problems.

- Look for lack of motivation.

- Check stress levels.

- Identify employees resistant to changes.

✔ Fix the problems.

- Speak with anyone who may be resistant.

- Correct misconceptions.

- Recognize individual successes.

Dealing with Minds That Are Difficult to Change

Katy was a great salesperson. She loved working with customers and never had a problem making sales. When her company switched computer programs and every sale had to be entered in the computer at the time of the sale, Katy rebelled. After an onsite training, all of the other employees caught on to the system right away. Katy still made sales, but she had to have another employee do her computer work.

Katy was confronted by her employer. She admitted that she was afraid of making mistakes. She needed practice and confidence, and so her employer set up some time for her to practice, and practice, and practice. Finally, she became confident enough to make the change.

Resistance to change is a problem with some employees. While some employees look at change as an opportunity, others may see it as a punishment. For those who find that learning new skills or procedures is a problem, as their leader you must decide whether they still belong with your organization, whether you can do further training, or whether you can find another position for them that doesn't require the change.

Looking for solutions

When information has been ingrained in the brain for years and years, it is much harder to change. Sometimes employees feel totally stuck when they find themselves in a pattern that they can't get out of. In this situation some leaders would say, "My way or the highway." But a good leader takes a closer look at his employees. If what you see is loyalty, a strong work ethic, and talent that has contributed to more than just your bottom line, perhaps you need to offer this person a different opportunity.

You have probably put a lot of time and money into this employee. Training employees can become a huge expense. Loyalty is a hard commodity to find these days. You may try some of the following:

✔ Determine whether you're dealing with a real skill problem.

✔ If skills are there, check out the employee's attitude.

✔ Examine your expectations of this employee.

✔ Verify that the employee understands those expectations.

✔ Check out the employee's personnel file.

- Find out what positions the employee has held.

- Verify his productivity over the past several years.

✔ Look at other positions that are available within the company.

- Locate an open spot where this employee might fit in.

- Find another employee with whom this employee could switch positions.

Crossing digital and generational divides

The Boomer generation and the Traditionalists who came before them may be reluctant to take on some of the latest technology. These employees may have a hard time redesigning their brains with the latest digital media. You may need to approach any training that pairs workers of these generations and technology in a different format than you would other kinds of trainings. I suggest a "Before, During, and After" training format.

Before

Veteran employees used to the low-tech way of doing things are not against using technology. Rather, they feel that technology is often thrown at them, which gives them a sense of having no control over their work.

Ease them into possible changes and give them a chance to talk with you or their team leader about impending change. They may feel threatened by the younger generations' ease with technology. Casually introduce them to the program or process you're interested in having them learn. Then discuss the possibility of training to use the technology. Let them see the program in action at your company or at another place of business. Show them video presentations online. Be sure they understand how this new technology can help both the company and themselves.

Make sure the training includes a lot of coaching. Some experts agree that by the end of the day of training, many of the memories are gone; interacting with a coach may help retention. Make continual connections between the training and the individual participant's jobs. Remember that some well-used networks need to be changed, which requires a slower pace and a lot of repetition.

After

These workers need mentoring or coaching as they apply new technology to their jobs. Bringing in the younger generations to assist works with some employees, but those who feel threatened may not gain any new understanding from Gen X or Gen Y coaching. You may want to ask a peer who has learned the process to offer support. The thought may be, "If she can do it, so can I!"

If no peers have reached the level of proficiency for coaching, you may want to reinforce learning through online tutorials, by calling on peers from other departments who could check on the newly trained, or by holding some small group meetings with a trainer. In groups, the older generations may feel less threatened by a younger coach.

Chapter 20

Conducting Meetings That Matter

. . . .

In This Chapter

▶ Eradicating meetings that miss

▶ Giving the brain what it needs in meetings

▶ Getting your post-meeting message across

▶ Meeting one-on-one with employees

. . . .

*W*hen I speak to employees at most organizations, they say that nearly all of their meetings are a huge waste of their time and the company's time. But when they talk about specific meetings, they discover that for the most part meetings really do matter. The problem is that the few meetings that weren't worthwhile became memorable because of the bad feelings that they brought forth.

Worthwhile meetings usually have two significant qualities: They last for short periods of time and they have clear objectives.

If you have one specific target or problem that requires a meeting, making it short and getting straight to the point are often appreciated by team members if they don't believe that the problem relates to their job personally. Therefore, sometimes you have to add some short, engaging activities to point out how the team is a unit and that every member has a choice to make: Am I an insider or an outsider? Everyone in an organization needs to understand what others do and how all jobs are interdependent.

In this chapter, you discover how to create meetings that are compatible with how the brain works, how to communicate with different types of employees, and how to keep your vision in sight at all times.

Why You Should Toss the Old Meeting Model

Just the sound of the word *meeting* can make some employees and leaders wince. Everyone has had bad experiences at meetings. In fact, people make up all kinds of excuses to miss meetings — just like kids who show up at school without their homework. (Anyone on your team have about six dead grandmothers?)

Take a survey at your organization, and you're likely to find some of the following reasons that meetings get such a terrible rap:

- Meetings never start on time.
- There was no agenda.
- The agenda wasn't followed.
- It was too long.
- It was too short — not worth it.
- A memo (e-mail, text message) would've been sufficient.
- Too much time was wasted talking about unimportant items.
- People talked during the whole meeting; I couldn't hear a thing.
- The room was too hot (cold, warm, dark, bright, crowded . . .).
- Not enough people were there.
- Too many people were there.
- The supervisors weren't there.
- Reports were read aloud; I know how to read.
- The refreshments were stale.
- There were no refreshments and I was starving.
- I couldn't concentrate because cell phones kept ringing.
- The content had nothing to do with my job.
- Nothing was accomplished.
- People could have been making sales instead of wasting time.

And the list goes on and on. The only solution to the problem is to reconstruct how meetings are held. Some organizations call them *non-meetings,* but that joke gets old. Use your brain and grab the attention of the brains in your organization by making your meetings matter.

Meeting with the Brain in Mind

For meetings to matter, they have to appeal to those diverse brains in your organization. You can't differentiate a meeting for a lot of different intelligences and personalities, but you can address the universal needs that every brain has:

- The **survival brain** needs to be calm and open to new information.

- The **emotional brain** needs an emotional hook to hold onto the information and mark it for memory.

- The **thinking brain** needs challenge and choice to appeal to its ability to problem solve and make decisions.

The upcoming sections give you ideas for meeting these needs.

Bringing continuity with ritual

Most meetings contain procedures that are followed to keep the agenda running smoothly. For example, meetings often begin with a welcome and a review of the minutes from the previous meeting. *Procedures* are established methods of getting things done. They are usually done at a specific time or in a particular order.

Rituals are acts that provide a sense of security and continuity. Whereas procedures don't elicit much feeling, rituals tend to bring forth warm feelings, such as a feeling of belonging. Adding rituals to meetings makes them more interesting, memorable, and fun.

You can weave rituals into meetings in various ways and make them much more pleasurable. The possibilities are endless, but here are some rituals to consider for your meetings:

- Take the first several minutes at each meeting to "unload" and put stress on the back burner:

  - Have participants find a partner.

  - Give each partner two minutes to share something that may be causing tension. (The work they should be doing instead of attending the meeting, for example, or the projects they need to work on after the meeting — maybe a head cold or flu coming on.)

  - After sharing is complete, ask each person to put concerns on the back burner during the meeting because the meeting is going to be worthwhile.

✔ Have music playing while people enter the meeting. You might choose a theme song for the event. For instance, Queen's "We Will Rock You" may be a great tune for the sales team's meeting.

✔ Address special occasions. Acknowledge a birthday, for example, by playing The Beatles's "Birthday" song and presenting the team member a gift — even something as simple as a pencil with the organization's name or logo.

✔ Celebrate success. When a goal has been met, have confetti and horns to blow, play a sound effect like a drum roll, or have a special treat.

✔ Ask for the "story of the week" and allow participants to share interesting or funny incidents that occurred since the last meeting.

✔ Use novel ways of getting people interested in the agenda, For example, sell the agenda. Like a carny who sells the acts at the carnival, ask participants to step right up and participate in the greatest show on earth as you hear from the most knowledgeable people in the company . . . .

✔ Conclude each meeting in the same way. You might

- Ask participants to pair up and review the meeting's important points.

- Ask participants who they feel contributed the most and give that person a round of applause.

- Play music, like the theme from the movie *Rocky*.

 Rituals give meeting participants something to count on. Wouldn't it be nice for your employees to look forward to a meeting because they know it will be more than just another meeting, that it will be filled with fun, fanfare, and frivolity along with data, discussion, and decisions?

Sharing control

Employees may not get to choose whether they attend a meeting, but you can work choice into meetings so that they feel included and have some control over the meeting. Perhaps the group can discuss which agenda items are important and in what order they should be addressed. Sometimes, however, not all team members agree, but you can work with a consensus.

As soon as the first employee arrives, the meeting has begun. Rather than having early arrivals sit around worrying about what other things they could be getting done, offer them a choice of what to do. It can be as simple as getting a refreshment to helping you distribute literature or writing information on the whiteboard or flipchart. They get a bit of a heads up on the meeting content and get some time to consider how they feel about it. When others enter and see their teammate helping, many act as they did in grade school: they want to help the teacher, too! Soon everyone is coming early, anticipating what they can do to be part of the meeting.

You may add this idea as a ritual to your meetings: "Hit and Miss" is one way to attack the agenda as a team. What are the hits — the important or timely items you need to talk about? The misses are those items that should not be included in this particular meeting. If team members help redesign the agenda through a vote, you're sure to cover the points important to them within the allotted time.

At problem-solving or decision-making meetings, ask employees to choose how they want to attack the issue. Perhaps they want to get into smaller groups and discuss the issue on a more detailed level and then bring the ideas from each group together. Brainstorming may be a better way to attack the subject. Those who have few ideas to contribute initially may feel much better and become more knowledgeable through brainstorming.

Soliciting feedback

Exit cards — simple index cards on which the participants answer some pertinent questions about the meeting content — are an excellent feedback mechanism. (I talk about them also in Chapter 3.) You can use them just as easily at the beginning of a meeting. These cards provide valuable information that can be scanned quickly and easily if the meeting is not too large. For large groups, exit cards may be more useful.

If you use these cards at the beginning of a meeting, you can get an idea of each person's feeling about the agenda you are about to cover. Use them after a meeting to find out how much employees understood and get their feedback.

After employees have index cards in hand before a meeting, ask them to respond to the following statements, which you display on a flipchart, whiteboard, or PowerPoint slide:

> *The last meeting left the following problem unresolved*
>
> *I would like the following issue to be addressed at this meeting*
>
> *The most important item on the agenda to be covered is . . .*
>
> *The most important item not included on the agenda is . . .*
>
> *Two areas that need to be included on future agendas are . . .*

Using scorecards to focus on goals

Scorecards can add fun, keep employees focused on goals, and encourage participation before, during, and after the meeting. Creating a scorecard is a team project. The team, along with the leader, decides which categories should be tracked and how, and then creates a scorecard. Table 20-1 shows a sample scorecard.

A scorecard is a self-assessment tool, and so each team rates itself, often on a scale from 1 to 10 or by percentage for goals reached. You might want to write the team's goals at the bottom of the chart.

Table 20-1	A Sample Scorecard			
Team Categories	**Meeting #1**	**Meeting #2**	**Meeting #3**	**Meeting #4**
Participation	8			
Meetings on time	9			
Individual work accomplished	10			
Team work accomplished	10			
Fun	8.5			
Team average	9.1			
% of goals reached	33%			

Goals set: 1. Increase sales by 5 percent

2. Increase new customers 10 percent

3. Complete new product data distribution

After assessing themselves on the scorecard, team leaders share how the team determined the scores, including the percentage of goals reached. Then the team decides which category needs to be worked on for the next meeting.

While teams are getting their scorecards out and assessing themselves, play music such as "Celebration" by Kool and the Gang or "With a Little Help from My Friends" by The Beatles. Doing so adds to the fun and celebration.

Getting Your Message Across

In order to get everyone on board, you need to find the best way to express your vision, your mission, or your dream. The brain likes stories, emotions, pictures, and facts. Using what the brain likes to remember makes getting your point across much easier.

Offering facts

According to some research, most individuals really like facts. People love television shows such as *Jeopardy!*, and Trivial Pursuit is a popular game for people of all ages. Storing trivial information and sports facts is a popular hobby. Facts can be impressive to the general public. The public has been taught to respect data.

The facts your employees and all of your stakeholders want are the facts about what's happening in your company. The brain is curious, and especially in tough economic times, the brain needs to be reassured. When you present facts, you meet both of these needs.

For instance, you might say to your employees:

> "A very productive business similar to ours in a city nearby had to close its doors because of high overhead."

That statement doesn't have the impact of the following:

> "Lancaster's in Bloomington had to close down because the overhead was up 45 percent over last year."

Details make the second statement more memorable.

Adding emotion

Adding emotion gives the story a more personal feeling. A store closing is sad, even when a competitor is closing. In troubled times, no leader wants to see another business fold. When times are good, they are often good for everyone.

To make the story even more memorable, make it more personal:

> "Thirty-three employees are out of work in Bloomington because Lancaster's went under. That's right, they closed their doors on Wednesday without even telling anyone, including their employees. When Bob Larson, the former president of the company was finally reached, he broke down as he shared with me, 'I couldn't pay the bills. Our overhead was one of the main problems. We should have cut back last year; it's not like we didn't all see this coming. We were so far behind. I haven't taken a paycheck in four weeks. I can't even pay any severance to the great people who worked for me. I'm off to see an attorney about bankruptcy right now.' So, I'm just telling all of you right now, this could mean more business for us, or it could be some handwriting on the wall.

We have to keep costs down if we want to make it in this economy. Turn off the lights when you leave a room. Don't make unnecessary road trips at the expense of the company. Meet your customers for coffee instead of lunch. Let's see if we can make it through this economic downturn."

The story calls up surprise, sadness, and fear — strong emotions that imprint a sturdy memory in the brain. Those employees are going to remember what their leader told them.

Humor is also a wonderful way to convey a message. When you express yourself using humor, you relieve stress in your audience. Their smiles cause the release of dopamine as a reward, and they look forward to what you have to say.

Creating connections with symbols

If I tell you I had a really bad day and give you no further information, your brain creates a mental picture of what you think that bad day was like. Perhaps you see me stranded at the airport, having a flat tire, or losing my credit card. If I don't give you the picture, you create your own.

So it goes with sharing your vision or your mission. Making certain that your language is as symbolic as it is emotional and factual makes your message more compelling. Concrete symbols create an instant connection between giver and receiver. Such is the case with the pink ribbon symbol for the Komen Foundation and its fight against breast cancer. Avon and Dr. Susan Love have their Army of Women who are going to beat breast cancer. Symbols and symbolic language are both shortcuts to the message.

Your symbol may be your logo, an anecdote, a metaphor, a song or a story. Make your symbol or symbolic language a shortcut to a message. The previous story about the closing of Lancasters becomes a symbol for your company. Whenever teams are thinking about spending money, the ritual statement is always made, "Remember Lancasters." This puts spending into perspective: can the expenditure really help the company?

Leaders use their company symbols to keep the vision in sight. The logo is on the wall, the stationery, the uniforms, and the trucks. When the leader speaks using facts and emotions, the symbol is present. She shares it, shows it, and conveys it through her message.

Symbolic language in action:
"I'm so glad you got to meet me"

My father, Lee Broms, dropped out of high school to get a job and make a living. It was 1939 and he wanted a trade. Dad went to work for a furrier. He learned to cut skins and sew them together to look like the wonderful coats and stoles he had designed. The fur business was a good business in those days. When Dad started working for Jack, he was promised "a piece of the business" one day. And that was his dream. To own and run his own business.

Time passed. Dad married Mom and had two little girls. That "one day" in which Dad would own part of the business never seemed to come. When Dad would ask, Jack would say, "Business just isn't that good right now, Lee. But soon. Very soon." Dad waited.

When Mom became pregnant for the third time (that would be me), Dad asked Jack one more time to fulfill his promise. Jack said no and Dad knew he had to start looking around. By this time the fur salons were showing up in the nicer department stores. Not having monster. com or any other fast form of communication, job opportunities usually came through friends, relatives, and people in the business.

With Mom getting closer and closer to her due date, Dad packed up the family and left the only town he knew, Minneapolis, and headed down to Peoria, Illinois, where Bergner's department store was opening up a fur department. Dad walked in to apply for the job. Several others waited to be interviewed, so Dad knew he had to be memorable.

The interview went very well — after all, Dad had a lot of experience. But how could he be remembered? When the interview was about to conclude, Dad, who always had a great sense of humor, shook the interviewer's hand and said, "I just want you to know that no matter who you hire, I'm glad you got to meet me!"

He left the man speechless. Later that night, Dad got a phone call. "Mr. Broms," the interviewer said, "of all the people I interviewed for this job, as I sat down to consider each person you kept popping into my head. I couldn't get that last line out of my mind. How soon can you start?"

That would end the story, except that line became a staple for the salespeople in Dad's department. When a customer left, whether she bought a fur or not, the salesperson always said, "I'm glad you got to meet me." A smile and sometimes a wink (politically correct in those days) accompanied the "line." It became the symbolic language of the department. People thought it amusing, and more importantly, they thought about their experience in that fur department.

It sent a message not only to the customers but also to every person working in the department and eventually in the entire store. They wanted every single customer to know that their job was to make each experience pleasant enough to end with that somewhat cocky statement. And most people responded back, "I'm glad I got to meet you, too!"

Keeping the Conversations Going

Meetings end, but the work keeps going. You need to remind your team about the discussion, the decisions, and the camaraderie. You have a lot of options for communicating with employees, and how you choose to do so has a lot to do with the needs and styles of the people who work with you. The upcoming sections outline some of the methods for getting out your message.

Updating employees with a memo or newsletter

A newsletter or memo (printed or sent by e-mail) can be an effective vehicle for keeping up the team spirit. You may use such a communication for reporting meeting minutes, or you may want to produce a lively newsletter complete with team accomplishments and upcoming celebrations, holidays, or other events. The upcoming list gives you ideas for items you might want to include:

- ✔ Tips or suggestions for carrying out tasks discussed at the meeting
- ✔ An agenda for the next meeting
- ✔ Updates about how specific projects are going
- ✔ Personal information that may interest meeting participants (birthdays, accolades, and so on)
- ✔ Current goals and how they're being met

Putting together a newsletter can be time-consuming, but you can keep it simple and get your point across.

Sending your message electronically

After a meeting, you can send an e-mail or text message or write a blog entry that employees can access within minutes to reinforce meeting information, give reminders, or even make a few corrections.

Keeping Gen X and Gen Y workers in on the team conversation often involves more high-tech communication. Some may think that the newsletter sent via e-mail is okay but certainly low-tech.

Options for communicating electronically include

- ✔ **Text messages:** Sent via your cell phone, a text message enables you to contact individuals quickly, especially if they need a reminder to do a specific job that must get done quickly or if you have a correction to make specifically for one person.

- ✔ **Blogs:** A blog is basically an active online journal. A leader may post pertinent company information on his blog, which is available for all employees to read, and employees can read and respond to it.

- ✔ **Facebook pages:** Facebook is a social networking tool similar to a blog, but only those whom you designate can access your Facebook page and comment on what you write. This communication tool provides interaction among users.

- ✔ **Intranet:** A private computer network, such as Google Sites or Microsoft Share Points enables you and your employees to create personal sites with information, pictures, videos, and goals. You can communicate with employees, sharing announcements, data, newsletters, and gathering feedback through surveys. Your team can also create a site for the project or goal that it's working on. You can control who has access to your site and use it to interact with other businesses, as well.

- ✔ **Twitter:** This short blog enables you to let others know what you are doing at any given time. It is limited to 140 characters, so you can't give much information in one *tweet* (message on Twitter). When you sign up for Twitter, you can decide whether to restrict who can read your tweets. Once you are signed up, others can search for you and ask to *follow* you (the term for communicating with others on Twitter). Your team can sign up and exclusively tweet each other.

Supporting Employees through Personal Meetings

Employees want the opportunity to be listened to and understood. The brain reacts to this interaction by releasing neurotransmitters that help with focus, attention, and memory. These chemicals also make a person feel happy. Happy employees are more motivated and productive. So think of personal, one-on-one meetings as a real opportunity to help your employees do their best work for you and for the company. These personal meetings also create relationships and bonds based on unspoken or spoken promises. Leaders promise leadership, resources, opportunity, security, compensation, and a future. Employees promise their loyalty, talents, and skills.

The Chief Effervescent Officer

Charlie Cowell is the CEO of a pharmaceuticals company in the southeast. Charlie lets everyone know that his job is not Chief Executive Officer; he is Chief Effervescent Officer. Charlie bubbles over with excitement about his job, his vision, and his mission. Whenever he speaks to anyone in the building, his bubbling personality and his passion about Cowell Pharmaceuticals spills over the conversations.

Ask Charlie what his job description is, and you will find it unique among other leaders. Charlie's job is to "make the fizzy feasible for everyone." He conjures up in the minds of his employees, customers, and other stakeholders "fizzy liquid solutions" (a vision of his pharmaceuticals) that make their way into homes and hospitals

to make people feel better. Charlie loves his employees, and when he meets with them — whether in individual or company wide meetings — you can bet he's offering a sparkling solution as a refreshment. Charlie holds up a glass and toast his workers because they are making a difference in people's lives.

Are the drugs he makes fizzy, you might ask? No. But fizzy is as fizzy does, Charlie says. If everyone in his employ would effervesce, they would have high spirits and be animated. That's how Charlie is, and his high spirits have spread throughout the company. Everyone who leaves a meeting with Charlie is a bit happier and a big believer in his solutions.

Sharing your vision; living your vision

Five years from now . . . *what?* As a leader you have created a picture in your mind of what your organization will look like in the future. It is so vivid, that when you speak of it, you assume that others see it. But your job is to make undeniably certain that your employees see and feel your vision. The passion that you must share is a contagious emotion that can spread throughout your company with your assistance, persistence, and insistence!

Your senior leadership team should be living your vision on a daily basis. Their behaviors and actions should radiate and reinforce what that vision means. The key is alignment. Can you align your vision with the personal dreams and goals of your employees? Can you convince them that you are all here for the same reason? If you can do that, you have a dream you can share.

Begin each personal meeting with your vision statement, "Five years from now our company will be . . . ." The key word here is *our.* Make your employees feel that they are part of something big. And then talk about how this employee will contribute to this vision.

Each and every time you share your vision, you help your employees store it in their brains. When your employees are asked about their work, that vision is easily accessible and can become part of the conversation. And every time a memory is retrieved, the easier it is to remember again and the faster it comes to mind in various situations.

No leader did a better job in sharing his vision than Walt Disney. When he pre-pared to make his first animated film, many people thought he was crazy. But he went as far as acting out the entire movie for his animation staff. He wanted them to see what he saw, a quality full-length animated film that would keep the audience's attention. And he was relentless. He made his team work hard and cut much of their other work to keep them focused on the goal. Because he made them feel that this was an opportunity to hone and to share their tal-ents, they stayed with him and created a box-office success.

Showing the whole picture

Because of the way the brain works, it is easy to leave out certain information when you are explaining something that has been stored and rehearsed many times. You assume that the person you're speaking with sees what you see and understands what you understand. As a result, you likely assume that your message is clear and complete even when it isn't.

Even worse, of course, is not sharing the vision with the team and the indi-viduals who make up that team. This is one reason personal meetings are so important. The second is the possibility of building really strong relation-ships with your employees, much like Walt Disney did.

Giving the whole picture may require the following in group meetings:

- ✔ **Many repetitions:** Even though the information is in your long-term memory, it's not in theirs.

- ✔ **Visuals:** Add a picture, chart, or any visual that represents what you want them to see.

- ✔ **Emotion:** Your passion goes a long way.

- ✔ **Stories:** A story or metaphor may help them see what you see.

Find out in personal meetings whether your employees can share the com-pany vision with you. Ask them to write it down for you or to create a visual to help others. All of these suggestions can tell you whether you're clearly communicating your vision. Walt Disney's employees were drawing his vision, and so he knew that they were seeing what he saw. You may not have that same opportunity, but if you want everyone to be able to spread the word and get it right, you have to check for any misconceptions.

Building better relationships

Whether you're meeting with employees, customers, or other stakeholders, keep in mind that your optimism is contagious. The more positively you speak as you share your vision and their participation in that vision, the more likely you are to receive positive responses. People who get to know each other on a personal basis accomplish more tasks and solve more problems.

Every meeting is an opportunity to create relationships that keep your employees aligned with your vision. Most meetings are conducted in a very procedural manner. This does save time, and you can quickly go through an agenda and check things off as completed. When you meet with individuals, the shape of the meetings is very different.

When you work on these personal relationships, you build trust. Take the risk of exposing a little of your personality, and be willing to accept feedback. Meet with employees on equal ground. This can be anywhere from meeting them on the plant floor to taking a walk or going to a restaurant. Thank your employee for her contribution to the vision and show her again how it fits into the big picture. Let her know what your expectations are and how much you appreciate the manner in which she is meeting (or getting close to meeting, or exceeding) those expectations.

When the meeting is over, keep the relationship going. Send a thank-you note and say you are looking forward to future meetings. Thank him again for his contribution.

Meeting employees in the middle

Ben is given the lead position at a Southwest assembly plant for a modular home manufacturer. When he takes over the plant, the end product is of poor quality, and morale among employees is low. There is also a large turnover in help. A company meeting is called to introduce Ben to the work force. Ben walks in front of the group wearing a work uniform and his carpenter tool belt. He starts off with a story about a young family buying their first new house, which was built by their plant. He explains that this family is much like the families of the people working in this plant. He then tells them all of the problems that the poor quality issues caused this family and asks them all to think about how they would feel if this happened to their own families. Ben tells his co-workers that with their help he is going to change the assembly plant to a "home creation center" so that young families can buy homes in which they live happily ever after.

Ben starts by holding meetings with each team and having them list the problems they are having. Ben helps them pick the three highest priority problems. Even if Ben already has the solution, he asks the team for ways to solve the problems. Most of the time the teams come up with the best solutions, but when they don't they're more willing to use Ben's suggestion because they've had the opportunity to provide input. When problems arise, Ben meets with the team involved and addresses the problem in an unthreatening way. Ben always emphasizes that he isn't interested in reprimanding the person who caused the problem; he is interested in adjusting the procedure to eliminate the problem. Ben has the teams keep a self-assessment scorecard of new and old problems so that they can see how they are doing. In less than a year, Ben eliminates the quality issues and brings up the company's morale.

Part V
The Part of Tens

The 5th Wave   By Rich Tennant

THE NEXT EVOLUTION IN PALM-TOP ORGANIZERS

The PatchPilot

Delivers a preset amount of data into your bloodstream which quickly rushes it to your brain and subconscious.

I have to go now. I suddenly got the feeling I'm supposed to be at a meeting in 10 minutes.

In this part . . .

The chapters in this part give you quick bits of information that you can easily put to use. I give you the truths behind ten common myths about the brain, tell you ten ways to incorporate neuroscience into your leadership practices, and ten strategies for keeping your brain in tip-top shape.

Chapter 21

Debunking Ten Brain Myths

In This Chapter

▶ Finding the facts behind the rumors

▶ Discovering more about how the brain really works

▶ Laying to rest mistaken ideas about the brain

*T*he brain is full of mystery. Even today, a lot remains unknown about the inner workings of this 3-pound organ. And with mystery comes myth. It's natural for the brain to make up stuff about itself as it tries to figure itself out — snippets of information cause people to wonder, and because the brain tries to make sense out of things, the snippets become stories and the stories become legends.

In this chapter I share ten persistent myths about the brain and the truth as it is known today.

You Use Only 10 Percent of Your Brain

People argue about whether you use even 10 percent of your brain. On some days, you might feel like your brain isn't working at all. But the fact of the matter is, you use all of your brain! If that makes you feel dumb, don't let it.

Your brain really is a use-it-or-lose-it organ. Those little nerve fibers I talk about in Chapter 2 either bloom as you learn new things and use that learning, or they are pruned away if you don't use them.

But your entire brain contains electrical and chemical activity at all times. Even when you sleep. Granted, sometimes the electrical and chemical activity is quite low in areas that aren't being actively used, but from moment to moment those areas are ready to fire up if needed.

You Are Either Left-Brained or Right-Brained

This myth feels like it should be addressed by my left brain, because that is where you would find my logic. Years ago, when researchers discovered that the brain hemispheres have separate functions, some unknowing people took that information and decided that you use only one of your hemispheres. That notion isn't logical. Worse, the idea that more women are right-brained and men left-brained got appended to the myth.

This myth is really a no-brainer. Everyone uses both hemispheres of their brains as long as they have both hemispheres. (There have been cases in which a hemisphere has been surgically removed for medical reasons. If that happens at an early age, the remaining hemisphere takes over the functions of both.)

Your left hemisphere controls the right side of your body and the right hemisphere controls the left side of your body. If you used only one hemisphere, you would have physical difficulties with one side. More proof that this is a myth.

Drinking Alcohol Kills Brain Cells

First things first: There is little doubt that alcoholics hurt their brains and may cause permanent damage.

You probably have heard the "alcohol kills brain cells" myth several ways. My favorite is, "Every time you have a drink, you kill 50,000 brain cells." But the myth can be even scarier: for every ounce of alcohol you drink, you lose one million brain cells!

I personally like the buffalo theory as hypothesized by the character, Cliff, on the TV series *Cheers*. His story is that just like in a buffalo herd, the slowest runners are the ones who get killed, slow brain cells are the ones that die off from alcohol. According to Cliff (who always hangs out at the bar), drinking kills off weak brain cells, and so when you drink you feel smarter!

The fact is, you do lose some brain cells every day. And "You may as well have a good time doing it," as educator and researcher Dr. David Sousa said at a conference on the brain. But alcohol doesn't kill brain cells. Excessive drinking may damage parts of cells, but moderate drinking isn't a problem.

Adults Don't Grow New Brain Cells

For decades, scientists believed that you were born with one hundred billion brain cells and lost some throughout your life but never got any new ones. In 1992, I was telling people that as a fact. But research proved it wrong.

Neurogenesis is the word used to describe the growth of new cells in the brain. New cells are produced in such structures as the hippocampus, which is responsible for assisting in the storage of long-term memories. The research that cinched this was performed by injecting a dye into cancer patients. The dye would attach itself only to new cells. Autopsies of these patients revealed that they indeed had grown new brain cells.

You can get new cells from learning something new, exercising, and eating nutritious foods. Stress, on the other hand, can prevent the birth of new neurons.

There Is No Difference Between Male and Female Brains

This ongoing argument about male and female differences should be coming to an end with the latest research proving that males and females use different parts of their brains for various functions.

The facts are clear when you look at statistics rather than at individuals. Females tend to remember details, especially in connection with more emotional memories, and so they use their left hemisphere (which remembers facts) more than males. Males tend to remember the big picture, and they call on their right hemispheres to do so.

Typically, females handle emotion differently and remember emotional events quickly and intensely; the emotional center of the brain, the amygdala, is larger in men than in women.

Males have more gray matter; females more white matter. As a result of these typical differences, males and females working together complement each other. Males work in a more localized area of the brain, which is helpful for things like computation. The white matter in females enables faster interaction between widespread areas of the brain like those for speech and reading body language.

Most studies suggest that the band of fibers connecting the two hemispheres is larger in females than in males, which may be why females tend to do many things at one time while males tend to do only one thing at a time.

IQ Is Fixed

The more you understand about the brain, the more you realize that a person's IQ staying the same throughout her life has to be a myth. Recent research has proven that the brain can change at any age. Increasing intelligence throughout your life is possible and likely.

Genetics doesn't play as big a part in determining intelligence as researchers once thought. Environment and experience are bigger factors than genetics in determining intelligence, but nature and nurture work together.

In short: If you keep trying new things, you improve your intelligence.

Subliminal Messages Work

Years ago a study was done in which pictures of Coke and popcorn, and the words "Drink Coke" were flashed intermittently on the screen in a movie theater. These "messages" appeared too briefly for viewers to notice them. They were meant to reach the unconscious mind and make moviegoers go to the concession stand and buy Coke and popcorn. The study was done by a man named James Vicary, who claimed that sales of Coke went up about 20 percent and popcorn sales over 50 percent.

The study caused advertisers to consider using these messages for their products. Books were written about how to use subliminal messages in advertising. But a few years later, Vicary admitted to lying about the study. Further studies produced no difference in sales using subliminal messages.

Brain Damage Is Always Permanent

The neuroplasticity of the brain serves two purposes: One is to make new connections for learning and memory and the other is to rewire to help repair brain injury. There have been many heartfelt stories told of the ability to reconnect brain pathways to overcome damage from accidents, strokes, and brain disease.

The older the brain is, the slower it can repair itself, but the possibility of forming new pathways after a stroke that affects the language centers, for example, is good. It requires therapy and much repetition, but many people respond well after brain injury.

The Brain Gets New Wrinkles When You Learn Something

You're born with as many wrinkles as you are going to get — at least, in your brain.

Shortly after conception the brain begins to grow. It starts out very smooth, and by the time a baby is born, her brain is wrinkled — just as much as an adult's. The wrinkles are a result of the brain growing. Neurons are produced and migrate to different brain areas. They also grow dendrites and axons that make the brain larger. The brain just wouldn't fit into our skulls if it weren't folded. If you unfolded the top layer of your brain, the folded part, it would be about the size of a large dinner napkin! The birth canal isn't large enough for a brain that size!

Your brain does change when you learn something, but not by adding wrinkles. New neurons develop, dendrites sprout, and axons grow. It's a wonderful process.

Your Memory Worsens As You Age

You simply are not doomed to fading memory as you age. Because the brain continues to change as you learn new things, you form new memories. If you activate your old memories by reminiscing, talking to old friends, and looking at pictures, you can keep those old memories active, as well. Hanging around with interesting people and trying new things improves your cognitive abilities and adds new memories, too.

The more active you remain, the more likely your memory is to stay strong. Exercise increases blood flow and oxygen to your brain. The more sedentary you are, the more likely you are to experience memory deficits.

Good nutrition also keeps memory strong because it provides the brain with what it needs to produce the chemicals to help you store memories. Sleep also helps: The brain stores information at night while you sleep.

Chapter 22

Ten Tips for Brain-Based Leadership

*T*hroughout this book I talk about how understanding the brain and applying brain research help you become a better leader. In this chapter, I offer ten tips to keep you using your head as you lead.

Hire Leaders

When you're surrounded by others with leadership qualities, you receive better advice and better decision-making strategies, and you can take your business where you want to go in a shorter period of time.

As a leader you need to

✓ Hire those who you feel have leadership abilities — those who listen well, are good communicators, are highly motivated, and know and share your values.

✓ Maximize leadership opportunities among your senior leadership team.

✓ Step back and let your leaders do what they do best. When you have employees who you feel are ready to lead, take a back seat and give them the opportunity to use their skills.

Maximize Digital Wisdom

Keep your organization technologically up to date by balancing the digital immigrants (those to whom digital technology is new) in your workforce with digital natives (those who grew up with digital technology). Take advantage of those tech-savvy employees who can teach others, including yourself.

The brain is changing as a result of the number of hours people spend working with digital gadgets. Learn how these brains are working, what their needs are, and how you can better lead both those who are very well acquainted with and rely on technology and those who need to learn more about it.

Bring People with You

Share your values, ideals, and vision with your followers. Use your passion and your influence to get others to believe in you. You do this by

- Acknowledging their value to the organization
- Recognizing and utilizing their strengths
- Praising their accomplishments
- Keeping them focused on the goals

Lead by Example

Mirror neurons ensure that whatever behaviors you model for your employees are recreated in their brains. In other words, when someone watches how you treat a customer, the same connections your brain makes as you actively interact are being made in the brains of those who observe you. Make sure that you

- Model how customers should be treated.
- Model how goals should be pursued.
- Just as Alexander the Great always led his soldiers into battle, make yourself visible to your workforce.
- Be optimistic and positive. Emotions are contagious.

Handle Conflict

Many leaders don't like conflict. Some ignore it and hope it goes away on its own. If you don't address conflict, employees lose their confidence in you. The good news is that you can take steps to handle conflict. Try the following:

- ✔ Ask questions to clarify the problem.
- ✔ Listen carefully to both sides.
- ✔ Resist taking sides.
- ✔ Find a way for the conflicting employees or teams to come to an agreement; lead them toward compromise.
- ✔ If compromise is unlikely, bring in a negotiator.
- ✔ Try for a win-win solution.

 Conflict can slow productivity and cause negativity to permeate the workplace. Try to create a climate of openness and trust so that employees are more likely to air their differences and find a solution.

Resist the Urge to Micromanage

You hired your employees because you knew they would be a great fit. They know their jobs. You can relax! If you second-guess employees, you squelch their motivation. Give them the chance to do what you hired them to do.

Be there for them. Ask whether you can help. But assume that you knew what you were doing when you hired them!

Value Emotional Intelligence

Pay attention to how employees interact with you and others. Knowing how to communicate with and read others has nothing to do with attending the best schools or getting the best grades. In fact, many of those valedictorians you went to school with aren't successful because they have academic skills but not people skills.

 Model your own emotional intelligence skills when you work with others and when you talk to them. If your work environment is filled with people using social skills, those few who lack them can learn through observation. If your workplace lacks models of emotional intelligence, institute training in these skills.

Give the Credit; Take the Cash

Many employees complain because they feel they haven't received credit for their work. They think their superiors are taking their ideas and their hard work to make themselves look good. This behavior may cause a heck of a lot of hard feelings. Give employees the credit. Let them feel good about themselves and the contributions they're making toward your goals.

The good news is that their hard work is making your business successful and improving your bottom line. Take the cash! Give employees the credit!

Provide Feedback

Feedback does two things: it gives your employees the opportunity to change the way they work so that they do a better job, and it raises the ability of your entire organization to be more successful. Every single person who improves his performance brings you closer to reaching your goals.

When you provide feedback make sure that you

- ✔ Make it specific. Cheerleading is not a bad thing, but specific feedback gives employees data that they can work with to improve.

- ✔ Suggest improvements. Positive feedback is easier to give, but you don't want your employees to become complacent. Mention an area where they could improve, so that they have something to work on.

- ✔ Connect feedback to the employee's job performance, and show the effect their performance has on the organization.

Seek feedback from your employees. If you listen to what they think you could improve upon, they're more likely to act upon your feedback.

When You Can't Decide, Run for It!

I hate those days when I can't make a decision or make a decision and then immediately change my mind. Indecision may have something to do with a lack of the neurotransmitter dopamine, which works in the executive center of your brain and helps eliminate other options after you have made a decision.

Movement is one quick way of getting a dopamine fix. If you can't make up your mind, get some exercise. A brisk walk or a run should jog your mind enough to help you decide. Another plus to exercise is that it helps rid your body and brain of stress chemicals that may also hinder your decision-making.

Chapter 23

Ten Ways to Build a Better Brain

In This Chapter

▶ Taking care of yourself

▶ Challenging your brain

As a leader who's eager to make a difference, you want to do all you can for your brain. The ten tips in this chapter get you started on a brain-healthy life.

Eat Nutritiously

If you really want high levels of cognition and the ability to learn new information more easily, begin with your diet. Your brain is about 78 percent water. Keep it hydrated for optimal performance. Make sure that you eat fresh fruit, nuts, vegetables high in antioxidants — the dark green, leafy kind — lean protein, complex carbohydrates, and good fats like omega-3 fatty acids in salmon, sardines, and tuna.

Your body turns food into the glucose that feeds your brain. Your brain can't store energy, so eating often is a good idea.

Balancing your diet should get you most of what you need, but talk to your doctor if you're considering supplements like a multi-vitamin or fish oil capsules.

Move It or Lose It

According to the research of Dr. John Medina, author of *Brain Rules* and director of the Brain Center for Applied Learning Research at Seattle Pacific University, exercise can increase your cognitive abilities in a matter of weeks. Aerobic exercise only twice a week for about 30 minutes increases blood flow and provides more oxygen to the brain — all of which means that new blood vessels are formed and old ones are renewed, keeping your brain cells healthy.

Exercise also gets rid of stress chemicals that have built up in your brain. Those chemicals can interfere with learning and memory. More exciting news is that exercise over time can decrease your risk of Alzheimer's disease by up to 50 percent.

The more exercise you do, the more the brain releases a chemical called *brain-derived neurotropic factor* (BDNF), which basically fertilizes your brain and helps neurons grow. Exercise also affects specific areas that help with learning and memory.

Rest

When you sleep, your brain is awake. Brain science believes that you learn while you sleep. Your brain repeats the connections that it made during the day as it was learning and having other experiences. The process is called *consolidation,* and interruptions to your sleep at specific times affect what you remember.

Get about eight hours of sleep and see whether you feel better, think better, and remember more.

Naps also increase performance. At about 3 p.m., most people really want to sleep. This is a great time for you and your employees to take a snooze. The nap can increase performance and attention!

Relax

A little bit of stress increases your memory, but a little bit more and you could be in trouble. According to some researchers, the stress hormones, such as cortisol, can actually disconnect a network of neurons in your brain. When that happens, you begin a thought and you can't remember how to finish it or start to do something and forget what it was.

To keep your stress low, try the following:

- ✔ Avoid stressful situations whenever possible.
- ✔ Exercise to rid yourself of built-up stress hormones.
- ✔ Seek treatment if you think you have depression.

Stress costs businesses money every year. If a great deal is expected of you at work, you need to feel in control. Knowing that you have the skills and the tools to do your work gives you this control.

Keep Your Memory in Shape

Put away your smart phone, your personal digital assistant, and your computer for a little while. Do you know the phone numbers of your friends, colleagues, or family members without having to look them up? If you want to improve your memory and your brain, you have to use it.

Memorize something. If you don't like memorizing numbers, try a poem or some funny stories. Are you the type of person who wishes you could remember jokes after you hear them? Go out of your way to memorize some jokes. These are great workouts for your working memory.

Over time you forget memory strategies; giving your memory a workout can give you the opportunity to reacquaint yourself with some of them. Keep working it!

Pick Up a Book

Have you read a good book lately? Reading is good for your brain. It also increases your vocabulary. Read something — fiction, nonfiction, poetry, whatever! — and then talk about it to someone. Better yet, join a book club, or start one yourself.

Reading helps you build new connections in your brain and may even cause new neurons to develop. It also gives you something to talk to people about. Building relationships is about finding common ground. A book might just be the perfect connection between you and someone you work with.

Be Upbeat

What makes you happy? Make a list and take a long look at it. Make sure you find time to do those things that truly make you feel good. Optimism in a leader builds confidence in employees and customers.

If you've always been a pessimist, find a book on optimism or on happiness. Read about how to change some of that thinking. You can train your brain to be more optimistic. Some research says that your brain is built for optimism. Take advantage of those natural tendencies to consider the future bright. Optimists know they have good brains, and they work to maintain them.

Make a Few Changes

Now is the time to break some of your routines. Try a new route to work or a new hobby. Breaking your routine causes you to be more aware of how your mind is working. If you've always wanted to learn to speak French, there's no time like the present. Get those neurotransmitters flowing.

So much of life is spent on autopilot that you may forget to take time to smell the roses. The brain likes novelty. Give it something new to think about, and you make some new connections.

Name That Tune

The brain likes music, and learning how to play a musical instrument excites your brain. Playing music activates several areas of the brain and so gets blood and oxygen flowing in various structures, making an overall healthier brain.

What about your old musical instrument? Is there an untuned piano in the basement or a guitar that could use some new strings in the back of the closet? If you don't play an instrument, at least play "Name That Tune." Someone hums the first few notes of a song and you try to guess the title. That can wake up a few sleepy cells!

Teach Someone Else

Research has suggested for years that teaching others is the number-one way to learn information yourself. Think about something you're good at and you haven't had much time for. Perhaps the chess board is missing a piece and you haven't picked up the game in years.

Replace that pawn and find someone who is interested in learning. You'll renew the chess patterns you previously stored, help someone else, and probably have a good time as well!

Teaching reinforces old connections, strengthens new connections, and strengthens social skills, too.

Index

• *F* •

• **N** •

iness/Accounting
ookkeeping
kkeeping For Dummies
-0-7645-9848-7

y Business
in-One For Dummies,
Edition
-0-470-38536-4

Interviews
Dummies,
Edition
-0-470-17748-8

mes For Dummies,
Edition
-0-470-08037-5

ck Investing
Dummies,
Edition
-0-470-40114-9

cessful Time
agement
Dummies
-0-470-29034-7

puter Hardware
ckBerry For Dummies,
Edition
-0-470-45762-7

nputers For Seniors
Dummies
-0-470-24055-7

ne For Dummies,
Edition
-0-470-42342-4

Laptops For Dummies,
3rd Edition
978-0-470-27759-1

Macs For Dummies,
10th Edition
978-0-470-27817-8

Cooking & Entertaining
Cooking Basics
For Dummies,
3rd Edition
978-0-7645-7206-7

Wine For Dummies,
4th Edition
978-0-470-04579-4

Diet & Nutrition
Dieting For Dummies,
2nd Edition
978-0-7645-4149-0

Nutrition For Dummies,
4th Edition
978-0-471-79868-2

Weight Training
For Dummies,
3rd Edition
978-0-471-76845-6

Digital Photography
Digital Photography
For Dummies,
6th Edition
978-0-470-25074-7

Photoshop Elements 7
For Dummies
978-0-470-39700-8

Gardening
Gardening Basics
For Dummies
978-0-470-03749-2

Organic Gardening
For Dummies,
2nd Edition
978-0-470-43067-5

Green/Sustainable
Green Building
& Remodeling
For Dummies
978-0-470-17559-0

Green Cleaning
For Dummies
978-0-470-39106-8

Green IT For Dummies
978-0-470-38688-0

Health
Diabetes For Dummies,
3rd Edition
978-0-470-27086-8

Food Allergies
For Dummies
978-0-470-09584-3

Living Gluten-Free
For Dummies
978-0-471-77383-2

Hobbies/General
Chess For Dummies,
2nd Edition
978-0-7645-8404-6

Drawing For Dummies
978-0-7645-5476-6

Knitting For Dummies,
2nd Edition
978-0-470-28747-7

Organizing For Dummies
978-0-7645-5300-4

SuDoku For Dummies
978-0-470-01892-7

Home Improvement
Energy Efficient Homes
For Dummies
978-0-470-37602-7

Home Theater
For Dummies,
3rd Edition
978-0-470-41189-6

Living the Country Lifestyle
All-in-One For Dummies
978-0-470-43061-3

Solar Power Your Home
For Dummies
978-0-470-17569-9

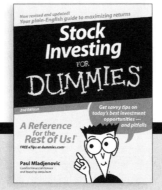

Internet
Blogging For Dummies,
2nd Edition
978-0-470-23017-6

eBay For Dummies,
6th Edition
978-0-470-49741-8

Facebook For Dummies
978-0-470-26273-3

Google Blogger
For Dummies
978-0-470-40742-4

Web Marketing
For Dummies,
2nd Edition
978-0-470-37181-7

WordPress For Dummies,
2nd Edition
978-0-470-40296-2

Language & Foreign Language
French For Dummies
978-0-7645-5193-2

Italian Phrases
For Dummies
978-0-7645-7203-6

Spanish For Dummies
978-0-7645-5194-9

Spanish For Dummies,
Audio Set
978-0-470-09585-0

Macintosh
Mac OS X Snow Leopard
For Dummies
978-0-470-43543-4

Math & Science
Algebra I For Dummies
978-0-7645-5325-7

Biology For Dummies
978-0-7645-5326-4

Calculus For Dummies
978-0-7645-2498-1

Chemistry For Dummies
978-0-7645-5430-8

Microsoft Office
Excel 2007 For Dummies
978-0-470-03737-9

Office 2007 All-in-One
Desk Reference
For Dummies
978-0-471-78279-7

Music
Guitar For Dummies,
2nd Edition
978-0-7645-9904-0

iPod & iTunes
For Dummies,
6th Edition
978-0-470-39062-7

Piano Exercises
For Dummies
978-0-470-38765-8

Parenting & Education
Parenting For Dummies,
2nd Edition
978-0-7645-5418-6

Type 1 Diabetes
For Dummies
978-0-470-17811-9

Pets
Cats For Dummies,
2nd Edition
978-0-7645-5275-5

Dog Training For Dummies,
2nd Edition
978-0-7645-8418-3

Puppies For Dummies,
2nd Edition
978-0-470-03717-1

Religion & Inspiration
The Bible For Dummies
978-0-7645-5296-0

Catholicism For Dummies
978-0-7645-5391-2

Women in the Bible
For Dummies
978-0-7645-8475-6

Self-Help & Relationship
Anger Management
For Dummies
978-0-470-03715-7

Overcoming Anxiety
For Dummies
978-0-7645-5447-6

Sports
Baseball For Dummies,
3rd Edition
978-0-7645-7537-2

Basketball For Dummies
2nd Edition
978-0-7645-5248-9

Golf For Dummies,
3rd Edition
978-0-471-76871-5

Web Development
Web Design All-in-One
For Dummies
978-0-470-41796-6

Windows Vista
Windows Vista
For Dummies
978-0-471-75421-3